BEFORE DALLAS

The U.S. Bishops' Response to Clergy Sexual Abuse of Children

NICHOLAS P. CAFARDI, JD, JCD

Paulist Press
New York/Mahwah, NJ

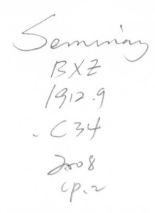

Jacket and book design by Lynn Else
Jacket photo by Nancy M. de Flon

Library of Congress Cataloging-in-Publication Data

Cafardi, Nicholas P.
    Before Dallas : the U.S. Bishops' response to clergy sexual abuse of children / Nicholas P. Cafardi.
        p. cm.
    ISBN-13: 978-0-8091-0580-9 (alk. paper)
    1. Catholic Church—Clergy—United States—Sexual behavior. 2. Child sexual abuse by clergy—United States. 3. Clergy—Sexual behavior. I. Title.
    BX1912.9.C34 2008
    261.8'327208828273—dc22

                                                                                    2007024145

Published by Paulist Press
997 Macarthur Boulevard
Mahwah, New Jersey 07430

www.paulistpress.com

Printed and bound in the
United States of America

Dedication

This book is dedicated to the
Most Reverend Donald W. Wuerl, STD,
archbishop of Washington, D.C.
and former bishop of Pittsburgh.
He did the right thing right the first time.

Acknowledgment

I would like to acknowledge the help and support of Rev. Michael Carragher, OP; Rev. Dean Francisco J. Ramos, OP; Rev. Jan Sliwa, OP; and the faculty of Canon Law at the Pontifical University of St. Thomas Aquinas. I would also like to thank Rev. Lawrence G. Wrenn, Rev. Louis F. Vallone, Dr. George Worgul, and Joseph A. Katarincic, Esq., as well as Dean Donald J. Guter, Marie Zagrocki, and Donna Schneider of the Duquesne University School of Law. Thanks also to Rev. Lawrence Boadt, CSP; Rev. Michael Kerrigan, CSP; Paul McMahon; and the invaluable staff at Paulist Press. Most of all, I would like to thank my wife, Kathleen A. Shepard, MD, who as a caring pediatrician helped me to understand the terrible, lifelong harm caused by the sexual abuse of children.

N.P.C.

CONTENTS

CONTENTS

CONTENTS

INTRODUCTION

This is an historical synopsis and canonical analysis of the American bishops' original response to the sex abuse crisis that convulsed the Church in the United States from 1984 to approximately 1994. It covers the period well before the Dallas Charter and Norms of 2002, which significantly changed the canonical ground rules for how the bishops could deal with sexually abusive priests. As an original member of the United States Conference of Catholic Bishops (USCCB) National Review Board for the Protection of Children and Youth, I was deeply involved in the bishops' post-2002 response. I have ended this work well before the time of the Dallas Charter and Norms.

Chapter 1 summarizes the long history of the canonical crime of the sexual abuse of a child by a priest. Chapter 2 is a brief restatement of the major cases that brought the problem to the national stage in the United States. Chapter 3 is an in-depth analysis of the canonical response to this crisis—what the canonists were saying, what advice they were giving the bishops. Chapter 4 deals primarily with the response of the national bishops' conference to the crisis, within a canonical framework—what the bishops knew, when they knew it, what they did. Chapter 5 explains the therapeutic option that most diocesan bishops took in dealing with sexually abusive priests, analyzed from its canonical aspects. Chapter 6 is a summary, not of the facts or analyses that precede it, but of the canonical lessons that the Church needs to take from this crisis, if any good is to come of so much pain. While the first five chapters proceed chronologically, in order to help the reader synthesize the information of these chapters, I have provided a timeline of events in an appendix.

BEFORE DALLAS

A few introductory notes are in order, primarily on vocabulary. First, I consistently speak of the victims as children. Some have questioned whether the victims would not be better described as minors. Nothing good can come of soft-pedaling what happened in the Church in the United States in the second half of the twentieth century, and describing the victims as minors and not children does just that. The victims were not underage persons in a bar seeking to purchase alcohol, nor were they persons in line for a provisional driver's license. They were, by and large, children. According to the report compiled by the John Jay College of Criminal Justice from figures provided by the American dioceses, under the supervision of the USCCB's National Review Board, which covered the years 1950–2002, the largest group of victims, over half (50.9 percent) were young persons between the ages of eleven and fourteen. They were children, plain and simple. Less than 15 percent of victims were sixteen to seventeen. The description of this crisis as primarily one of psychologically and sexually immature priests focusing on physically mature, but underage, victims is a fantasy.

Second, I consistently speak of the clerical child sexual abusers as priests, even though Canon 1395, §2 speaks of clerics, not just priests. The term *cleric* includes bishops, priests, and deacons. I chose to use the term *priest* simply because, according to the John Jay numbers, more than 98 percent of perpetrators were priests. Bishops (who are, of course, priests) and deacons, transitional or permanent, accounted for only 1.6 percent of the abusers. Since the abusers were, with very few exceptions, priests, they are identified as such throughout this work.

Third, when I speak of "the bishops" in this text I am invariably speaking of the local ordinary or diocesan bishops, those men who head American dioceses and who are described in Canon 381, §1 as having all ordinary, proper, and immediate power over a diocese. There are other kinds of bishops, for example, auxiliary bishops and retired bishops, but they do not govern dioceses, and while they may have assisted in the decision making described in this work, my focus is on the decision maker, the diocesan bishop or local ordinary, who actually made the choices about what to do with priests who sexually abused children in the United States. Hence every reference in this work to "the bishops" should be understood as meaning the American diocesan bishops. I also speak of "the bishops" as a group, and rarely individuate the hierarchical response to this crisis. In individual instances that is unfair, because there were some American diocesan bishops who consistently applied the canon law (though usually not the penal process) to keep sexually abusive priests out of ministry. That was hardly the majority response of the bishops, however, and this work deals with the majority response.

Finally, I genuinely hope that this work will be helpful in the years to come, not only to understand the tragedy that engulfed the Church in the United States in the period right after 1985, but also to prevent its reoccurrence. As George Santayana famously said, "Those who do not know their history are doomed to repeat it." The year 2002 was a sad replay of the lessons that the bishops should have learned no later than 1993. The fact that these problems occurred at all proves the truth of Santayana's observation. I earnestly pray that, years from now, no one will be able to say that the bishops have forgotten the painful lessons of 2002, lessons they ought to have learned at least a decade earlier.

A LIST OF ABBREVIATIONS USED

CDF is the Congregation for the Doctrine of the Faith.

CIC is the *Codex Iuris Canonici,* the Code of Canon Law. There are two of them, the 1917 Code and the 1983 Code that replaced it.

CLSA is the Canon Law Society of America.

NCCB is the National Conference of Catholic Bishops.

USCC is the United States Catholic Conference.

USCCB is the United States Conference of Catholic Bishops.

On July 1, 2001, the NCCB and the USCC merged to become the United States Conference of Catholic Bishops (USCCB). During the time period covered by this text, the American bishops' conference was known as the NCCB.

1

THE CANONICAL CRIME OF THE SEXUAL ABUSE OF A MINOR BY A CLERIC: AN HISTORICAL SYNOPSIS

A. THE NEW TESTAMENT

From the very beginning of the Christian tradition, the sexual abuse of a minor has been decried in various ways. In Matthew's Gospel, Jesus condemns those who would lead a child astray, adding an unusually violent warning that their punishment will be worse than death by forced drowning.[1] In his First Letter to the Corinthians, the apostle Paul writes that wrongdoers such as fornicators, adulterers, male prostitutes, and sodomites will not inherit the kingdom.[2] In his Letter to the Ephesians, Paul also writes that no fornicator or impure person will inherit the kingdom, adding that "because of these things, the wrath of God comes down on those who are disobedient."[3] This phrase, "sins because of which the wrath of God descends on the disobedient," will become important in the canonical history of the crime of the sexual abuse of minors.

B. THE FATHERS

In the second century of the Christian era, the Didache specified, "Do not murder; do not commit adultery; do not practice pederasty, do not fornicate."[4] Also in the second century, Polycarp wrote in his Letter to the Philippians, "the younger men must be blameless

1

in all things, caring for purity before everything and curbing them-selves from every evil....neither whoremongers nor effeminate persons nor defilers of themselves with men and boys shall inherit the kingdom of God."[5] In 177, Athenagoras of Athens deemed pederasts to be ene-mies of the Church.[6] With the fathers, the more general prohibitions of Matthew and Paul start to be particularized around concepts of sex with young boys.

C. THE EARLY COUNCILS

The Council of Elvira, held in Spain in AD 305–306, addressed sexual crimes in a number of canons. Canon 71 of the council con-demns "stupratoribus puerorum," rapists of little boys.[7] The Council of Ancyra, in Canons 16 and 17, condemned "those who have been or who are guilty of bestial lusts," a reference to male homosexual activ-ity.[8] Under Canons 9 and 10 of the Council of Neocaesarea (314–325), and Canon 9 of Nicea (325), men who had sinned against chastity, even if the offense occurred before ordination and even if absolution had been obtained, were not permitted to exercise their orders.[9]

D. THE MIDDLE AGES

An important source of canonical practice from the sixth to the eleventh centuries was the books of Penitentials, authored primarily in the Irish monasteries, which provided lists of suggested penances for individual sins. While these Penitentials are not authoritative, and while there is no uniform version of them, they do provide a window on the Church's canonical practices during the time in which they were in use. As the scholar of legal history James A. Brundage has written, "Prescriptions drawn from the penitentials quickly infiltrated collec-tions of canon law and penitential writers came to rank as canonical authorities."[10] The Penitentials of David (525), Columban (600), Cummean (650), Theodore (690), and Bede (early eighth century) list homosexual crimes committed by clerics as sins.[11] The Penitential of

Bede, from eighth-century England, lists effeminacy and sodomy as capital sins, with penalties that increase based on the sinner's status in the Church: seven years for deacons, ten years for priests, and twelve years for bishops.[12] Brundage thinks that the emphasis in the Penitentials on homosexual activity and masturbation "mirrored the experience and concerns of the monastic environment in which most penitential writers received their spiritual and intellectual formation."[13]

Toward the end of the time of the Penitentials (end of the sixth to the beginning of the eleventh centuries)[14] the sexual abuse of minors by clergy was condemned by Burchard of Worms. Burchard, bishop of Worms, was the author of a twenty-book collection of canon law. Begun in 1008 and finished in 1012, the collection, which is called Burchard's *Collectarium Canonum* or *Decretum,* was a primary source for canon law for over a century, up to and including the time of Gratian in 1140. In book 17, at chapter 35 of his *Decree,* Burchard wrote:

> A cleric or a monk who is a perverter of young boys or ado-lescents, who has been caught kissing or in another occasion of base behavior with young boys or adolescents, shall be whipped in public, shall lose his crown (tonsure), and so basely shorn, shall have his face spit in, shall be bound in iron chains, shall waste in prison for six months, and for three days of each week, shall be fed only on barley bread at evening time. After this, for another six months, he is to be kept apart in an enclosure, under the watch of a spiritual elder, intent on manual labor and prayer, subject to vigils and prayers, and he is always to walk under the guard of two spiritual brothers, not being allowed to engage in private speech or counsel with any young men.[15]

Also in the eleventh century, in his work, *The Book of Gomorrah,* writ-ten in 1051 and endorsed by Pope Leo IX, Peter Damian deals exten-sively with clerical sexual abuse.[16] Damian held "that those who are addicted to impure practices should be neither promoted to orders nor, if already ordained, should be allowed to continue."[17] Damian was rather graphic in his description of the sexual misconduct of clerics, specifying four types of homosexual "criminal vice." "There are some," he wrote, "who pollute themselves; there are others who befoul one another by mutually handling their genitals; others still who fornicate between the thighs and others who do so from the rear."[18] He also quotes the section of Burchard of Worms, excerpted above, that specifically condemns clerics who sexually abuse boys and adolescents.[19]

E. THE *CORPUS IURIS CANONICI*

In his *Concordantia Discordantium Canonum*, Gratian lists sexual acts "contra naturam" as a canonical delict or crime.[20] He also identifies unnatural sex acts with young boys as a canonical delict.[21] He condemns the sexual abuse of young boys under the caption *de extraordinaribus criminibus*. Although these injunctions against unnatural sex and sex with young boys apply to both laypersons and clerics in Gratian, he does make a point, in a number of places, to enjoin a life of chastity upon all ranks of the clergy.[22]

A decree of Pope Alexander III, issued at the Third Lateran Council in 1179, condemns unnatural sex acts of both laity and clergy as "that unnatural vice for which the wrath of God came down upon the sons of disobedience."[23] This decree was later collected in the Decretals of Gregory IX and became a part of the *Corpus Iuris Canonici*.[24] This euphemism was, as noted above, taken from Paul's Letter to the Ephesians, referring to sins of sexual misconduct. At the Fourth Lateran Council in 1225, a decree of Pope Innocent III ties Paul's phrase specifically to the actions of the clergy for the first time: "In order that the behavior and actions of the clergy may be reformed to the better, let all, especially those who are constituted in Orders, strive to live in continence and chastity avoiding every lustful vice especially the vice for which the wrath of God descends from heaven upon the sons of disobedience."[25] This decree, too, was collected in the *Corpus*.[26]

F. FOLLOWING THE *CORPUS*

At the Fifth Lateran Council in 1514, Pope Leo X, in his apostolic constitution, *Supernae dispositionis,* basically repeats the words of Alexander III's prior decree, referring to both laity and clergy, but now adds language of specific penalty: "If in fact anyone, lay or cleric, shall be convicted of the crime for which the wrath of God came down on the sons of disobedience, he is to be punished respectively according to the sacred canons or with the penalties imposed by the civil law."[27] The Council of Trent condemned sexually active priests, without specifically dealing with the sexual abuse of children. The council's decrees required bishops to punish sexually active priests, including depriving them of their office.[28] Pope Pius V in his 1566 apostolic constitution, *Cum primum,* repeats this general prohibition, but with language intensifying the penalty for clerics: "If anyone perpetrates the nefarious crime against nature, because of which the wrath of God comes down on the sons of disobedience, he is to be handed over to the secular arm to be punished, and if he is a cleric, he is to be fully degraded from all orders, and subjected to a similar penalty."[29] The same prohibition was repeated by Pius in his apostolic constitution, *Horrendum,* two years later in 1568.[30] Once Pope Alexander III introduced St. Paul's phrase, "the sin or crime against nature because of which the wrath of God comes down on the sons of disobedience," into the Church's jurisprudence, it was adopted by his successors. This euphemism almost certainly included the sexual abuse of a minor, by a cleric or by a layperson, and, more specifically, the homosexual abuse of a minor, since there is a clear refrain of "unnaturalness" in this usage.

This interpretation is validated by a case decided in the eighteenth century by the Sacred Congregation for the Council.[31] In that case, a priest who had sodomized young boys was convicted of the "crime against nature" and sentenced to the galleys. This sentence was never carried out, however, and the priest ended up serving his sentence by working at a hospital instead. The priest petitioned the Congregation for permission to say Mass again, something not allowed to priests who had been sentenced to the galleys. Since the priest had not in fact served in the galleys, he argued that this prohibition ought not to apply to him. The Congregation for the Council did not agree, finding that the infamy of his sexual crimes with minors was such that he could not say Mass again, whether he had actually served in the galleys or not. This decision creates a jurisprudence that the matter of some sexual crimes by priests with minors is so serious as to forever afterward prevent their ability to function as priests.

G. THE EIGHTEENTH AND NINETEENTH CENTURIES

In the age of the great commentators one euphemism gave way to another. What had previously been referred to as "a crime against nature, for which the wrath of God comes down on the sons of disobedience," was now considered together with other sins of the flesh as being *contra sextum*, a crime against the sixth commandment of the Decalogue. This usage of this term in canon law evidently started with Franz Xavier Wernz, who wrote in his *Ius Decretalium* that "carnal sins considered globally are understood to be those grave and external sins against the sixth commandment of the Decalogue, committed either with others or with public scandal."[32] In his characterization, Wernz was relying on the work of moral theologians, especially Alphonsus Ligouri and the manualists, who in turn based their work on the Roman Catechism issued by Pope Pius V in 1566.[33] In his work, Wernz listed as canonical offenses against the sixth commandment the crimes of fornication, stuprum, concubinage, lenocinium, rape, incest, carnal sacrilege, adultery, sodomy, and bestiality.[34] Without belaboring the point, the sexual abuse of a minor is undoubtedly covered in Wernz's list.

H. THE 1917 CODE

Wernz's influence was so substantial that when Cardinal Gasparri and his collaborators on the 1917 Code of Canon Law came to list canonical crimes, they departed from the decretalists' Pauline euphemism about "sins against nature because of which the wrath of God comes down on the sons of disobedience," and instead used Wernz's designation, *contra sextum,* for these and other sexual crimes.[35] Canon 2359, §2 of the 1917 Code states that clerics "who have committed an offense against the sixth commandment of the decalogue with minors under the age of sixteen...shall be suspended, declared infamous, deprived of every office, benefice, dignity, or position that they may hold, and in more grievous cases they shall be deposed."[36] It has been argued that this usage is just as much a circumlocution as the language of the decretalists.[37] If it was a circumlocution, however, it was a circumlocution that was unambiguous. As the Canon Law Society of America has stated in a recent publication, "A common element among commentators on the 1917 Code is that 'an offense against the sixth commandment' refers to 'crimes of lust.'"[38]

I. BETWEEN THE CODES

"Prior to the promulgation of the revised code, competence over certain forms of sexual misconduct by clerics was granted to the then Holy Office."[39] On March 16, 1962, the Holy Office issued an instruction, *Crimen sollicitationis,* which dealt not only with the crime of solicitation of sex by a priest in the confessional, but also dealt with what it referred to as the *crimen pessimum.* In a continuation of the Church's use of euphemisms in its description of unnatural sex acts by its clergy, *crimen pessimum* was a reference to acts of homosexual sex, including pederasty, by the clergy.[40] "In order to avert these...delicts, the Supreme Sacred Congregation of the Holy Office...established a manner of proceeding in such cases, inasmuch as judicial competence had been attributed exclusively to it, which competence could be exercised either administratively or through a judicial process. It is to be kept in mind that an instruction of this kind had the force of law since the Supreme Pontiff, according to the norm of can. 247, §1 of the *Codex Iuris Canonici* promulgated in 1917, presided over the Congregation of the Holy Office, and the Instruction proceeded from his own authority, with the Cardinal at the time only performing the function of Secretary."[41]

J. THE 1983 CODE

The 1983 Code does not differ substantially from the language of the 1917 Code in describing the crime of the sexual abuse of minors by clerics. The relevant canon is 1395, §2, which states that "a cleric [who has] committed an offense against the sixth commandment of the Decalogue…with a minor below the age of sixteen,…is to be punished with just penalties, including dismissal from the clerical state if the case warrants it."[42] The language is again a bit of a circumlocution, but one that the commentators have no trouble understanding as referring to any sin of sexual impurity that a cleric commits with a child.[43] Such crimes may vary from the viewing of pornographic materials in which children are the subjects to the performance of the various forms of sexual copulation with a minor. The entire gamut of these sexual sins with minors is covered by 1395, §2, and it provides the precise meaning of "sexual abuse" as it is used throughout this work: "Sexual abuse of a minor includes sexual molestation or sexual exploitation of a minor and other behavior by which an adult uses a minor as an object of sexual gratification."[44]

This prohibition in the Code reinforces the priestly obligation, also imposed by the Code, to observe "perfect and perpetual continence."[45] Sexual continence has been defined as "the non-use of the sexual faculties."[46] The clerical obligation to continence is "perfect and perpetual."[47] "They are not to use their sexual faculties with anyone of either sex, for life."[48] Priests are bound by their ordination vow to a life without any form of sexual activity. In order to meet their obligation of continence, the Code further requires clerics "to behave with due prudence towards persons whose company can endanger their obligations to observe continence or give rise to scandal among the faithful."[49] As the New Canon Law Society of America commentary states, "In view of the terrible scandals occasioned by child abuse, clerics must avoid any physical contact with minors that would provoke legitimate comment from reasonable people, such as hugging, tickling or wrestling. Clerics should not invite children to their rooms or allow them to stay overnight in the rectory. It would also be very imprudent for clerics to go on outings, field trips, or vacations with children unless the parents or other adults were present. The civil law in most jurisdictions defines a minor as one under the age of eighteen."[50] It should also be noted that "because of a cleric's special role in society and in the Church, the canon law has a greater concern about his misconduct."[51] Canon 1326, §1, 2° provides that "a person who has been established in some dignity or who has abused a position of authority or office" can be punished with a more serious penalty. As James Provost has noted, "This would be especially true of a cleric who used his relationship of trust in the community to engage in sexual misconduct, or who committed the misconduct while engaged in ministry as a cleric."[52]

K. SUMMARY

There has not been an era in the Church's long history when it was not aware of the evil of the sexual abuse of children, especially by its clergy. It is clear from this brief synopsis that the Church's law early on recognized the sexual abuse of a child as wrongful, and that it dealt with the sexual abuse of a child by a priest as particularly wrongful. This condemnation was repeated throughout the ages, which indicates that the sexual abuse of children by priests has been a problem throughout the Church's existence. Yet even though they had this highly developed legal system in their hands to deal with clergy's sexual abuse of children, the bishops of the United States did not, by and large, turn to it. What did they do? To understand the nature of the bishops' response, it is first necessary to understand the scope of the problem.

2

THE SCOPE OF THE PROBLEM: AN HISTORICAL SYNOPSIS

A. THE DIOCESE OF LAFAYETTE, LOUISIANA, 1984

The first serial sexual abuse case against a Catholic priest that went to criminal trial in the United States in the second half of the twentieth century involved Father Gilbert Gauthe, a priest of the Diocese of Lafayette, Louisiana. In 1984, Father Gauthe was indicted on thirty-four counts of sex crimes against children.[1] Gauthe eventually pled guilty to molesting eleven boys and admitted to victimizing dozens more.[2] He was sentenced to twenty years in prison.[3] There is no question that Father Gauthe's ecclesiastical superiors had known about his abuse of children for years. He had been sent for therapy in the 1970s, but he refused to stay in treatment and the diocese simply reassigned him.[4] Monsignor Alexander Larroque, who handled Father Gauthe's case, said that they simply did not understand pedophilia then, and did not know how to treat it.[5]

B. THE ARCHDIOCESE OF SANTA FE, NEW MEXICO, 1991

The Servants of the Paraclete operated a facility at Jemez Springs, in the Diocese of Santa Fe, New Mexico. Originally founded in 1947 to assist priests with problems of alcohol addiction, in 1976 it opened "the first treatment center in the world for psychosexual disorders."[6] Treatment costs averaged $4,500 a month.[7] The Servants accepted troubled priests for treatment from dioceses all over the country. In the late 1960s and early 1970s, a top administrator at Jemez Springs facility was himself a convicted sexual abuser.[8] As a part of the therapy for the priest-patients, they were allowed to leave the facility to celebrate Mass on weekends at nearby parishes. In 1991, litigation revealed that a number of priests who had been sent to the Servants for the sexual abuse of minors had continued their abusive conduct at their weekend parishes, injuring countless dozens of youngsters.[9] The center was closed in 1994, and the remaining patients were sent to a Servants' facility outside St. Louis, Missouri.[10] The Santa Fe Diocese, whose own archbishop, Robert Sanchez, resigned in 1993, after admitting that he had had sexual relationships with at least five young women in the 1970s and 1980s,[11] barely escaped bankruptcy as a result of the tort claims filed against it by abused children and their families.[12]

C. THE DIOCESE OF FALL RIVER, MASSACHUSETTS, 1992

It was revealed in 1992 that James Porter, when he had served as a priest of the Diocese of Fall River, had molested between fifty and a hundred youngsters.[13] At the time of the disclosure, Porter was married and living in Minnesota, where he had gone on to molest the babysitter of his own young children.[14] After complaints by parents at three different parishes in Fall River,[15] Porter had been sent by his bishop to the Servants of the Paraclete facility at Jemez Springs, where on weekend release, he had abused youngsters in local parishes.[16] He was assisted by the Servants to find a new parish assignment in Bemidji, Minnesota, where he also molested.[17] Porter was extradited to Massachusetts for criminal trial on child abuse charges, pled guilty to forty-one charges, and was sentenced to eighteen to twenty years in prison.[18]

D. THE DIOCESE OF DALLAS, TEXAS, 1997

In 1997, the many victims of Father Rudolph Kos became national news when eleven of them brought civil suit against Father Kos and the Diocese of Dallas.[19] Father Kos had been married and divorced, and had entered the seminary in Dallas after obtaining an annulment.[20] If the diocese had talked to his former wife or his siblings, they would have discovered that Kos had serious child sexual abuse problems.[21] One priest who lived in the same rectory as Kos was so concerned about the many young boys whom he saw in Kos's bedroom that he began to keep a log that he turned over to the bishop.[22] Kos was cycled through the Servants of the Paraclete Center in Jemez Springs for treatment, where, while on furlough, he continued his sexual abuse.[23] He was convicted of multiple acts of child sexual abuse and sentenced to life in prison.[24] There is no doubt that his bishop had been previously aware of Father Kos's conduct, but did nothing to protect the children of the diocese from him. The bishop testified, under oath, that he had warned Father Kos three times not to allow boys to stay overnight in the rectory.[25] A civil law verdict of $119.6 million was rendered against the diocese for its negligence, although it was subsequently reduced to $31 million.[26]

E. THE ARCHDIOCESE OF BOSTON, MASSACHUSETTS, 2002

Even though the Porter case had erupted ten years earlier in the neighboring Diocese of Fall River, the Archdiocese of Boston had, on active duty, two predator priests, John Shanley and John Geoghan, well after 1992.[27] In both cases, there was no doubt that the archdiocese was aware of the sexually abusive conduct of these priests against the young people in their care.[28] When civil suits were filed against the archdiocese for the actions of both men, their archdiocesan personnel files became public. Shanley's file contained information on his activity in the North American Man-Boy Love Association, a pedophile organization,[29] and Geoghan's contained a remonstrance by an auxiliary bishop, dating from 1984, that he should not be reassigned because of his "history of homosexual involvement with young boys."[30] Father Geoghan was killed in prison while serving a nine-year sentence on a child sexual abuse conviction and while he was awaiting trial on more charges.[31] Father Shanley is currently in prison, serving a twelve- to fifteen-year term, convicted of sexually abusing an altar boy.[32] In September 2003, the Archdiocese of Boston reached a settlement of $85 million with 550 victims of sexually abusive priests.[33]

F. THE NATIONAL PICTURE

The entire history of the number of priests who abused young children in the United States could not ever be fairly summarized. The dioceses referred to above are the ones that attracted nationwide attention because of the number of victims of the predator priests and because of the apparent lack of concern of the dioceses, which kept these priests in ministry long after their sexual aberrations were known to their bishops. From the revelations of the predations of Father Gilbert Gauthe in Lafayette in 1984, to the implosion in Boston once the Geoghan, Shanley, and other cases became public knowledge in 2002, it seemed as if the Church in the United States could not go through a five-year period without dealing with the clergy child sexual abuse crisis on the national stage. One commentator has described these years as "akin to watching a person falling down the same flight of stairs over and over again."[34] Eruptions in dioceses across the country raised serious questions about the national scope of this problem.

In 2003, the National Review Board for the Protection of Children and Youth of the United States Conference of Catholic Bishops engaged the John Jay College of Criminal Justice in Manhattan to conduct a nationwide study of the scope of clergy child sexual abuse in the second half of the twentieth century. The study, in which 97 percent of the dioceses in the United States and 60 percent of men's religious orders participated, gave a reasonably accurate national view of the problem.

According to the John Jay Report,[35] in the 1950–2000 period, at least 4,392 priests and deacons nationwide, who constituted 4.3 percent of those who served during that time, had allegations of sexual abuse lodged against them with the diocese or religious order. The total number of alleged victims was 10,667. Of these allegations, 50.9 percent involved victims between the ages of 11 and 14,[36] 27.3 percent involved victims between the ages of 15 and 17,[37] 16 percent between the ages of 8 and 10,[38] and 6 percent were age 7 and under.[39] By far, most of the victims were boys—81 percent,[40] and boys between the ages of 11 and 14 constituted 40 percent of all victims.[41]

G. SUMMARY

This is a sad record, one that raises the very obvious question of what went wrong. How did so much clerical abuse of so many children go on for so long? What did the bishops of the United States do as they were faced with this problem? The first step in answering this question must be a consideration of the canonical landscape in the United States as these instances of abuse were surfacing. This is the topic of the following chapter. Only after an understanding of the canonical situation in which the bishops found themselves can one begin to comprehend the response of the bishops to the burgeoning problem of the sexual abuse of minors by their priests. What did the bishops know, when did they know it, and what did they do? "In fact, the bishops' corporate failure to address the issue seriously at that time underlies much of the continuing criticism of episcopal non-accountability in this area."[42]

3

THE CANONICAL LANDSCAPE: THE FAILURE OF THE PENAL SYSTEM

A. INTRODUCTION

One thing that the bishops did not do was to rely on the clear law of the Church and treat these actions as canonical crimes. Very few priests who were accused of the sexual abuse of a minor underwent a canonical penal process based on the allegations against them. There were a number of reasons given for this failure. As the eminent canonist Francis Morrisey has written, "As the first cases came to light, there was confusion, consternation, and at times even panic in chancery offices and religious institutes. What was to be done?"[1]

A number of reasons have been hypothesized as to why there was what appears to be an almost complete breakdown in the Church's legal system over the problem of the priestly sexual abuse of minors. These reasons have been explained as:

1. A penal process (whether judicial or administrative) was not favored in the law.
2. The penal process was not adequate to the problem.
3. American canonists lacked training and experience in the canonical penal process.
4. The crimes were covered by prescription.
5. The canonical penal process would have been useless since the priest's mental defects made the ultimate penalty of dismissal from the clerical state unavailable.

6. The rights of the accused priest, including his appeal rights, would trump the canonical penal process.
7. The cooperation of the victim could not be counted on and was not sought.
8. Civil lawyers strongly advised against a canonical penal process because of the discoverability of the acts.

This chapter examines each of these reasons, but before doing so it would perhaps be useful to offer a brief explanation of how a penal process against a priest accused of the sexual abuse of a minor would have proceeded in the timeframe before the Dallas Norms. The following summary of the penal process regarding the crime of the sexual abuse of a minor by a cleric describes the process as it was in place in the United States during the period before Dallas. On April 30, 2001, this process was modified by the apostolic letter *Sacramentorum sanctitatis tutela*.[2] And, of course, the Dallas Norms made even greater changes.

B. A DESCRIPTION OF THE CANONICAL PENAL PROCESS

Every penal process starts when information is received by the diocesan bishop that an ecclesiastical crime may have been committed. At that point, the bishop is to commence a preliminary investigation to determine whether a canonical penal process is called for.[3] The language of the Code would appear to allow no discretion here.[4] Upon receipt of believable information of a canonical crime, the bishop must start the investigation. This investigation can be carried out by the bishop or his delegate.[5] If the evidence collected in the preliminary investigation indicates that a penal process is appropriate, that is, that there is a certain truth or verisimilitude to the charges, the bishop is next to consider whether, in light of Canon 1341, a canonical penal process should be started against the accused. Canon 1341 makes the canonical penal process a last resort. It is to be pursued only if there is no other way to "repair the scandal, restore justice, [and] reform the offender."[6] If the bishop, in spite of the preferences of the Code against

16

a penal process, decides to go ahead with a penal process, the accused is to be notified.[7] Oddly enough, the accused does not have to be notified of the earlier preliminary investigation.[8]

Another precondition to the canonical penal process is the statute of limitations, called "prescription" in canon law.[9] For most of the time before the Dallas Norms, it was thought that the sexual abuse of a minor by a cleric was subject to only a five-year statute of limitations.[10] That is to say, the canonical prosecution of the crime of the sexual abuse of a minor by a cleric had to begin within five years of the abusive event, or in the case of serial events, within five years of the last incident of abuse.[11] Minors were defined in the Code as those persons under sixteen years of age.[12] Since the gap between the time when a minor is abused and the time when the victim is psychologically able to deal with the abuse so as to be able to tell a third party about it is, in most of the literature, approximately twenty years,[13] a five-year statute was unrealistic from the start. In 1994, this statute was increased to ten years after the last abusive event, and the age used to define a minor was raised to eighteen.[14]

Once a decision has been made to start the penal process, the bishop can proceed either with an administrative penal process or a judicial penal process. The administrative penal process is much less formal than the judicial penal process. In the administrative penal process, the accused is informed of the charges and is given a chance to respond.[15] Having heard his response, the bishop, with the help of two assessors, makes a decision as to whether guilt has been proved.[16] This decision, along with the penalty imposed, is to be issued in a decree that follows the norms of Canons 1342–1350, and that summarizes the law and the facts upon which the decree is based.[17] "Just causes" must exist, however, for the bishop to use an administrative, as opposed to a judicial penal process,[18] and an administrative process can never be used to impose a perpetual penalty, such as dismissal from the clerical state. That can only be done in a formal judicial process under the 1983 Code.[19]

The formal judicial process is a full canonical trial of the matter, with witnesses, experts, and documentary proofs, weighed by a panel of three judges.[20] The accused must be represented by an advocate,[21] and the promoter of justice of the diocese acts as the prosecutor.[22] If guilt is established, there are a number of mitigating factors that the Code says the judges must consider in imposing a penalty. One of these mitigating factors is "the imperfect use of reason."[23] Another is "a disturbance of mind" that impairs the use of reason.[24] Another is drunkenness during the commission of the crime.[25] Another is "grave heat of passion."[26] In the presence of these mitigating factors, an ultimate penalty, such as dismissal from the clerical state, is not to be imposed.[27]

Once the penal process, whether administrative or judicial, has ended and the cleric has been found culpable of the alleged crime and a penalty has been imposed on him, the cleric has a right of appeal. In the administrative penal process, this appeal is to the bishop's hierarchical superior, which is the Holy See.[28] In the judicial process, a case heard in the first instance before the tribunal of a suffragan bishop is appealed to the metropolitan tribunal, while a case heard in the first instance before a metropolitan tribunal is appealed to the stably designated appellate tribunal for the metropolitan court.[29] A third level of appeal from the provincial tribunal is to the Roman Rota, although a direct appeal to the Rota from the original decision at the diocesan level is possible, bypassing a provincial appeal.[30] A criminal sentence that is under appeal is suspended until the appeal has been heard.[31] Further, since a penal laicization involves the "status" of the priest, some canonists hold that it is never "case closed" or *res judicata*.[32] This would mean, in effect, that a penal laicization could be challenged at any time in the future, should "due cause" exist.[33]

C. THE REASONS WHY THE CANONICAL PENAL PROCESS WAS NOT USED

Despite the existence of this highly evolved canonical penal process, and despite the fact that the sexual abuse of minors by clergy was undoubtedly the material of a canonical crime, the bishops of the United States failed to make use of this process to deal with sexually abusive priests. The literature of the time provides eight different reasons for this failure, which we now consider.

    1. A penal process (whether judicial or administrative) was not favored in the law.

    Prior to Dallas, the American bishops did not turn to the canonical penal process, even when they had reason to believe that accusations against a cleric of the sexual abuse of a child were true. One reason for the bishops' failure to use the penal process may lie in the law itself. By its own terms, the Code of Canon Law apparently disfavors the penal process. Specifically, Canon 1341 establishes certain preconditions for the use of the penal process that many canonists thought could not be met in the clerical sexual abuse area.[34] Rather early in the crisis, for example, John G. Proctor wrote:

> In guiding the bishop's decision on this matter, c. 1341 lists, non-taxatively, some conditions to be considered. Penal procedure is to be used *only* when scandal cannot be sufficiently repaired, when justice cannot be sufficiently restored, and when a miscreant cannot be reformed in any other way. Specifically, penal procedure is to be used when fraternal correction, rebuke, or "other ways of pastoral care" have been ineffective. It is hard to imagine all of these techniques being ineffective with any given offender (particularly with reference to accusations of misconduct under c. 1395) and yet full imputability still being attributed to him, not to speak of being judicially maintained.[35]

    Proctor was hardly alone in this position. Writing in the Canon Law Society's first commentary on the Code of Canon Law, James H. Provost of the Catholic University of America canon law faculty said:

> Book VI provides a number of norms that must be observed in imposing sanctions in the Church. No sanction can be imposed unless a person has externally violated a law or pre-

cept, has done so gravely, and is personally imputable for the act (c. 1321, §1). A sanction can be applied by using either a judicial procedure or an administrative one—only, however, after it is clear that nothing else (e.g. fraternal correction, warning or pastoral solicitude) will repair scandal, restore justice or lead to change in the problematic way of acting (c. 1341).[36]

Francis G. Morrisey of the Faculty of Canon Law at St. Paul's University in Ottawa held much the same opinion. In a 1991 presentation to the Canon Law Society of America he said that "the imposition of penalties, and particularly of a return to the lay state, should be a last resort, a measure not applied until all other possibilities have been exhausted."[37] Morrisey did state, however, in the same presentation, "I am very reluctant at this time to recommend using the penal process whereby priests are returned to the lay state. However, I recognize that in some exceptional cases it might be necessary."[38] A year earlier, in her presentation to the Canon Law Society of America Convention, Elizabeth McDonough, a member of the canon law faculty at Catholic University, had pointed out that "the competent ordinary must first take cognizance of canon 1341 which…certainly seems to present use of penalties as a last resort."[39]

It is fair to say that this opinion concerning the impropriety of using the penal process in cases of the sexual abuse of children by clergy, except as a last resort, was nearly unanimous. Even after Dallas, an eminent scholar of the Church's penal law, Thomas J. Green of the Catholic University of America canon law faculty, wrote, "Even if a penal process is possible, is it *expedient* (2°)? A key canonical principle is that penalties are a last resort in handling a problematic situation. Can scandal be repaired, justice restored and the offender reformed without a penal process (c. 1341)?"[40]

This prevalent canonical mindset helps to explain the American bishops' apparent failure to use the canonical penal process in the face of the sexual abuse of children by their clergy. As explained by then-Bishop of Green Bay Adam J. Maida:

Also, under our penal process, when a priest expresses sorrow, it derails the process. If he seeks reconciliation, in Canon Law we may give him absolution and say, "sin no more." But every civil lawyer knows that what is between God and his conscience does not satisfy either the victims (or the potential victims) or the civil law. In Canon Law we are limited because a diocese cannot proceed to a final determination of laicizing a priest, which is the ultimate way of bringing about that excardination and severing the legal bond between bishop and priest.[41]

The bishops were being advised by their canonists that the penal process was not the proper way to handle the issue. Other measures were more appropriate. Based on their reading of Canon 1341, and its requirements of fraternal correction and pastoral solicitude for the wrongdoer, most canon lawyers were recommending to the bishops that the bishop's first response should be pastoral and not punitive. As yet another eminent canonist stated in the early days of the crisis, "the code recommends the therapeutic and pastoral approach."[42]

An immediate reaction to this response is, of course, what about the bishop's pastoral solicitude for the victim? Where does the victim fit into this canonical scenario? In what is perhaps a blind spot in the Code of Canon Law, especially given modern sensibilities to the great harm perpetrated by the sexual abuse of a child, solicitude for the victim is not mentioned in the penal process. In the penal equation, the pastoral solicitude of Canon 1341 is solely for the perpetrator.[43] This unfortunate equation often meant that the bishop never even talked to a victim or the victim's family. As noted in the report of the National Review Board,

> Time and again, bishops informed the Board that they did not fully comprehend the horror of sexual abuse and the damage it wrought until they had met with a number of victims. As one said, "Anyone should have seen the horror of it. But unless you listen to victims, survivors, you don't really have the sense of that horror." Another bishop said that

21

there was "a disconnect whereby for some reason at a pastoral level bishops and priests did not grasp how horrified the average parent would be over the thought that his or her child would be sexually abused by a member of the clergy."

The failure to meet with victims often resulted in bishops making decisions based on a one-sided version of events. As one bishop said to the Board, "Bishops are human: Sometimes they get diffident about walking into situations where they don't know what's going to be waiting for them there, so they back off and say, 'Well maybe I won't go there; but here, I know this priest and I'll talk to him.'" It should have been obvious that talking only to priests about allegations against priests was unlikely to provide an adequate basis for determining the validity of allegations and responding to a problem of enormous magnitude.[44]

In the situation described in the report, and given the clear language of Canon 1341, it is rather easy to see why canon lawyers favored a non-penal approach, and why pastoral solicitude was only offered to the priest-perpetrator and not to the victim or the victim's family. It is also rather easy to see why the bishops so eagerly took that advice. It avoided conflictive situations, either with the priest-perpetrator or with a hostile victim's family that the quoted bishop described above. It was all too human a reaction. John Proctor stated the advice of most canonists, the advice the bishops took: "In summary, it is hard to imagine the desirability of the penal process in matters of alleged clerical misconduct. The law itself seems to have a reluctance to use the penal process."[45]

2. The penal process was not adequate to the problem.

Not only did canonists think that the canonical penal process was disfavored in the case of the sexual abuse of a child by a cleric, they also thought that the canonical process, even if it were to be used, was not up to the task. As Francis Morrisey said, "Once Church authorities began to turn to the canon law for assistance—particularly in trying to terminate the ministry of a problem priest—they began to realize that the legislation was not drafted with this particular situation of criminal responsibility and civil liability in mind."[46] And "when bishops began to address the issue, they came to realize that the laws of the Church had not been written in the perspective of such cases, especially given the serious financial and public relations consequences arising from criminal and civil proceedings against the offending priest as well as against the diocese or religious institute to which he belonged."[47]

There was also a concern that the penal process was simply too detail-oriented and time-consuming for the task. "The penal process, as described in the *Code of Canon Law,* is perceived by many as being 'too hard,'" wrote Patrick R. Lagges. "That is, it is seen as too bulky and unwieldy for situations which require quick action. There are warnings that must be given and certain time periods which must be observed."[48] And as the eminent canonist John Beal noted, "This prompt and decisive action often cannot be achieved through the Church's penal process."[49]

To be fair, it must be pointed out that the 1983 Code of Canon Law was being written at a time when clerical sexual abuse of children was not on too many radar screens. As Thomas Green noted, "One must remember that the code was drafted and promulgated in the 1970s and early 1980s, somewhat prior to the notable emergence of the scandal of clerical sex abuse of minors in the United States and elsewhere. At that time church authorities and canonists were much less aware than today of the broad and complex implications of this tragic development."[50]

There is also another problem with the canonical penal process that bears mentioning. Not only is the process "bulky and unwieldy," the fact is that the canonical penal process is presented in the Code of Canon Law in a rather disorganized fashion. It is spread over two books of the Code, Book VI on sanctions and Book VII on processes, and its application requires jumping back and forth between books and among canons that are not even placed in chronological order, in the sense that the canons that tell you what to do next come after the canons that tell you what to do first. Elizabeth McDonough has found the order of the canons on the application of penalties so confusing that she has proposed a "friendly revision" to make the process more understandable and accessible.[51] In this friendly revision, the canons governing the canonical penal process are restated in chronological order, beginning with Canon 1717 and ending with Canon 1361!

There was also a resistance among canonists to use the penal process, especially to avoid what they feared would be a witch hunt to drive an accused priest from ministry. Francis Morrisey has written:

> We must recognize that the law does not provide for imme-diate dismissal from the clerical state. Canon 1341 considers this process as the final stage in a process of correction. Furthermore, canon 696, when speaking of cases perpetrated by religious involving minors, specifically states that dismissal need not be applied if provision can be made in some other way for the amendment of the member, the restoration of justice and the reparation of scandal. So, although there are people clamoring for the dismissal of priests, the Code takes another approach.[52]

Or, as Morrisey wrote in the same article, "Law is not always the most appropriate means whereby such matters should be treated."[53] This position of the canonists was not without support in higher circles. Patrick Lagges noted that "the Holy See has acknowledged the difficulty of applying the canons on penal process to clerical sexual misconduct cases."[54]

In addition to its bulkiness and unwieldiness, another reason why the canonical penal process was judged not suitable to the task of handling clergy who had sexually abused children was that it only would have dealt with part of the problem. It punished the cleric, but did nothing else.[55] As Francis Morrisey has written, "Those who have been involved, though, in trying to apply penalties, have generally found that such remedies do little to address the deeper issues at hand. In spite of a certain sensitivity for the dignity of the priesthood, sometimes the victims, and more especially their families, wish to see the offending priest removed perpetually from ministry. But we must recognize that this approach does not resolve many of the personal issues at stake."[56] Thomas Green is in agreement: "At times the most beneficial approach may be pastoral and therapeutic in character rather than penal, especially if the cleric's imputability is notably diminished. Concerns about his dignity, well-being, and future ministerial options are key legal-pastoral considerations."[57]

Additionally, the way the 1983 Code defined the canonical crime of the sexual abuse of a minor by the clergy was problematic. Since a minor was defined in Canon 1395, §2 as anyone sixteen years of age or under, it did not criminalize sexual acts by clergy with minors who were under eighteen, but who were older than sixteen. "Canon 1395, §2 of the revised code provides for the penalty of dismissal from the clerical state for clerics guilty of sins against the Sixth Commandment of the Decalogue with minors 'below the age of sixteen,' but not for such sins with older minors. However, many, perhaps the majority of the victims of clergy sexual abuse in the United States have been sixteen or seventeen years old when the abuse occurred."[58]

Whether it was because the penal process of the Code was bulky and unwieldy, whether it was because it was seen as treating only one part of the problem, whether it was because the penal process was seen as too harsh on priest perpetrators and unnecessarily distancing of them from the Church, or whether because too many victims were thought to be minors over the canonical age of sixteen, the American bishops turned away from the Church's legal process in the treatment of clergy sexual abuse. The law was seen as simply not being up to the task. This was a decision that would bring unwanted repercussions in the not too distant future.

3. American canonists lacked training and experience in the canonical penal process.

It is fair to conclude from the two previous sections that American canonists were uncomfortable with the canonical penal process. One reason for that discomfort may have been their lack of training and unfamiliarity with the penal process. As one canonist experienced in the area of the clerical sexual abuse of minors has written:

As professionals in the field of canon law, we have to acknowledge that to some degree we have failed to utilize effectively the penal procedures which the Church has entrusted to us. This failure is not necessarily due to a lack of good will or honest efforts on the part of those who have been involved in penal cases of this nature. It is due, rather, to a general lack of experience and specific training in using the penal process which is quite different than the much more familiar process used in adjudicating questions surrounding the nullity of marriage.[59]

A Canadian who has trained many highly regarded American canonists, Francis Morrisey admitted in 1991 that "I...have learned much canon law over the past couple of years—a law that was not necessarily the one I studied when I was in class, but one which had to be applied today."[60] And on the application of the penal law in clergy sexual abuse cases, he said, "We are traveling in largely uncharted waters."[61]

John P. Beal of the Catholic University of America canon law faculty has said much the same thing. "First, the process itself is complex, cumbersome and time-consuming and few tribunals in the United States, whose almost exclusive mission has been the expeditious processing of marriage nullity cases, have experience in using it."[62] Beal also notes that "dealing with sexual misconduct cases by the penal process has been hampered by an almost total lack of penal jurisprudence and by an almost equally total lack of experience with the process in the local churches."[63] Thomas P. Doyle, onetime canonist at the Apostolic Nunciature in Washington, D.C., stated flatly in 1990, "Canonical penal trials are rare to the point of being non-existent in this country."[64] John J. Coughlin of Notre Dame University Law School has written, "From a purely anecdotal perspective, I am unaware of a single case in the United States during the past several decades in which a priest was dismissed from the clerical state as a result of the diocesan penal process stipulated in canon law."[65]

Acknowledging canonists' lack of familiarity with the penal process, Elizabeth McDonough wrote that "canonists are encountering a variety of problems in implementing the revised canons on sanctions. Theoretically there appears to be some general reeducation needed in relation to the purpose of the penalties and to their use as a last resort."[66] Her reeducation solution would be accompanied by better training and practice aids: "A major problem confronting canonists today in the area of sanctions seems to be that there are simply not yet any readily available and workable summaries of procedures, or practical examples of decrees, or data bases for case experience (and the like) that could provide valuable basic information and serve as a handy reference for those dealing with penalties."[67]

It is remarkable that so many highly qualified canon lawyers, many of them professors of canon law, would admit, in print, that lack of training in and unfamiliarity with the Church's penal law led to its disuse in the cases of clergy sexually abusing minors. But that is exactly what occurred. There was by all accounts, at the time the clergy sexual abuse crisis broke, and as it continued to grow in the United States, a huge lacuna in the Church's canon lawyers' ability to handle it.

In defense of the canonists, a major reason for this lacuna in their knowledge is that, prior to the 1983 Code and the changes that it made in the penal process, especially in recognizing the rights of the accused, a penal process was not necessary to deal with a sexually abusive priest. A bishop had a number of other canonical tools, besides a penal trial, to adequately handle this type of conduct. In both their studies and their practice, then, there was very little reason, juridically, for canon lawyers to focus on the penal process. This goes a long way to explaining their lack of familiarity with the penal process and their admitted inability to give any form of coherent advice to the American bishops on this issue.[68]

A number of the canon lawyers interviewed by the National Review Board offered the same conclusion. As the report of the board notes:

Canon law has proven to be an inadequate method of dealing with cases of sexual abuse of minors for many reasons. First, the canonical tribunals in dioceses simply did not have the expertise to handle laicization cases. These tribunals dealt almost exclusively with annulment cases. The canonists in the tribunals had little training in the canons and the procedures relating to the punishment of clerics, including Canon 1395. The Board interviewed several individuals with degrees in canon law, and the remarks of one regarding laicization provisions captured the views of many, "This was seen as something very extreme and so you probably wouldn't be using it very much. At least that was the impression that I got when we were studying it."[69]

4. The crimes were covered by prescription.

The reasons why the canonical penal process was not used by the American bishops in their response to the sexual abuse of minors by their clergy are not limited to weaknesses in the law itself or to those trained in the law. Even if the penal law were to have been applied, there is a good chance that priest-perpetrators would have escaped canonical prosecution due to the interpretation of the canonical statute of limitations then in use in the United States. In canon law, the statute of limitations is referred to as "prescription." Canon 1362 establishes the prescriptive period for canonical crimes. It specifies that the prescriptive period or statute of limitations for the sexual abuse of minors by clergy is five years from the abusive event.[70] In the case of serial abuse, the date of the last abusive incident is the time from which the prescriptive period would run.[71]

The Ad Hoc Committee on Sexual Abuse of the National Conference of Catholic Bishops noted this fact in one of their very first reports on the crisis: "As noted, many of the claims coming to the attention of U.S. bishops were beyond the five year time of prescription in the Code of Canon Law. At this time, most claims involve conduct that occurred many years ago."[72] No matter how valid the accusations against the cleric were, if they involved sexually abusive conduct that was more than five years old, canonists saw no point in a canonical penal prosecution. This was the case even when the civil law statute of limitations on such crimes had not run. "Thus, no matter how civil jurisprudence with regard to the statute of limitations for child molestation may develop, a cleric must be summoned for judgment in an ecclesiastical forum within five years of the commission of this crime or the penal action is extinct."[73] Francis Morrisey admitted this same fact, although he seems to indicate that in at least some egregious situations the statute of limitations was being ignored:

> Can a cleric be suspended or removed from office if the events which have now come to light took place fifteen or twenty years ago and there has been no repetition of the acts? This is especially important in cases where the cleric has carried out excellent ministry in the intervening years. There are statutes of limitations in the Code, but the current climate is such that people tend to overlook them because of the social consequences.[74]

The situation was perhaps best summarized by John Beal:

> Prosecution of clerical sexual misconduct cases may be rendered impossible because of prescription. In most civil jurisdictions, the statute of limitations for the crime of sexual abuse of minors begins to run when the minor reaches his or her majority. In many states, the running of the statute of limitations is suspended when the potential defendant is physically outside the state's jurisdiction. Because of the traumatic effect sexual abuse has on children, in some jurisdictions the time from which the statute of limitations for civil suits begins to run has been set at the point when the victim can consciously appreciate the wrongness of the abusive acts and is psychologically capable of facing the meaning of these acts. Canonical prescription of a penal action for sexual misconduct with minors by clerics is much less flexible. After five years have elapsed from the time the offense was committed, the canonical penal action for sexual misconduct with minors is extinguished. When those five years have elapsed, no penal action can be brought even

if full proof both of the commission of the offense and of the cleric's imputability have become available.[75]

As John Beal noted in another article, prescription prevented the canonical prosecution of a cleric for crimes older than five years even when the priest was still a danger to commit more sexual crimes against minors. "At other times, the penal action has been extinguished by prescription, but the cleric remains at serious risk of future misconduct because of an underlying psychological disorder."[76]

There is no question that American canonists, during the entire clergy sexual abuse crisis, thought and advised that incidents of the sexual abuse of children more than five years old could not form the basis for a canonical prosecution of a cleric. But what if there was an alternative statute, one that the canonists were not familiar with? A strong argument could be made that, after the Holy Office's instruction *Crimen sollicitationis* was issued on March 16, 1962, giving the Holy Office (later the Congregation for the Doctrine of the Faith) jurisdiction over the *crimen pessimum,* yet another euphemism for the sexual abuse of minors,[77] the statute of limitations or prescriptive period for clerical sexual abuse of a minor was abolished. This follows from the fact that crimes reserved to the judgment of the Holy Office were not subject to prescription according to the 1917 Code of Canon Law in effect in 1962.[78] This exception to prescription for crimes reserved to the Holy Office was preserved in the 1983 Code. There Canon 1402 states that the procedural norms of the Code, which would include such norms as prescription, do not affect the separate norms of the tribunals of the Apostolic See, which would include the tribunals of the Congregation for the Doctrine of the Faith.[79]

If this analysis is correct, then the use of the five-year prescriptive period of Canon 1362, §1, 2° as a basis to avoid the canonical prosecution of a cleric for the sexual abuse of a minor when the abuse occurred after March 16, 1962, was wrong. While that statute may have applied to canonical penal prosecutions that remained at the diocesan level, perhaps all that had to be done to avoid the statute was for the diocese to refer the crime to the Holy Office (now Congregation for the Doctrine of the Faith) for prosecution. Once the crime was referred or reported, the reserved jurisdiction of the Congregation would have become applicable and prescription did not run against these crimes reserved to the Holy Office (Congregation for the Doctrine of the Faith).[80] This means that many abusive priests may have escaped canonical prosecution because of an honest confusion about the applicable statute of limitations.

In defense of the canonists, the problem may lie with how the instruction *Crimen sollicitationis* was promulgated in 1962. It was never published in the *Acta Apostolicae Sedis* or other definitive source for the Church's legislation. Rather, it was mailed to all of the bishops in the world with the instruction that it was to be kept in the secret archives of the diocese.[81] So by the late 1980s and early 1990s, when the clergy sexual abuse crisis was at its peak, most of the bishops who had received the instruction were either dead, were retired, or had forgotten the communication, and most canonists had never even been made aware of it.[82] In any event, the five-year statute of limitations of Canon 1362 was, even if erroneously, enforced during this critical time in the history of the Church in the United States, leaving many bishops without what would have been a critical tool to deal with the sexual abuse of a child by a cleric that came to light more than five years after the abuse.

The problem of the short statute available to diocesan tribunals was partially solved in 1994 when, at the request of the National Conference of Catholic Bishops, the Apostolic See granted a derogation for the United States on the five-year statute of limitations imposed by Canon 1362. As Thomas Green explains, "in 1994 John Paul II authorized two key derogations from the Latin Code for five years for the United States: a) the age for sexual abuse victims (c. 1395, §2) was raised from sixteen to eighteen; b) the period for prescription for pursuing a criminal case was no longer five years after the alleged delict prescinding from the alleged victim's age (m. 1362, §1...) but rather his or her twenty-eighth birthday."[83] These derogations on the age of the victim and on the prescriptive period were renewed by the Holy Father on November 30, 1998, for an additional five years until

April 25, 2009. The apostolic letter *Sacramentorum sanctitatis tutela* of April 30, 2001, extended these derogations to the universal Church.

It is obvious why American canonists were unaware of *Crimen sollicitationis*. That was due to the secret manner of its promulgation. But what rationale can be ascribed to the Apostolic See for simply not reminding the American bishops of its existence and the potential of prosecuting these crimes outside the statute by referring them to the Congregation for the Doctrine of the Faith? Why go to all the "who-struck-John" of negotiating changes in the prescriptive period with the American bishops when all that had to be done was to dust off *Crimen*? Could the Apostolic See have forgotten about the document as well? That answer is appealing, but then there is Cardinal Ratzinger's clear statement in *De delictis gravioribus* in 2001 that *Crimen sollicitationis* was *"hucusque vigens"*—in effect until now, that is, until 2001. There is no easy answer to this question, but it does indicate that the secret promulgation of legal norms can only cause trouble in a legal system.

5. The canonical penal process would have been useless since the priest's mental defects made the ultimate penalty of dismissal from the clerical state unavailable.

American canonists viewed the canonical penal process as bulky and unwieldy, as not really adequate to the problem, and as something almost foreign to them, an area of the law that they were ill-equipped to handle. Yet the Code of Canon Law clearly provided, in Canon 1395, §2, that a cleric who has offended against the sixth commandment with a minor "is to be punished with just penalties, not excluding dismissal from the clerical state if the case so warrants." And this had been the longstanding jurisprudence of the Church.

At the same time the Code criminalized this conduct, however, many canonists thought that the Code's language on imputability made it difficult, if not impossible to use the penal process to separate a sexually abusive priest from ministry on a permanent basis. Canon 1321, §1 states that "no one is punished unless the external violation of a law or precept, committed by the person is gravely imputable by reason of malice or negligence." While Canon 1321, §3 does create the presumption that an external violation of the law is imputable to the actor, "unless it is otherwise apparent," Canon 1323, 6° provides that a person who completely lacks the use of reason is considered incapable of a delict; in other words, the delict is not imputable to him. Canon 1324, §1 adds that "the penalty established by law or precept must be tempered or a penance employed in its place if the delict was committed: 1° by a person who had only the imperfect use of reason; 2° by a person who lacked the use of reason because of drunkenness or another similar culpable disturbance of mind; 3° from grave heat of passion." As Thomas Doyle has explained, "It is not enough that there is proof of a canonical crime. Other factors must be considered such as the state of mind of the accused, the circumstances under which the crime was committed and the ultimate purpose to be served by imposing a penalty."[84]

The sexual abuse of a child by an adult very often indicates that the adult perpetrator is a mentally disturbed individual although the depth of the mental disturbance will vary from individual to individual. If the sexual abuse perpetrated by a priest on a child was due to one of the possible paraphilias, such as pedophilia[85] or ephebophilia,[86] then it could be argued that the priest was not operating with his full mental capacities. This, in turn, meant that under the Code sections just cited, the ultimate penalty of dismissal from the clerical state was not available in the penal process because there could not be full or grave imputability for the priest's wrongful acts.

This point of view came into prominence very early in the crisis. As John Proctor wrote in 1987:

> A variety of conditions and/or factors affect imputability. Most of these conditions/factors would be recognizable by modern medical practice as psychological problems. The list would include: insanity, fear, ignorance, psychological impairment, alcoholism and drunkenness (even if drunkenness is deliberate), drug use or addiction, senility, affective or psychosexual disorders, provocation, judicial invention, and cultural or local circumstances. Although the law presumes imputability in the occurrence of an external viola-

tion, this presumption can be overturned, something which will frequently happen in these circumstances.[87]

In summarizing the position of those canonists who thought that the sexual passion involved in canonical crimes *contra sextum* invariably limited imputability for such crimes, a position with which he did not sympathize, Bertram F. Griffin explained:

> Other canonists argue that sins against the sixth commandment of the Decalogue are "sins of the flesh" and should be treated as *crimes passionel* in the continental sense. A crime of passion is not exempt from a penalty for transgression of a law but the penalty set by the law must be tempered unless of course, the passion totally impedes the use of reason (in which case no penalty is applicable) or the passion is voluntarily stirred up or fostered (in which case full imputability is presumed). Some would argue that the heat of sexual passion at the time of any sin against the sixth commandment excuses from the full rigor of the law though of course, not from all penalty.[88]

Francis Morrisey's approach to the problem was very humanistic. In 1991, he wrote:

> Even if [the priest] did commit the act, the question of imputability must also be examined carefully. At times, we may be placing too many burdens on priests' shoulders, or leaving them in impossible living conditions, and they simply snap under the pressure. For some the break could be manifested by an abuse of alcohol; for others, problems with money; for others, sexual difficulties with various categories of persons, and so forth. Without overlooking the existence of sin and evil, it would be important to determine whether the priest is solely to blame for what happened, or whether other factors have been quite significant in leading up to the events.[89]

A year later, in 1992, John Beal explained the canonical paradox in detail:

> Canonical penalties can only be imposed when an offense is "seriously imputable" to the person (c. 1321, §1). Imputability is presumed whenever an external violation has occurred "unless it appears *(appareat)* otherwise" (c. 1321, §3). However, this presumption of imputability may be rather easily rebutted in clerical sexual misconduct cases. Sexual disorders are often characterized by a high degree of compulsivity that may diminish or extinguish an offender's freedom. Moreover, sexual misconduct is often associated with drug or alcohol abuse or addiction. In fact, the more treatment an offender has received for sexual misconduct, the more evidence there is likely to be that he acted with diminished capacity. If an offender's imputability is wholly extinguished, he is not liable to any penalty (c. 1323).[90]

Beal concluded that "a cleric's diminished capacity may render it impossible for the judges to impose the most severe penalty of dismissal from the clerical state of a cleric guilty of sexual misconduct."[91] William H. Woestman, of the St. Paul University canon law faculty, emphasized the praxis of the Apostolic See when he pointed out the difficulty of a penal process against a mentally disturbed priest: "The practice of the Holy See is to impose non-voluntary transfer from the clerical state, only if the cleric has been convicted in an ecclesiastical tribunal of serious crimes. However, such conviction can be difficult to obtain because of diminished responsibility caused by psychological illness."[92]

In the midst of the crisis, the American bishops seem to have accepted the canonists' position that, due to the alleged diminished mental capacity of a sexual abuser of a minor, the canonical penal process would not be worth the trouble, inasmuch as at the end of it, the full penalty of dismissal from the clerical state could not be imposed on the abusive priest due to his likely defense of diminished mental capacity.[93] In his report on this topic, which was discussed at the

November 1992 meeting of the bishops' conference, Thomas J. Reese, editor of *America* magazine, described the bishops' belief:

> The code of canon law has numerous provisions protecting priests from dismissal by authoritarian bishops. Psychological illness, which is prevalent among priest abusers, would be grounds for dismissing a case against a priest. The law is aimed at protecting psychologically sick priests from simply being dumped by their bishops. This makes it almost impossible for bishops to dismiss priests for sexual abuse....[94]

> As the bishops' own Ad Hoc Committee on Sexual Abuse reported in 1993, "In addition, because these claims involved psychological incapacity on the part of clerics, there was some question whether a sentence of dismissal from the clerical state could be sustained."[95]

This problem with the Church's penal process was also noted in the report of the bishops' National Review Board: "The canon law process for dealing with sexual abuse cases was impeded further by the concept of 'imputability,' which provided that the penalty of laicization could not be handed down if the priest or his advocate were able to show that the priest was not completely responsible for his actions because of an illness or some other psychological condition. Thus, the worst predators, who actually had been diagnosed as pedophiles or as suffering from some other 'illness,' paradoxically were the most difficult to laicize under canon law."[96]

In steering the bishops away from canonical criminal processes against sexually abusive priests, because it was thought that full imputability could not be established, canonists did not leave the bishops without an alternative. Just as the inadequacy of the canonical process was thought to point the Church's response to the clergy's sexual abuse of children toward a nonjudicial, therapeutic approach, so, too, the diminished imputability of a "mentally disturbed" priest also pointed in this direction. In 1987, James Proctor wrote: "Both the pastoral nature of Church law and its requirements for establishing full imputability in the penal process argue at least implicitly (if not explicitly) for the desirability of non-penal models when misconduct associations are found to have some merit."[97] And "furthermore, because of the almost certain presence of diminished (if not totally mitigated) imputability, it is difficult to envision the usefulness of the penal process. A therapeutic model is definitely to be preferred."[98] As history demonstrates, this therapeutic model was the alternative that the bishops fastened onto.

> 6. The rights of the accused priest, including his appeal rights, would trump the canonical penal process.

In the canonical penal process, the accused person can appeal not only a finding of guilt and the imposition of a penalty, he can also appeal a finding of guilt even when no penalty is imposed.[99] An appeal or recourse from a judicial sentence suspends the execution of the sentence.[100] Since an appeal suspends the sentence, a priest found guilty of the sexual abuse of a child in a canonical penal process in which the judges have imposed on him the penalty of dismissal from the clerical state remains a priest, with all of the rights of a priest, until the appeal is decided. As Michael O'Reilly has written:

> Often priests and deacons who have been guilty of crimes mentioned in canon 1395 refuse to seek spontaneously permission to return to the lay state, rendering it necessary to institute a penal judicial process. On the other hand, by reason of the canonical norms, such processes are inevitably long, especially in the case of an appeal, when the priest or deacon still remains in the clerical state. This causes serious scandal among the faithful and casts a shadow on the image of the Church, as well as causing very serious material harm to the Church in different countries.[101]

The fear that Rome would reverse them on appeals by priests who had been found guilty in diocesan tribunals of the sexual abuse of a child resonated with the American bishops. As was reported by the National Review Board:

In addition, process often took precedence over substance. Under canon law, some convictions could be reversed by tribunals in Rome years after the fact because of a failure to follow all technical procedural requirements, injecting the potential for inordinate delays into cases that did go forward. One bishop told us that his fellow bishops avoided recourse to canon law because they "weren't sure where Rome would come down," adding that "it was extremely hard to press your case in Rome and be sure that you would be heard." Another [bishop] told the Board, "We were all very hesitant to do a canonical trial because if there's any procedural flaw in it you can easily be overturned on appeal to Rome."[102]

Canonical penal processes are complicated proceedings, and just as in criminal prosecutions by the state, the rights of the accused must be respected. Given that American canonists had already expressed the fear that they were not adequately trained in the penal process, the idea that they would be error-prone in carrying it out is not difficult to accept.

In the midst of the clergy sexual abuse crisis, there appeared to be affirmation that Rome would indeed favor the rights of accused priests over those of the diocese. In a notorious case involving a Pittsburgh diocesan priest who was charged with child sexual abuse, Rome in fact did overturn the judgment of the diocesan bishop that the man was unfit for ministry. The priest had been criminally charged with the sexual abuse of a minor in 1978, but the charges were dropped when the youth and his family chose not to go forward with them.[103] In 1988, another young man came forward with similar charges in a civil suit against the priest and the diocese.[104] After a psychiatric evaluation and the priest's refusal to undergo further treatment, the bishop decreed him impeded from ministry due to a psychological infirmity, under Canon 1044, §2, 2o.[105]

Pursuant to Canon 1737, §1, the priest appealed this decree of the bishop to the Congregation for Clergy, which upheld the bishop.[106] There then followed an appeal by the priest from the decree of the

Congregation for Clergy to the Supreme Tribunal of the Apostolic Signatura under Canon 1445, §2.[107] This case proceeded administratively, and not judicially, since a canonical penal process was not instituted against the priest. But the analogy to the canonical penal process is apt in terms of gauging Rome's response to a diocesan bishop's treatment of a sexually abusive priest. In fact, it should be noted that, in a canonical penal process, an accused priest actually has more rights than he would have in an administrative process. As John Beal has pointed out, an administrative process "does not demand for the legality of actions of administrators the same scrupulous observance of formalities of procedural law that are required in judicial processes."[108] In other words, it is easier to err in a criminal process than in an administrative process.

The Apostolic Signatura, much to the shock of American Catholics, ordered the priest to be reinstated, finding that the diocesan bishop had not met his burden in the administrative process of demonstrating the priest's lack of fitness for ministry.[109] This decision was all the more difficult for the diocese to accept, given the fact that it was not a party to the appeal of the priest to the Apostolic Signatura. The parties in the second appeal, after the Congregation for Clergy had upheld the diocesan bishop, were the priest and the Congregation for Clergy, and not the diocese. In fact, the diocese was not even aware of the substance of the priest's appeal to the Signatura, and found out about the Signatura's decision reinstating the priest by reading about it in the Pittsburgh newspapers after the priest's civil attorney, contrary to the rules of the Signatura, had released a copy of the Signatura's decision to the press.[110]

This is no way to run a railroad, let alone a Church trying to deal, under extreme public scrutiny, with the very serious problem of the sexual abuse of minors by its clergy. Whether the impression was correct or not, this case reinforced the fear of many American bishops and their canonists that Rome was set to overturn them in a heartbeat when they dealt with sexually abusive priests. The Signatura's decision became public in March 1993, and it was the topic of unofficial discussion at the June 1993 national meeting of the American bishops. A report of the June 1993 meeting stated, "Every ranking bishop questioned recalled the case immediately and expressed concern over it. 'I certainly felt it was a most unfortunate thing to do,' Cardinal John O'Connor of New York said."[111] In the same report, Cardinal Joseph Bernardin is quoted, "I've expressed concern about it to many people since I heard it," and Cardinal Anthony Bevilacqua said, "I think every bishop is concerned."[112]

The thought of the American bishops and canonists was, "If this is the burden a diocese must sustain in an administrative case, dealing not with dismissal from the clerical state, but a suspension for psychological reasons, then penal cases against priests will be even harder to sustain on appeal to the Apostolic See." Although it is not known how many times priests suspended by their bishops because of child sexual abuse claims made successful appeals to Rome during this time, a legitimate inference is that it happened in more cases than the one reported from Pittsburgh.[113] Monsignor Francis Maniscalco, official spokesperson for the bishops' conference, is on the record stating that "some suspended priests have won reinstatement from the Vatican, and others went back to work with the consent—sometimes even the insistence—of [Vatican] congregations."[114]

7. The cooperation of the victim could not be counted on and was not sought.

When a minor or a minor's family brought to the attention of the Church the claim that a priest had sexually abused the minor, the last thing that the minor or the family wanted was to be drawn into a lengthy ecclesiastical penal process. The raw emotions of such a claim do not easily admit to channeling into a matter of sworn statements and depositions that the Church's legal system requires. The family typically wanted fast action, "getting rid" of the priest so that he would not harm other children, and it did not matter how that fast action occurred, as long as it happened and happened quickly.[115] As John Beal has described the situation: "When victims or their families approach church authorities with accusations of sexual misconduct, their immediate concerns are often that they be taken seriously and that the church official act promptly and responsibly to insure that the accused cleric does not victimize others."[116]

To a certain extent, this created a double bind for the bishops, since a canonical penal process is anything but quick. As Francis Morrisey has described the problem, "Experience shows that the Church has to be able to act quickly when such painful situations arise; yet at the same time it must act prudently and wisely so as not to deprive the person against whom the allegations are made of the right to a fair trial."[117]

In a canonical penal process, the first stage is a preliminary investigation to determine if a basis exists in fact for a canonical penal process to go forward. The charges must have at least the appearance of truth.[118] Only after a preliminary investigation is complete may an accused priest be removed from his assignment.[119] As part of this preliminary investigation, the child victim will have to make some form of a statement to the investigator that can constitute the basis of charges against the priest. If the investigation determines that there are grounds to proceed, then a charge (a *libellus*) is drawn up against the accused by the promoter of justice. There is the normal notification and so forth, but eventually in a judicial penal process, which was the only way to seek the penalty of dismissal from the clerical state,[120] the promoter of justice would have to substantiate the charges against the priest before a panel of three judges with appropriate proofs.[121] These proofs will necessarily include the testimony of witnesses.[122] Children below the age of fourteen are not allowed to be witnesses in canonical processes, unless a judge were to rule their testimony expedient.[123] In an abuse situation, very often the child will be the only witness of what happened, which of course would render the testimony more than expedient.

This obviously creates a situation of some delicacy. Normally, witnesses are to testify in front of the tribunal,[124] which in cases of priestly sexual abuse of a minor would be a panel of three priest judges.[125] The child, who has alleged sexual abuse by one of the Church's priests, must now talk to not one, but three priests, with yet a fourth priest acting as notary to take down the testimony.[126] Under canonical process, the accused priest cannot be there, unless the judges have decided to admit his presence, but his advocate who might be a fifth priest can be there.[127] At the tribunal, only the judges can question a witness.[128] Canonical penal trials, unlike American criminal trials, do not permit the witnesses to be cross-examined. The promoter of justice and the advocate for the accused priest do not have a right to question any witness, although either side may suggest questions to be asked by the judges.

There is a way around some of this unpleasantness for a child witness. Canon 1558, §1 states, "Witnesses must be examined at the tribunal *unless the judge deems otherwise*" (emphasis added). In the case of witnesses who are children, it would seem possible, then, for one priest-judge from the collegiate panel and a priest-notary to take the child's testimony outside of the actual hearing, or even for a delegate of the judge to do so, perhaps someone expert at interviewing children.[129] But even this lower-keyed approach to involving the child and his family in the penal process is not without its difficulties. As John Beal has written:

> If the initial assessment leads to a further investigation in preparation for a penal process, it may be necessary to translate the victim's story into the form of a sworn denunciation. It may also be necessary to take depositions from family members and others with knowledge of the misconduct. In the emotionally charged context of these cases, both intimating the need for depositions and actually taking the testimony require the utmost sensitivity and discretion.[130]

This again points out the double bind that the bishops found themselves in: the need to proceed on serious charges against accused priests while at the same time not seeming to put pressure on the alleged child victims. As James Provost said, "Bishops also have a special responsibility towards victims and their families. Given the trauma they have experienced through a cleric's misconduct, they may be reluctant to turn to the usual sources of pastoral care, or may be even incapable of doing this."[131] If victims and their families had trouble accepting pastoral care from the diocese that had injured them, how much more difficult would it have been to accept that same diocese's invitation to participate in a contentious legal process, a legal process staffed by priests of the diocese, where the judges were chosen by the diocesan bishop, who himself holds full judicial power?[132] The question barely survives its statement. It seems too much to ask, or, at least, so it was thought by those who ought to have done the asking.

An excerpt from the response of the Archdiocese of Philadelphia to the report of the investigating Grand Jury illustrates this situation. Although it speaks of the abused minor's participation in a state criminal proceeding, the Church's concerns would be the same in a canonical penal process:

> The situation when a minor is sexually abused is complex. The initial reporting decision is controlled by the parents. It has been the experience of the Archdiocese that many parents do not wish to subject their children to questions by police, do not wish to have their children cross-examined at preliminary hearings or at the trial of the accused; they prefer instead to seek counseling to treat the damage to the child and put the events behind the child and its family.[133]

Added to the natural reluctance of making a child relive his or her sexual abuse by participating in a canonical penal process, there was the advice of attorneys working to defend the Church that drove the bishops away from any contact with alleged victims. As the report of the National Review Board states, the views of one bishop on relying on attorneys are instructive:

> We made terrible mistakes. Because the attorneys said over and over "Don't talk to victims, don't go near them," and here they were victims. I heard victims say, "We would not have taken it [further] had someone just come to us and said, 'I'm sorry.'" But we listened to the attorneys.[134]

With their lawyers telling them not to talk to victims, it was difficult for bishops to ask victims to participate in a canonical penal process against the accused priest. And without the participation of the victim, who was often the only witness to what were, by their nature, private actions involving perpetrator and victim, there was no direct proof against the priest on which to base a finding of guilt. As outlined in the report of the cardinal's commission in Chicago in a description of civil trials, but true also of canonical processes: "In child sexual abuse cases, there are usually no witnesses to the alleged misconduct, at least no witnesses willing to come forward into the public arena of the courtroom. It is often difficult for young victims to testify."[135]

Seeing the situation this way, the bishops took the path of least resistance and did not seek the victim's assistance in a penal process against the accused priest, assistance that they were in no way assured of, but, instead, turned to extrajudicial means to address the clergy's sexual abuse of minors.

8. Civil lawyers strongly advised against a canonical penal process because of the discoverability of the acts.

As Francis Morrisey wrote, in the area of clergy sexual abuse of a minor, there was "the renewed propensity of certain people to have recourse to the courts each time there was a complaint, legitimate or not. The litigious characteristic of some people spilled over into Church matters."[136] Not only did this litigious characteristic spill over, there are those who would say that it was allowed to hijack the canonical penal process. Were a bishop to proceed against a cleric on charges of the sexual abuse of a minor under Canon 1395, §2, there is little doubt that the "acts" of the canonical penal process, that is to say, the written redactions of the testimony of the witnesses, the accuser, and the accused, together with any other documents used as evidence and the briefs filed by the promoter of justice and the advocate for the accused cleric, would be "discoverable" in civil law.

The Code requires that such acts be kept in writing,[137] and that they be "published," which means that they are available to the parties for their review.[138] No assertion of confidentiality would protect these documents from the subpoena of a civil lawyer who had commenced a lawsuit against the diocese on the basis of the cleric's misconduct. It was thus advised by some civil lawyers who worked on behalf of American dioceses, or rather who worked for the insurance carriers of American dioceses, that a canonical process should not be pursued, since it would, by virtue of the "discoverability" of the acts, "hand a case to the plaintiff." There is no doubt that fear of civil litigation stilled a number of bishops' hands.[139] As Francis Morrisey warned, "If there is a possibility of civil litigation, the dioceses or institute should obtain the advice of its lawyers to ensure that its civil position is not jeopardized by steps taken in pursuance of the canonical procedure."[140]

This issue was also lamented by Elizabeth McDonough: "Particularly problematic of late has been an apparent preference for following purely or primarily American civil law advice in penal cases, sometimes even to the exclusion or violation of canonical requirements."[141] In that same presentation, she also said, "the canonical legal system certainly should not be ignored or abused by canonists and competent ecclesiastical authorities in preference to civil law advise *(sic)* in seeking to avoid 'deep-pocket' consequences."[142] In his report of the bishops' discussions at the November 1992 meeting of the bishops' conference, Thomas Reese wrote, "There is also some fear [among the bishops] that those involved in an ecclesiastical trial would be subpoenaed for civil and criminal trials."[143]

The same point was made ten years later by Gregory Ingels in an April 2002 presentation to the National Federation of Priests' councils: "It also appears that those in authority are being guided by civil attorneys, insurance companies or others not familiar with canonical rights or procedures."[144] Or as explained in the report of the National Review Board, "As a general matter, as one bishop observed, 'the Church has not always been served well in a legal way.' Indeed, it appears that many dioceses and orders made disastrous pastoral decisions relying on attorneys who failed to adapt their tactics to account for the unique role and responsibilities of the Church."[145]

D. SUMMARY

On its own, perhaps none of the above eight reasons was suffi-cient for the bishops to turn away from the Church's legal system in their attempts to confront the problem of the sexual abuse of children by their priests. But these rationalizations were not at work individu-ally. They were all part of a set that effectively describes the canonical landscape in the United States as this crisis was breaking. Each influ-enced and gave weight to the others and together they created a mind-set among the bishops that the canonical penal system simply was not worth the trouble. Not only was it cumbersome, it was not apt for the problem and probably would not provide the results sought. Worse, it could even cause additional trouble for the bishop in terms of aggra-vating victims or encouraging their litigation against the Church.

The sky was falling, and there appeared to be no source of sup-port in sight. But what the bishops missed in all of this was the true value of the canonical penal system, and its ability to protect the Church from harm by dealing honestly with offenses when they occurred. As John Beal reminded the bishops at the time, "What church officials can do to shore up the falling sky is to follow the Church's own canon law when faced with allegations of clerical sexual misconduct."[146] At this critical time, the Church in the United States was deprived of the benefits of its own legal system, a system centuries old, that provided a sure, time-tested way to handle the crime of the sexual abuse of a child by a priest, namely a penal process with the pos-sibility of the penalty of dismissal from the clerical state if the charges against the priest were proven. As Cardinal Julian Herranz, president of the Pontifical Council for Legislative Texts, has said, canon law "'provides all the trial and punishment tools necessary' to mete out jus-tice and protect the community in clerical sex abuse cases."[147]

4

WHAT DID THE BISHOPS DO?

A. EARLY REACTIONS AND THE MANUAL

While the National Conference of Catholic Bishops reported receiving information from two unnamed dioceses regarding the sexual molestation of children by priests as early as 1982,[1] the dam did not break nationally until the Gauthe case. Following the indictment of Father Gauthe in the Diocese of Lafayette in 1984, things began to unravel rather quickly. Other victims of other priests came forward, and Lafayette was soon facing charges involving at least three of its priests.[2] The original Gauthe story was picked up and amplified by the national media.[3] Among all the national publicity, the National Conference of Catholic Bishops put the topic of the sexual abuse of children by clergy on the agenda for its June 1985 meeting in Collegeville, Minnesota.

The Apostolic Nunciature in Washington, D.C., had been monitoring the crisis in Lafayette through Father Thomas P. Doyle, OP, a canonist on the delegation's staff. Father Doyle had put F. Ray Mouton, the lawyer defending Father Gauthe, in touch with Father Michael Peterson, the head of St. Luke Institute, a psychiatric treatment facility near Washington, D.C. When Mouton came to Washington to discuss the possibility of Gauthe's admission to St. Luke's for treatment in January 1985, a face-to-face meeting of Doyle, Mouton, and Peterson was quickly arranged. As Doyle describes it:

> The three of us were of the opinion that now that the Gauthe case had become public and received so much publicity from coast to coast, that the entire issue would no longer be able to be contained by Church leaders....We

47

decided, on our own, to try and write something to give to the bishops to assist them in dealing with the cases that we predicted would start to appear with increasing regularity....The original idea was to compose a manual containing information about the issue from different approaches: canon law, civil law, criminal law, insurance, pastoral practice, medical. The manual would be given to the NCCB in hopes that they would take some kind of action. We were not commissioned to write it and did so entirely on our own with no backing, financial or otherwise, from anyone.[4]

The coauthors discussed their ideas with Bishop A. James Quinn, auxiliary of Cleveland, a civil and canon lawyer who had been asked by the apostolic nuncio to keep an eye on things in Louisiana and who, Doyle says, encouraged the project, urging the authors to use a question-based format that would cover as many aspects of the problem as possible.[5] Once completed, the name given to this report by its three authors was "The Problem of Sexual Molestation by Roman Catholic Clergy: Meeting the Problem in a Comprehensive and Responsible Manner," although it has since become known simply as the Manual.

Doyle had sent draft sections to John Cardinal Krol of Philadelphia, who, Doyle says, was in favor of the project. Cardinal Krol, according to Doyle, took up the report with Bernard Cardinal Law of Boston, who promised to get the report assigned to a subcommittee of the National Conference of Catholic Bishops' Committee on Pastoral Practices and Research, of which he was chair, for further action. A final draft was completed on May 14, 1985, and later that month, Doyle, Peterson, and Mouton met with Archbishop William Levada, then of Portland in Oregon, who was the secretary of the Pastoral Practices and Research Committee, and who, says Doyle, "was positive about progress."[6] Shortly after their meeting, however, Doyle says that Archbishop Levada telephoned him to say that another committee of the National Conference of Catholic Bishops, not Cardinal Law's committee, would deal with the matter. Doyle had heard that this might be the National Conference of Catholic Bishops'

Committee on Priestly Life, but when Doyle met that June with Bishop Anthony Bevilacqua, then of Pittsburgh, and three years later to become archbishop of Philadelphia, he got the impression that "no committee and no action was planned. It was merely a PR move to announce it."[7]

Although the Manual had been prepared by its authors with the evident hope that it would be presented to the National Conference of Catholic Bishops at its June 1985 meeting as a part of the bishops' discussion of the clergy sexual abuse crisis, it was not. Rather, in their executive session, the bishops were briefed on the topic by Richard Issel, a psychologist-consultant for the Archdiocese of Chicago; Bishop Kenneth Angell, auxiliary of Providence, Rhode Island; and attorney Wilfrid Caron, the general counsel for the National Conference of Catholic Bishops.[8] No action was taken by the National Conference of Catholic Bishops on the matter, however. The briefing was for informational purposes only. As the Bishops' Ad Hoc Committee on Sexual Abuse described that meeting:

> In 1985, for the first time, sexual abuse claims were also discussed in a closed meeting of diocesan attorneys and in executive session of the National Conference of Catholic Bishops. That latter meeting, held in Collegeville, Minn., featured a presentation by a psychiatrist, a lawyer and a bishop on aspects of the problem of child molestation. It offered basic information to bishops and allowed for discussion to be held with, and questions to be asked, of the panel. Although this meeting was closed to the press and the public, media reports offered some insight into the difficult nature of the problem there discussed. For the first time, bishops were facing a most horrific and difficult problem, seeking guidance of experts and proposing tentative approaches.[9]

Almost from the moment it first saw the light of day, the relevance of the Manual to the bishops' future handling of claims of the sexual abuse of minors by their clergy has been a matter of some contention and not an unimportant part of the canonical history of those times. In a 1989 sexual abuse lawsuit brought in the U.S. District Court for the Southern District of Mississippi, Monsignor Daniel Hoye, then-general secretary of the National Conference of Catholic Bishops, submitted an affidavit regarding the Manual. In it, he stated:

> Only a limited number of copies of that report were ever distributed in June 1985 at the Collegeville meeting. The total number is likely to have been less than 20, although I have no way of knowing the exact number. The report was not generally available to all bishops, was not on their agenda for discussion, was not raised by anyone for discussion, and thus was never the subject of any vote of approval or disapproval. More importantly, it was neither offered nor adopted as the basis for national policy at that or any other time.[10]

In their committee report on the actions of the bishops, the National Conference of Catholic Bishops' Ad Hoc Committee on Sexual Abuse described these events as follows:

> During the Collegeville meeting, the report was circulated to a handful of bishops, it is believed, largely for comment. When the Collegeville meeting nonetheless featured presentations by other experts on how best to respond to claims, the gist of the report, to a certain extent, became overtaken by events. The conference was facing the problem directly.[11]

Peterson spent the summer of 1985 writing an Executive Summary to the Manual. On December 9, 1985, Father Peterson sent each bishop in the United States a copy of the revised Manual, with the Executive Summary, as a mailing from St. Luke Institute, which he headed.[12] The Manual was marked "Confidential," and included the following statement at the start of the Executive Summary:

> *CONFIDENTIAL NOTE:* Please treat the contents of this document as confidential. Further, it is my opinion that the contents of this document are my professional and personal

remarks and should not be construed as a national plan for the National Conference of Catholic Bishops, for Major Superiors of religious communities. The professional and personal opinions are given individually to each person who has possession of this document for their personal reaction and for one psychiatric approach to dealing with this complex moral, legal, and psychiatric problem. [Signed, Rev. Michael R. Peterson, M.D.]

The bishops' Ad Hoc Committee on Sexual Abuse reported these events as follows:

In the fall [of 1985], Father Michael Peterson, one of the report's authors, sent a copy of the text as an appendix to a document prepared by St. Luke Institute describing some of the medical issues presented by child molestation. Each diocesan bishop received a copy of that report. As explained in the report itself, it was not prepared as a proposal to the NCCB and never offered by its authors, or by Father Peterson subsequently, as the definitive text of an approach to dealing with child molestation....Subsequent press characterizations of the report as a proposal to the conference that had been either summarily ignored or rejected are inaccurate.[13]

In August 1986, Peterson wrote to all of the bishops yet again, this time forwarding to them certain changes that Doyle had made in the canonical section of the Manual. While in the original draft, Doyle had advised suspension of accused priests while charges were being investigated, he now was advising "administrative leave."[14]

Despite its supposedly confidential nature, the contents of the Manual were soon leaked to the press with the implication that, by ignoring it, the bishops had failed to take effective collective action to address the problem of the sexual abuse of children by its clergy.[15] It is thus rather important to examine the contents of the Manual to determine exactly what advice it did provide to the bishops.

The Manual "consisted of four main parts, covering civil law, canon law, criminal law, and insurance and medical considerations. Among the key proposals were the immediate removal from [assignment] of a priest accused of sexual misconduct, pending investigation; the creation of a national team of experts to help in that investigation; and a fundamental challenge to bishops who viewed such priests through the prism of sin alone, rather than psychology and law."[16]

With its turn to psychology, the Manual is an unabashed endorsement of the therapeutic approach to the problem of clergy sexual abuse of minors, as one might expect from one coauthor who was head of a treatment facility and another who was a defense lawyer who had tried to have his priest-client plead guilty and serve his time, not in a prison, but in a psychiatric care facility.[17] As the Manual states, "The Ordinary should re-assure the priest or cleric that he will support him legally and financially and that he will also help him to obtain evaluation and treatment for his problems."[18] And "as soon as the Ordinary has ascertained that there is some truth to the allegations of sexual abuse by a cleric, arrangements should be made the same day or the following day at the latest for the priest's transfer to an evaluation center."[19] And "the priest must clearly be seen as one suffering from a psychiatric disorder that is beyond his ability to control."[20]

To be fair, there is much in the Manual to commend it. Certainly its prediction of a billion dollars in tort liability for the Church in the United States has come true, as have its dire predictions for the public embarrassment of the Church and the diminution of its moral authority should this problem not be dealt with in a comprehensive fashion. Its recommendation that joint action by the bishops was the only way to address the crisis was also correct, something that the bishops did not comprehend until 2002. The Manual is also clear that for some priests who have sexually abused children there is "the real possibility that they are almost totally unfit to be priests."[21] To its credit, the Manual also reminded the bishops that "failure to report information regarding sexual molestation of a child by a priest when such information is available or in the possession of the Ordinary, is considered a criminal offense in some states. Secondly, to allow a priest to continue to function, endangering the health of children, following the receipt of private, confidential knowledge that this priest victimized a child is considered to be 'criminal neglect' (a crime in many states)."[22] The Manual also rejected out of hand the suggestion, later made by Bishop Quinn from Cleveland, that sensitive documents regarding priest-abusers be sent to the Vatican Embassy in Washington, D.C., where they would be beyond the reach of civil authorities. "In all likelihood," the Manual states, "such action would ensure that the immunity of the Nunciature would be damaged or destroyed by the civil courts."[23]

The canonical section of the Manual, authored by Doyle, correctly points out the difficulties of the canonical penal process:

> Although the law includes dismissal from the clerical state (laicization) as a possible penalty for the offenses mentioned in canons 1387 and 1395, this penalty may not always be imposed on those guilty of sexual crimes not excluding pedophilia. Canon 1324, 1, 1°, 2°, 3° indicates that the penalty prescribed by law or precept must be diminished if the culprit had only imperfect use of reason; lacked use of reason because of culpable drunkenness or other mental disturbance of a similar kind; acted in the heat of passion, which, while serious, nevertheless did not precede or hinder all mental deliberation and consent of the will, provided that the passion itself was not deliberately stimulated.

> As is obvious from the above paragraph, it is possible to dismiss a cleric from the clerical state if he committed canonical crimes involving sexual misconduct. Yet if he acted under the influence of one or more of the conditions mentioned in canon 1324 it is not possible to impose the extreme penalty allowed, namely dismissal.[24]

In such situations, the canonical section states that:

> It may happen that situations arise when dismissal is seen to be the only viable course of action but when, at the same

time, a court process is ill-advised or impossible. In such cases only the Holy See has the power to issue a rescript whereby a priest or deacon is reduced from the clerical state. It is possible for the Holy Father to *ex officio* laicize a man when it appears that no other course of action is advised. In such cases, the cleric's local ordinary should prepare the petition for laicization and send it, together with all pertinent material, to the Congregation for the Doctrine of the Faith. The relative urgency of the case will determine the alacrity with which the case is handled in Rome.[25]

But the Manual is not nearly strong enough on the critical issues of transparency and openness to the faithful that would eventually begin to solve this problem. It speaks, for example, of "pleadings to protect the confidentiality of the process" in court cases, and of "suppressing or quashing subpoenas for Diocesan Records."[26] Further, in its legal section it does not address the tort theories of negligent supervision and negligent entrustment that eventually led to massive diocesan legal liability for the acts of its priests.[27] In its canonical section, it mentions a form of *ex officio* laicization that was not available in 1985, and, as noted above, its canonical advice of suspension without warnings or of "administrative leave" for accused priests is problematical.[28]

Although the assembled bishops did not hear the authors of the Manual, other audiences did. In May 1986, Doyle and Mouton and Dr. Stephen Montana, a psychologist at St. Luke Institute in Washington, were featured speakers at the Eastern Regionals of the Canon Law Society of America held at Morristown, New Jersey. As reported by the *New York Times,* Mouton told the assembled canonists that "the Roman Catholic Church cannot credibly exert moral authority externally in any area where the public perceives it as incapable of maintaining moral authority internally."[29] Doyle was quoted as saying that "when a case of abuse has been proved church officials should disclose it to parishioners rather than secretly shuttle an offender to another parish, as…they often did in the past," and "that the desire to avoid publicity, coupled with 'extreme moral judgmentalism in matters of sex,' hampered efforts to solve problems with sexual abuse, which he said were inevitable."[30] Doyle also "cautioned against trying to bully a family into dropping a complaint. 'You don't send some imperious cleric out there to show them how bad they should feel about dragging the church's name through the mud,' he said."[31] A year after the Manual was written, this is a different tack than the original document, which seems to endorse the use of confidentiality agreements and the protection of confidential Church records.

In July 1987, the Canonical Affairs Committee of the National Conference of Catholic Bishops prepared and sent to the bishops a document entitled, "Dismissal from the Clerical State in Cases of Sexual Crimes Against Minors."[32] The text is a very comprehensive canonical "how-to" on the dismissal of sexually abusive priests using the canonical penal process. In their text, the Canonical Affairs Committee states clearly, "Canon 1395 #2 provides for a just penalty, even to the gravity of dismissal from the clerical state if the cleric has violated the sixth commandment with a minor below the age of sixteen."[33] The committee also notes, however, that there is a very short period in which to charge a cleric with this crime. "Prescription or the statute of limitations in canon law applies to a penal process for crimes mentioned in Canon 1395. If the situation is that of pederasty or statutory rape, the procedure and trial must be initiated by the promoter of justice before the period of 5 years has passed from either the commission of one action or the cessation of a series of actions."[34]

In terms of the application of Canon 1341, the committee states:

> If the certitude of a crime of pederasty or statutory rape is there, various options are open to the diocesan bishop. Removal from office, mandatory counseling and therapy, and if necessary, suspension should precede other penal actions and should attempt to encourage a change of behavior.

> Before initiating action for dismissal, the diocesan bishop should attempt to encourage the cleric voluntarily to petition the Holy See for a rescript of laicization. Dismissal from the clerical state is always a last resort (Canon 1341) and

imposed only because of obstinate persistence by the perpe-trator or because the requirements of justice and the repara-tion of scandal cannot be achieved in any other manner.[35]

In their assessment, the bishops' Canonical Affairs Committee was on the same page as their academic colleagues. As did the professors of canon law, the committee saw the problems with prescription, or the short, five-year canonical statute of limitations. The committee also saw the problems caused by Canon 1341, which makes penal action the last resort against an offending priest. The committee also repeats the prevailing wisdom that therapy and a chance to reform the offender should precede any attempt to penalize the priest. This document is a fair description of the canonical conundrums in which the bishops saw themselves in 1987, in their attempt to deal with the burgeoning clergy child sexual abuse crisis.

In executive session at their November 1987 meeting, the bish-ops heard a presentation from the chair of the Canonical Affairs Committee, then-Bishop Adam J. Maida of Green Bay, Wisconsin, entitled "A Focus for Canonical and Civil Law Issues in Pedophilia Cases." In his talk, Bishop Maida, a highly experienced civil lawyer and eminent canonist, explained how the two legal systems under which dioceses in the United States act, the Church's own canonical system and the civil legal system, treat the crime of the sexual abuse of minors. He first explained to the assembled bishops the canonical means for dealing with priests who sexually abused youngsters. He described the administrative process in which an abusive priest can himself request a decree of laicization from the Congregation for the Doctrine of the Faith. He then described the praxis of the Apostolic See when the abu-sive priest himself will not make the request:

When a priest is a pedophile and refuses to seek a decree of laicization, the Congregation for the Doctrine of the Faith will not act unilaterally in laicizing him. Why? To reduce a priest to a lay state against his will is a penalty. Penalties are normally imposed pursuant to the criminal procedure as laid down in the Code of Canon Law. The Congregation has no present authority to impose such a penalty in an administrative process. Consequently if the pedophile refuses to request the decree of laicization and dispensation from celibacy, the Congregation will not act unilaterally.[36]

In such situations, Bishop Maida said, "the diocesan bishop will have to ascertain whether criminal conduct under the canon law is involved and whether he should proceed according to the criminal procedure in the Code of Canon Law. Ultimately if the accused is found guilty, the competent tribunal could impose the penalty of laicization."[37]

While Bishop Maida did hold out the hope that some priests "with proper medical and psychiatric treatment, and counseling and ongoing supervision, [could] continue to function in society and in the Church in some capacity with limited risk to younger people,"[38] he recommended proceeding with a canonical penal process in the more serious cases. In so recommending, he knew that he was in disagreement with many other canonists:

> Some canonists observe that because a pedophile is a sick person, his culpability is diminished, and therefore it is improper to proceed in a criminal action against him. Some might even contend that a pedophile is incapable of committing a crime. However, in making the judgment as to whether or not to proceed in a criminal action, one must weigh the personal rights of the pedophile and his sickness and his culpability against the very serious potential harm to innocent victims, the great scandal to the Church, and the exposure to legal and financial liability to the diocesan bishop and diocese.[39]

Bishop Maida went on to explain how the civil law treats child sexual abuse, reminding the bishops that their diocesan attorneys had already received from the NCCB/USCC general counsel's office an explanation of the "five common liability theories used in these cases."[40]

57

B. A CHANGE IN THE LAW

Given the American bishops' perception of how difficult a canonical penal process was to use in the case of priests who had sexually abused children, it is no wonder that the next action of the American bishops, at first taken by individual bishops in the late 1980s, but then endorsed by the entire conference, was to seek a change in the law from the Apostolic See. Before examining these requests, however, it is important to understand where the bishops were coming from and what had been the law before the 1983 Code of Canon Law.

1. THE PRIOR LAW

a. Suspension *Ex Informata Conscientia*

The legal system that the bishops knew prior to the 1983 Code was one in which they had great discretion in their treatment of priests who had sexually abused children. Under the 1917 Code of Canon Law, when a diocesan bishop was aware that a priest had sexually abused a minor, he had the ability to suspend that priest *ex informata conscientia*, based on his own judgment that a canonical crime had been committed and without any further process. Edwin J. Murphy explains this procedure from the 1917 Code:

> The procedure *ex informata conscientia* is an extrajudicial procedure by which the Bishop, acting upon evidence fully satisfactory to himself,...suspends [a cleric] from the use of orders...on account of a crime known to the Bishop. It is called ex *informata conscientia* because it proceeds, as it were, directly from the informed conscience of the Bishop, which is solely responsible for it. It differs from the ordinary judicial sentence in as far as in the latter the judge must institute a trial according to the rules of canonical procedure; hear the witnesses for and against the accused; allow the accused to defend himself. The decision which he renders

58

must be based upon the evidence set forth in the trial itself, *ex allegatis et probatis,* and must be conformable entirely to the testimony which has been given. Now in the decree *ex informata conscientia* all these formalities of procedure are omitted; there is no trial; witnesses need not necessarily be heard; the defendant need have no opportunity to defend himself; guided only by his own judgment the Bishop pronounces the decree *ex informata conscientia.*[41]

This procedure dated to the Council of Trent, which "in the fourteenth session enacted a decree intended to enable the Bishop to cleanse the sanctuary from unworthy priests."[42] The procedure was included in the 1917 Code at Canon 2186, §1: "Ordinaries may, from their informed conscience, suspend their clerics from office, in whole or in part."[43] No sooner does it grant the diocesan bishop this power, however, than the 1917 Code puts some fences around it. Canon 2186, § 2 states that an ordinary can use this "extraordinary" power only when "grave inconvenience" prevents him from using the normal penal process.[44] In situations involving priests who have sexually abused young people, there is a need to act quickly, both to prevent the priest from hurting other children and to protect the good name of the Church, which cannot be seen to be harboring child sexual abusers among her ministers. Failure to act quickly creates exactly the kind of grave inconvenience of which the canon speaks.

Suspension *ex informata conscientia* was normally not to be used for delicts that were public or well known, however.[45] The preference of the law was that the suspension *ex informata conscientia* be used for "occult," that is, not well-known crimes, and that crimes known to the public should proceed by the normal canonical penal process. While well-known or public cases of child sexual abuse appear not to be covered by Canon 2186, the law did create certain exceptions. One exception was that the suspension *ex informata conscientia* could be used for public crimes where there were witnesses, necessary to the case, who had talked to the bishop but who were not available for a canonical process.[46] Abused children who ought not be retraumatized by a formal process certainly fit this category. Another exception that allowed the use of suspension *ex informata conscientia* in public crimes was when either the civil law or the danger of serious scandal created impediments to the use of the canonical penal process or to the imposition of a sentence.[47] Both of these impediments exist in child sexual abuse cases. A canonical process conducted simultaneously with a civil process is problematical. In seeking to speak with the same witnesses, those conducting a canonical process could be seen as obstructing the civil process. And leaving a priest in an assignment after his alleged abusive behavior becomes public would certainly give scandal to the faithful.

In a case of suspension *ex informata conscientia,* the bishop was to gather proofs of the crime on which he based his judgment that a priest should be suspended from ministry.[48] His judgment or sentence was to be issued in a written decree,[49] and hierarchical recourse against the decree by the suspended priest was possible.[50] If a suspended priest did take hierarchical recourse against the decree of suspension, then the bishop was required to send the proofs on which he had relied in making his judgment to the Apostolic See.[51] The priest remained suspended, however, and his appeal did not have effect on the suspension itself as long as the bishop had imposed the suspension as a form of censure.[52]

Obviously, the ability to suspend a priest against whom the bishop had solid proof of child sexual abuse, without the need for a warning or for a canonical process, was a major tool in the bishop's arsenal to handle the very serious problem of priests who had sexually abused minors. The 1983 Code of Canon Law, however, with its emphasis on the rights of individuals and its desire to deemphasize penalties, did not carry over this power of the diocesan bishop into the new law.[53] As a result, when the clergy child abuse crisis began to break in the United States after 1983, the bishops did not have the ability to suspend sexually abusive priests *ex informata conscientia.*[54]

b. Nonpenal Restrictions

The *suspensio ex informata conscientia* was, as noted, a form of penalty that could be imposed by the bishop when he was morally certain that a priest had committed a canonical crime. In situations where the diocesan bishop was not morally certain that a priest had sexually abused a minor, but strongly suspected that that was the case, or in situations where he knew the abuse to have occurred but the period of prescription had run so that a canonical process was no longer possible, the 1917 Code allowed the bishop to impose nonpenal restrictions on the priest. According to Canon 2222, §2 of the former Code, a diocesan bishop had not just the right, but the duty to avoid scandal by prohibiting such a priest from the exercise of sacred ministry and by removing him from office.[55] Canon 2222, §2 states that this action by the bishop was not a penalty. It was, rather, simply an exercise of the bishop's executive authority.

Canon 2222, §2 of the 1917 Code was not carried forward into the 1983 Code, with its emphasis on the rights of individuals and its desire to deemphasize penalties. As a result, when the child sexual abuse crisis broke in 1985, bishops were not able, as they had been in the past, to impose nonpenal restrictions on priests whom they had reason to think were child abusers, or whom they knew had sexually abused a child, but had done so in a timeframe outside the canonical prescriptive period.

c. The Administrative Rescript of Laicization

Under norms for the laicization of priests promulgated by the Congregation for the Doctrine of the Faith in 1971, the priest seeking laicization was foreseen as the normal petitioner for the rescript of laicization.[56] This was a revision of earlier 1964 norms, which had been established in a reserved secret circular letter, dated February 2, 1964, sent to all local ordinaries setting down certain norms for dealing with laicization cases.[57] Under the 1971 norms, "the form of enquiry was to be no longer the formal juridical one but rather a pastoral investigation, aimed, however, at diagnosing whether a sufficient reason for granting the dispensation...existed."[58] The 1971 norms, however, contained Section VII, "Cases Which Must Be Prosecuted Officially," which stated:

> While making due adaptations, what has been stipulated in these regulations for cases in which priests spontaneously

petition reduction to the lay state together with a dispensation from the obligations flowing out of sacred ordination, must be applied also in cases in which it seems that some priest because of depraved life, or doctrinal errors, or other serious reason, and after necessary investigation, must be reduced to the lay state and at the same time, out of mercy, must be dispensed lest he run the risk of eternal damnation.[59]

Under this section, the priest need not be the petitioner for the rescript of laicization. It allowed the diocesan bishop to be the petitioner, seeking the laicization of a priest in an administrative process when there was reason to do so because of the priest's "depraved life" or "doctrinal errors" or other "serious reason."

From 1971 until 1980, then, diocesan bishops had the ability themselves, without the cooperation of the priest involved, to petition the Congregation for the Doctrine of the Faith to laicize the priest for, among other things, leading a depraved life. Under this administrative process, a pastoral investigation conducted by the local diocese, which substantiated the priest's depraved life and was forwarded to the Congregation for the Doctrine of the Faith, was all that was needed to laicize a priest who had sexually abused minors. This was a major tool that a diocesan bishop could use in the case of a sexually abusive priest who himself could not be persuaded to seek laicization and that avoided the lengthy and complex procedure of a canonical penal process against the priest.

This administrative rescript process differed from the suspension *ex informata conscientia* in a very important way. While the suspension from the bishop's informed conscience also avoided a canonical penal process, at the end, the priest was only suspended. He remained in the clerical state, and the diocese still had obligations to him in terms of decent support.[60] Of the two, the administrative rescript of laicization was the most drastic remedy, since it removed the offending priest from the clerical state and severed any obligation that the Church had to support him.

The 1970s were years of tremendous loss to the priesthood. In 1975, alone, over three thousand priests worldwide left the priesthood.[61] When he became pope in 1978, John Paul II decided that the laicization process for priests needed to be rethought. On October 14, 1980, the Congregation for the Doctrine of the Faith issued new norms on laicizations that tightened up the previous procedures.[62] The 1980 norms also omitted any references to rescripts being sought by the diocesan bishop. With these 1980 changes, the diocesan bishops lost the ability to petition the Holy See for the administrative laicization of a priest who had sexually abused minors. After October 14, 1980, only the priest himself could request an administrative rescript of laicization from the Holy See.

d. Summary

It is truly ironic that, just as the clergy child sexual abuse crisis began to mushroom in the mid-1980s, the bishops in the United States (and throughout the world, for that matter) lost three highly effective ways to deal with priests who had sexually abused children. The suspension *ex informata conscientia* and the bishop's ability to impose nonpenal restrictions were eliminated by the 1983 Code of Canon Law. The administrative rescript of laicization was simply not carried over into Congregation for the Doctrine of the Faith's revised 1980 norms on laicization. It is a matter of no small conjecture whether or not the clergy child sexual abuse crisis would ever have become as serious as it did if the bishops had had more effective ways to deal with the problem.

These changes in the law also provide a basis for understanding why American canonists were so inexperienced in dealing with canonical penal processes. With these three tools in their armamentarium, American bishops seldom called on their canonists to conduct penal trials of sexually abusive priests. There simply was no need to do so because prior to 1983 these other alternatives existed to deal with this problem. But a new Code, a new emphasis on individual rights, and a deemphasis on penal processes, changed all that.

2. REQUESTS FOR CHANGES IN THE LAW

By the late 1980s, the bishops of the United States came to the conclusion that the canonical penal process was not up to dealing with the issue of the sexual abuse of minors by the Church's priests. There was an almost uniform decision that, if it was to be useful, the law had to be changed. Starting in the late 1980s individual bishops began asking the Apostolic See for an administrative, nonjudicial penal process to deal with priests who had sexually abused minors. Eventually this task of seeking a change in the law was taken on by the bishops' conference itself. As the Ad Hoc Committee on Sexual Abuse later explained it:

> NCCB/USCC officers and key staff began in late 1989 to discuss alternative approaches to existing provisions of canon law with representatives of the Roman Curia. There were concerns that the provisions of the Code of Canon Law on statute of limitations and culpability might preclude application of the Church's penal process in these cases. Discussions focused on ways to streamline the penal provisions of the Code of Canon Law and the possibility of an administrative process to remove a priest from the clerical state. Such discussions occurred periodically through 1990.[63]

The conference was focusing on the same areas of weakness that the Canonical Affairs Committee had pointed out, problems with prescription or the statute of limitations and problems of diminished culpability due to psychological illness. The negotiations that occurred between the American bishops and the Holy See on changes in the law occurred in five stages:

    a. Proposals for a Return to the Prior Law, in New Garb
    b. Proposals for an Administrative Nonpenal Procedure of Removal
    c. The Recommendation of the Joint Papal Commission
    d. Changes in the Law Proposed by the National Conference of Catholic Bishops
    e. Changes in the Law Approved by the Apostolic See[64]

These will be considered in order.

a. Proposals for a Return to the Prior Law, in New Garb

As explained above, the prior law gave the bishop much more flexibility in dealing with sexually abusive priests. John A. Alesandro describes it this way:

> For many years, especially during the pontificate of Pope Paul VI, bishops were able, in extreme circumstances, to petition the Holy See for the administrative (i.e., non-penal) laicization of a priest even without the priest's voluntary petition for such a dispensation. With the promulgation of the 1983 Code of Canon Law in 1983, the Holy See discontinued this practice. This left only two remedies for the grave cases in which we are interested: voluntary petition by the priest in question or penal dismissal of the priest from the clerical state by the use of the judicial process.
>
> Many bishops were under the impression that the "judicial process" was too cumbersome and unwieldy, replete with unnecessary delays, and difficult to employ. They sought some remedy. While hoping in reality for a return of the device of an *ex officio* (involuntary) laicization, the bishops seemed to think that this could be achieved by obtaining from the Holy See, in lieu of the judicial penal process, an *administrative process of dismissal from the clerical state....* The goal was to streamline the process and put it into the hands of the diocesan bishop.[65]

So the bishops' first requests to the Apostolic See were simply for a return to the prior law, allowing either the suspension *ex informata conscientia* or administrative laicization by rescript requested by the bishop.

These requests were taken seriously enough in Rome to be assigned to an interagency Vatican commission. One report of the American-Roman interaction on the bishops' first request for a restoration of their ability to move on the laicization of a sexually abusive priest describes it as follows:

> A meeting [of American bishops in Rome for their "ad limina" visits] with the clergy congregation dealt with the issue of clergy sexual misconduct. The bishops said Vatican officials made a real effort to understand the difficult legal, moral and psychological aspects of the problem in the United States. [Cardinal] Bernardin said that while curial officials listened, it was also evident that "they don't appreciate fully the situation, all the dimensions of the situation as we experience it." But the meeting helped, he added.

> A request by U.S. bishops for a simpler process for laicizing priests who sexually abuse minors is still under study by an interagency Vatican commission, the bishops were told. However, Catholic News Service reported March 24 [1993], several days after the "ad limina" visits, that a Vatican official had said a request by U.S. bishops for a simpler process to laicize priests found to be sex abusers is not allowed by current church law. Reducing priests to the lay state is only foreseen when the sacrament of ordination is nullified or after a judicial process, said Archbishop Geraldo Agnelo, secretary for the Congregation for Divine Worship and Sacraments. The congregation is directly involved in laicizations. "For now, according to canon law, we can do no more than that. It is not in our competence to do more," he said. For a bishop to administratively laicize a priest for sex abuse would be against "canon law," he told CNS.

> Agnelo said this negative judgment was expressed to the group of U.S. bishops during their "ad limina" visits. One bishop who attended the meetings, Bishop Joseph Imesch of Joliet, Ill., said the point made by Vatican officials was that "canonically, we cannot do such a process" and that the pope would be the only one with the power to change the

situation. Imesch said he thought this represented the Vatican's current thinking, not necessarily a final decision. Agnelo confirmed that an interagency commission is looking into the U.S. request. The main Vatican concern is that any simplification in the laicization process might not adequately protect the rights of priests and the value of the sacrament of ordination.[66]

The problem appears to have been, as Archbishop Agnelo explained, that the Apostolic See was concerned that diocesan bishops could not be trusted with their former powers inasmuch as they could be used to run roughshod over individual priests whom the bishop simply did not like. In addition, the American canonists in dialogue with the bishops over this proposal appeared to be at cross-purposes with the bishops. While the American bishops simply sought a return to the former, very expeditious state of affairs, American canonists were concerned that any new administrative procedure, even if it was simply a return to prior procedures in new garb, include "due process protections for the priest."[67] Discussions on an administrative penal procedure of dismissal soon came to naught.

b. Proposals for an Administrative Nonpenal Procedure of Removal

Unable to succeed in the restoration of the prior state of affairs, apparently over concerns that the old procedures trampled on priests' rights, the bishops then sought a form of administrative nonpenal removal from the priesthood of sexually abusive priests. Since their original requests had been criticized both by Rome and by American canonists as violative of an accused priest's due process rights, the insight of the bishops was to take an existing canonical procedure from the 1983 Code, the process for the removal of a pastor, and adapt it to the removal of sexually abusive priests from ministry.[68] The genius of this idea was that such an administrative procedure, based as it was on an existing Code process, could hardly be criticized by Rome or the American canonists as violating the priest's due process rights. If it violated the priest's due process rights, then so too did the existing Code procedure regarding the removal of pastors.

The procedure for the removal of pastors was also very apt to the current situation. Pastors are to be removed when their ministry becomes harmful or ineffective.[69] Priests who have used their ministry to sexually assault youngsters have certainly exercised a harmful ministry and, once their parishioners learn of their sexual abuse, the possibility of any effective ministry is over for them.

John Alesandro describes this next stage in the American bishops' response to the clergy sexual abuse of minors crisis: "the NCCB's Canonical Affairs Committee proposed for discussion a process not of 'dismissal,' but of administrative 'removal,' from the clerical state....In 1992, the Committee developed for discussion purposes a model based on the canons for the administrative removal of a priest from the pastorate." The proposed model did not have a period of prescription or statute of limitations, which many canonists saw as a problem with the canonical penal process, and it was based on "the bishop's considered pastoral judgment that the cleric's ministry had become permanently harmful *(noxium)* to the Church or completely ineffective *(inefficax)* in any reasonable ecclesial situation because of his past acts."[70]

Unfortunately, this attempt by the bishops to obtain the powers that they believed they needed to address the clergy child abuse crisis did not fare well, either. John Beal describes this stage of the bishops' response:

> In an effort to remove these obstacles to the use of the penal process, the National Conference of Catholic Bishops of the United States entered into discussions with the Holy See about possible derogations from universal law. An interdicasterial committee composed of representatives of the Congregation for Clergy, the Congregation for Sacraments and Divine Worship and the Apostolic Signatura was formed to discuss these issues with representatives of the American bishops. To rid the penal process of some of its complexity and clumsiness, the bishops proposed an admin-

istrative procedure modeled on the procedure for the removal of pastors (cc 1740–1747) that would allow diocesan bishops to impose the penalty of dismissal from the clerical state without a trial. Dismissed clerics would have had the right to make recourse to the Apostolic See against bishops' decrees of dismissal. The interdicasterial committee rejected this proposed administrative procedure as insufficiently sensitive to the rights of clerics.[71]

The failure of this second attempt by the bishops to deal with sexually abusive priests in ministry led to the next phase, which was a return to the formal penal process, but with some modifications.

c. The Recommendation of the Joint Papal Commission

The National Conference of Catholic Bishops takes up the narrative to describe how the Joint Papal Commission was formed and what it did:

> For several years, the representatives of the NCCB discussed with Roman officials the possibility of developing a more streamlined procedure to deal with such cases than that found in the Code of Canon Law. Serious consideration was given to a non-penal approach modeled on the administrative removal of a pastor and appropriately modified to safeguard the rights of the cleric. The personal intervention of the Holy Father in this dialogue led to the establishment of a joint commission of the bishops and four canonists from the Holy See and the NCCB to study the judicial process for the imposition of a penalty in the Code of Canon Law with a view to suggesting ways of facilitating its use rather than developing a completely new process.[72]

At their June 1993 meeting in New Orleans, the National Conference of Catholic Bishops discussed a letter sent to them by the pope in which he stated, "During the *ad limina* visits many times the conversation has turned to this problem of how the sins of clerics have shocked the moral sensibilities of many and become an occasion of sin for others."[73] In reference to the canonical issues involving such "sins of clerics," the pope added, "The canonical penalties which are provided for certain offenses and which give a social expression of disapproval for the evil are fully justified....As you are aware, a joint committee of experts from the Holy See and the bishops' conference has just been established to study how the canonical norms can best be applied to the particular situation of the United States."[74]

The Joint Commission established by the pope in May 1993 included, on the Vatican side, Bishop Julian Herranz Casado, secretary of the Pontifical Council for the Interpretation of Legislative Texts; Monsignor Raymond L. Burke, defender of the bond at the Apostolic Signatura; and Father Velasio de Paolis, professor of canon law at the Gregorian University; and, on the American side, Archbishop Adam J. Maida of Detroit; Monsignor John A. Alesandro, chancellor of Rockville Center; and Father John V. Dolciamore, professor of canon law at Mundelein Seminary in Chicago.[75] The Joint Commission was charged "to study how to apply the universal canonical norms governing judicial processes to the particular situation of the United States regarding the well-known problem."[76] The Joint Commission developed a brief thirteen-page report, suggesting how the universal penal law of the Church might be adapted to the clergy sexual abuse of minors problems of the United States.

The report was never published, but it evidently centered on the already discussed issues of prescription and imputability.[77] It may have also focused on the suggestion by Roman officials that the American bishops set up regional penal tribunals to act on clergy child sex abuse cases. It was reported by John Allen in the *National Catholic Reporter* that Father Joaquin Llobell of the canon law faculty at Santa Croce University in Rome made the following public criticism of the American bishops:

Llobell also took the American bishops to task for not pursuing canonical trials against abuser priests much earlier in the game. He charged that some bishops like to perform only the pleasant aspects of their job, leaving the pope or the Roman Curia to play the heavy. In fact, he said, the Roman Curia tried in the 1990s to convince the American bishops to set up inter-diocesan tribunals at the national level to process sex abuse cases, but nothing happened.[78]

The report of the Joint Papal Commission was provided to the Canonical Affairs Committee of the National Conference of Catholic Bishops for their further study. "The Canonical Affairs Committee, after reviewing the report of the joint commission, undertook to develop a set of guidelines or instructions to assist those called upon to apply the judicial penal process."[79] The Canonical Affairs Committee also took from the report of the Joint Commission three recommendations for changes in the universal law of the Church to deal with the clergy child abuse crisis in the United States. These three proposed changes dealt with the age of the minor, the statute of limitations, and the appeals process; these were then submitted for discussion to all the bishops.

d. Changes in the Law Proposed by the National Conference of Catholic Bishops

The recommendations of the Canonical Affairs Committee were presented to the bishops at their November 1993 meeting by Cardinal Anthony Bevilacqua, chair of the committee.[80] The first recommendation dealt with raising the age of the minor victim referred to in Canon 1395, §2 from sixteen to eighteen. Eighteen is the age of majority used in the Code itself at Canon 97, §1. The bishops evidently were of the belief that "the traditional limitation of such a delict to those under sixteen years of age set the cut-off at too early an age."[81] As a result, the first derogation from the universal law that the Canonical Affairs Committee suggested for the territory of the United States was to change the age of a minor victim of clergy sexual abuse from sixteen to eighteen.

The second recommendation of the Canonical Affairs Committee had to do with the prescriptive period for Canon 1395, §2 offenses as established in Canon 1362, §1, 2°. The period in the Canon 1362, §1, 2° is a short five years after the last sexually abusive act. As the bishops themselves admitted, "many of the claims that were coming to the attention of the U.S. bishops were beyond the five year time prescription in the Code of Canon Law."[82] The committee proposed lengthening the prescriptive period in two ways: (1) giving a bishop five years after the minor victim turned eighteen, that is, until the victim's twenty-third birthday, to bring charges of sexual abuse against an offending priest; and also (2) giving the bishop, after he receives credible information that a priest has sexually abused a minor, two years to bring charges, regardless of how long ago in the past the abuse occurred.[83] These two time periods within which a canonical penal process could be commenced against an accused priest were to be in addition to the five-year period already provided for in Canon 1395, §2.

The third recommendation of the Canonical Affairs Committee dealt with the appeals process of Canon 1444, §1, 1°. In order to prevent canonical penal processes from dragging on for years while appeals languished in Rome, during which time any penalty imposed on the priest-perpetrator was suspended, the committee proposed short-circuiting the Roman appeals process. They wanted to do this by limiting the first level of appeal to the local American appellate courts at the metropolitan or regional level. Their proposal allowed for appeal to Rome only when the appeals court or court of second instance did not agree with the trial court or court of first instance or when there were new proofs or evidence discovered. This third level of appeals was to be heard by the Roman Rota.[84]

These three proposals for changes or exceptions[85] to the universal law, on the age of the minor victim, on the statutory or prescriptive period, and on the appeals process made by the Canonical Affairs Committee, were adopted by the National Conference of Catholic Bishops at the same November 1993 meeting in which they were discussed. Oddly enough, in presenting these recommendations to the bishops for their adoption, Cardinal Bevilacqua, chair of the Canonical Affairs Committee, had "predicted that even under the new rules a judicial procedure against a priest who abused a minor would probably be rare. He said the judicial proceedings are cumbersome and time-consuming, and bishops still have other options."[86]

Following the adoption of these three proposals by the National Conference of Catholic Bishops, they were submitted to the Apostolic See on November 30, 1993.[87] The Apostolic See asked the Joint Papal Commission for its thoughts, and the commission made suggestions for further modifications in the American bishops' requests. Based on the modifications proposed by the Joint Commission, the Apostolic See granted the American bishops certain changes in the penal law for the United States.[88]

e. Changes in the Law Approved by the Apostolic See

The Apostolic See accepted some, but not all, of the proposals of the American bishops for changes in the Code of Canon Law in order to help them deal with priests who had sexually abused children. On the first requested change, regarding the age of the minor, the requested change was approved. A rescript of the Secretariat of State dated April 25, 1994, and effective for the next five years, stated that "with regard to canon 1395, §2, 2°: this norm is to be applied to delicts committed with any minor as defined in canon 97, §1 [i.e., under eighteen years of age] and not only with a minor under sixteen years of age."[89] This change was extended on December 4, 1998,[90] for an additional ten-year period, and became a part of the universal law of the Church in May 2001.[91] As Alesandro points out, "Since age is an element of the delict itself, the proposed derogation by the Holy See would be prospective in nature; it could not be retroactive."[92]

On the second requested change, extending the Canon 1362, §1, 2° statute of limitations or prescriptive period for child sexual abuse by allowing a bishop to bring charges against an offending priest until five years after the minor victim turned eighteen, that is, until the alleged victim's twenty-third birthday, or until two years after the bishop receives credible information regarding the offense, no matter when it occurred, the Apostolic See partially acquiesced. The new standards promulgated by the Apostolic See allowed an action to be brought until the alleged victim's twenty-eighth birthday as long as not more than one year had passed since the victim had reported ("denounced") the offense.[93] As was the case with the change in age of the alleged victim, this change in the law was prospective, that is to say, it only applied to offenses committed after April 25, 1994, the effective date of the rescript. The Apostolic See, however, did create a "transitory" norm for some offenses that were committed before April, 25, 1994. Under this transitory norm, charges of sexual abuse of a minor, using the old definition, that is, a youngster sixteen years of age or under, could be brought until the alleged victim's twenty-third birthday.[94] This means that for Canon 1395, §2 crimes committed before April 25, 1994, by priests on minors of age sixteen or less, the statute of limitations ran until the victim turned twenty-three.

On the third requested change curtailing the penal appeals process by limiting Roman involvement only to third-instance cases, the Apostolic See simply said no, and refused to make any changes in the applicability of Canon 1444, §1, 1° for the United States.[95] The right of immediate appeal to Rome after the initial trial phase or first instance of a case, penal or otherwise, was considered too basic a right to change. It is rare that a court system will agree to cede its authority, no matter what legal tradition one is dealing with, and the Roman ecclesiastical courts were no exception. To deal with the American bishops' fears that Roman appeals would be used by priest defendants to "string out" the process and delay their eventual punishment, there were evidently some representations that this would not be allowed to occur.[96]

f. Summary

By the spring of 1994, the American bishops had achieved their long-sought goal of changing the penal law for the United States. It was now easier to pursue the canonical penal process against an accused priest with a longer statute of limitations and a definition of minors that included youngsters until they reached the age of eighteen. But, strangely, these changes in the law did not open the gates on canonical penal processes against priests who were accused of sexually abusing youngsters. There were not appreciably more penal cases after April

1994 than there were before. The elephantine efforts of the American bishops to get the law changed seemed to have produced a mouse.

There are various reasons for this. First of all, except for the transitory norm on the prescriptive period, the changes in the law were prospective. They only affected offenses committed after the April 25, 1994 date of the rescript. Second, and perhaps more important, all of the other problems with the penal law we discussed in chapter 3 were still there. None of the changes in the law had affected these. Penal processes still were not favored in the law under Canon 1341. Canonists still doubted if the law was up to the task, and despite a number of seminars offered on the penal law at canonical gatherings in the late 1980s and early 1990s, few canonists felt familiar with the canonical penal process. Imputability under Canon 1321, §1 was still a major obstacle. The canonical penal process would have been useless if a priest's mental defects made the ultimate penalty of dismissal from the clerical state unavailable.[97] Since Rome had refused a change in the appeals process, the fear still existed that the rights of the accused priest, including his appeal rights, would trump the canonical penal process. And finally, there was still no guarantee that the victim would cooperate with a canonical penal process or that the acts of a penal process could not be used against the diocese in a civil or criminal proceeding.

There also remains the highly curious question as to why all of these negotiations with the Apostolic See were necessary if, as then-Cardinal Ratzinger said in 2001, *Crimen sollicitationis* was in effect during all this time.[98] That instruction from 1962 gave jurisdiction over the crime of child sexual abuse by priests to the Holy Office/Congregation for the Doctrine of the Faith, and crimes in their competence were not prescribable. For whatever reason, however, the American bishops were drawn into this long, extended process of proposal and counterproposal with the Apostolic See as to how American diocesan tribunals could proceed against priests who had sexually abused children, with results that hardly made their canonical prosecution more likely.[99] But, while these efforts of the American bishops to change the penal law did not bear much fruit, other efforts of the American bishops did.

C. CONTINUED ACTION BY THE NATIONAL CONFERENCE OF CATHOLIC BISHOPS

1. STATEMENT OF GENERAL COUNSEL, FEBRUARY 1988

In the late 1980s, "the general secretary [of the United States Catholic Conference] decided that the general counsel would become the conference spokesperson on [clergy sexual abuse of minors] cases."[100] The bishops' Ad Hoc Committee on Sexual Abuse says that this happened for two reasons: many questions being asked of the bishops involved ongoing civil litigation and they were fact-specific questions that required a lawyerly response.[101] In 1987, the general counsel was asked to prepare a public statement on the crisis. This statement was published by the general counsel on February 9, 1988,[102] and it was the first national statement on the clergy sexual abuse of children problem.

The general counsel of the United States Catholic Conference is a highly talented, highly principled individual, dedicated to the legal representation of the United States Catholic Conference and aided by a very capable staff. One has to question, however, the judgment of the bishops in asking their lawyer to take the lead on this issue. By so doing, they created a distance between themselves and the problem of the sexual abuse of minors by clergy. When they needed to be pastors and speak in strong moral terms, the bishops stood behind their lawyer.

The general counsel's statement explains the bishops' initial response to the crisis:

As public attention began to be focused on child abuse generally and pedophilia particularly, the U.S. Catholic Conference has taken strong and positive steps to educate, advise and guide. Because medical evidence shows that most offenders were themselves victims of abuse as children, the conference's efforts have been and will continue to be directed toward assisting those involved to break that cycle here and now, through positive programs of prevention and education.[103]

"Those involved" are, of course, priests who have sexually abused minors. Focus on priest-perpetrators, and what could be done to "rehabilitate the offender"[104] were the major concerns of the bishops in the early years of the crisis.

This does not mean that other concerns were not present. The general counsel's statement speaks of "commitment of the diocese to heal victims and their families,"[105] but any fair reading of the text detects a weighty emphasis on priest-offenders, how they will be helped to break out of the cycle, how they will be rehabilitated, and how they will be cared for. Even when the statement offers concern for victims, it speaks in parallel text, including both abuser and victim in the circle of concern. For example, it speaks of a "sensitive awareness to the pastoral implications for the accused and the victim" and of "commitment to the care and well-being of the individuals involved, especially children."[106] It is a carefully balanced, lawyerly statement written in an extremely difficult situation.

The statement also points out, one might even say bemoans, the fact that "the USCC is not a national governing board for the church in the United States. Under both church law and civil law, each diocese is separate and independent from every other diocese, and the conference may not direct that actions be undertaken by a diocese or other church-related institution."[107] The inability of the bishops' conference to create a nationally binding program for all dioceses was to become a constant refrain of the conference and its leadership during the early years of the sex abuse crisis.[108]

2. STATEMENT OF THE ADMINISTRATIVE COMMITTEE, NOVEMBER 1989

Almost a year and a half later, on November 5, 1989, the Administrative Committee of the National Conference of Catholic Bishops, which is the executive committee of the bishops' conference with over fifty bishop-members, issued the first joint statement by the bishops themselves on the clergy sexual abuse of children issue.[109] The Administrative Committee begins by seeking to put the problem in perspective, saying that "the problem of priests and child abuse is a serious one, but not a very common one."[110] It also makes the point that, "sadly, the most frequent offenders are found among individual parents and step-parents."[111] While arguably correct (there is a notable dearth of reliable statistics on levels of child abuse in the United States), this perspective of the bishops' Administrative Committee sounds an awful lot like the "Tu quoque" fallacy.

The most important part of the Administrative Committee's statement is what comes next. Whenever there is even a rumor of a priest sexually abusing a minor, "Church leaders are advised to investigate immediately, to remove a priest rapidly where the evidence warrants it, to seek appropriate treatment for the offender and to extend pastoral help to the victim of such a tragedy and to the victim's family."[112] Again, there is an endorsement of the treatment model for priest-perpetrators. There is no mention that the perpetrator's actions might be offenses against both canon and civil penal law. There is no mention of reporting a priest's abuse to the proper civil authorities. The earlier February 1988 statement of the general counsel did mention that the bishops' conference was providing the diocese with "guidelines governing the reporting of instances of abuse,"[113] and the November 1989 statement of the Administrative Committee does state that general counsel's statement "reflects the consistent approach by the conference."[114] However, a clear endorsement of treating the offending priest's conduct as a crime, either canonically or civilly, is woefully lacking in the Administrative Committee's statement.

3. STATEMENT OF THE OFFICE FOR MEDIA RELATIONS, FEBRUARY 1992

After the Administrative Committee's 1989 statement, there was no public action on the part of the bishops until 1992. In February of that year, the Office for Media Relations of the United States Catholic Conference issued the following brief statement:

POLICY ON PRIESTS AND
SEXUAL ABUSE OF CHILDREN

The policy of the conference, at the national level, is the strong and consistent recommendation to dioceses that they act in the following way: when there is even a hint of such an incident, investigate immediately; remove the priest whenever the evidence warrants it; follow the reporting obligations of the civil law; extend pastoral care to the victim and the victim's family; and seek appropriate treatment for the offender. This firm approach is evidenced in statements issued by the Conference's Office of General Counsel in 1988 and by the Administrative Board of bishops in 1989, as well as in the four sessions in recent years when the bishops have discussed the matter in general meetings. Though the Conference has no jurisdictional authority in such matters as a governing board, the fact is that the dioceses have used this guidance from the national level as a basis for founding their own explicit policies.[115]

This statement by the Office for Media Relations outlines what would have been a very effective way of handling the clergy child abuse crisis by those dioceses that did implement it: investigate the claim, remove the priest-perpetrator, report to civil authorities, and provide pastoral care to the victim and the victim's family. But note the continued endorsement of the treatment model and the repeated emphasis that the bishops' conference had no ability to ensure that every diocese was following these steps ("the Conference has no jurisdictional authority in such matters as a governing board").

4. EARLY DIOCESAN POLICIES, 1986-91

As the statement of the Office of Media Relations points out, individual dioceses had started to act. In 1986, the Archdiocese of Washington, D.C., adopted a policy of "swift action with regard to the perpetrator, compassionate outreach to the victim, cooperation with civil authorities and education for all church personnel and children in our schools."[116] "The Seattle Archdiocese broke ground when it crafted a new sexual-abuse policy, including the use of independent review panels, under then-Archbishop Raymond Hunthausen in the late 1980s."[117] In May 1990, Bishop William Weigand of the Diocese of Salt Lake City announced a child abuse policy that involved the establishment of an "assessment team" consisting of "a religious woman, a priest, a therapist, a medical doctor and an attorney who are professionally trained and knowledgeable in the subject of child abuse."[118] This assessment team was to weigh all charges of child abuse, including sexual abuse, made against any diocesan personnel, including priests. If charges against a priest were deemed "well-founded" by the assessment team, the priest was to be removed from ministry and sent for "appropriate" evaluation.[119] If he refused evaluation, or if the evaluation determined that the priest was "a real and present danger," or if the priest was convicted, then he was to be advised of his civil and canonical rights, "including the right to apply for laicization and also the right of the diocese to proceed with a canonical trial, which can result in canonical consequences up to and including laicization."[120] The policy also committed to reporting all such charges in accordance with the Utah Child Abuse Reporting Act. It also provided for pastoral outreach to victims and their families, and created preventive educational programs for all diocesan personnel. Finally, the policy required background checks on all diocesan personnel, including priests and seminarians, for evidence of prior incidents of child abuse.

In May 1990, Bishop Gerald O'Keefe of the Diocese of Davenport, Iowa, promulgated a diocesan policy regarding the sexual abuse of minors by clergy.[121] It created a review board, appointed by the diocesan bishop, of "three priests, a psychiatrist or psychologist and an attorney."[122] Oddly, this panel did not itself have the job of evaluating charges made against a priest. Rather, that would be done by the bishop and the bishop's delegate, but the review board was to "oversee all steps of the procedure for dealing with accusations and will...act as guarantor of due process for all parties." The delegate was to deal with civil authorities and the victims and victims' families. Iowa state mandatory reporting statutes were to be complied with by the delegate. The delegate was to see that the priest "receives psychological or psychiatric evaluation according to the recommendations of the review board and assure that the results of the evaluation be made available to the review board and the bishop."[123] If the bishop, based on the delegate's report, decided that the charges were credible, then the bishop would confront the priest and impose a leave of absence, except in situations where the charges were not current, in which case the review board would be convened "to determine appropriate further action."[124] The review board was also to be involved to determine, after "disposition or resolution of the incident," together with the delegate and the bishop, "whether further service in the Diocese of Davenport is possible."[125]

In September 1991, Bishop Jerome Hanus of St. Cloud, Minnesota, established a sexual misconduct policy for all personnel of the diocese.[126] Unlike the policies of Salt Lake City and Davenport, it was not focused solely on child victims, but dealt with "vulnerable persons," which could include vulnerable adults. Also unlike its predecessors, it did not establish any kind of a review board. It mandated that all diocesan personnel report to the diocese any "incident of sexual misconduct by any personnel of the diocese."[127] These allegations would be investigated "by the bishop or his designate."[128] Accused priests are to be informed of their civil and canonical rights, and if the claim is "substantiated or appears to be substantiable *(sic)*,"[129] they are to be removed from their assignment and placed on administrative leave. When guilt is established, the priest will be suspended and "further penal sanctions, including, but not limited to, dismissal from the clerical state, may be imposed pending the outcome of any civil/criminal actions, if any."[130] Priests who are not dismissed from the clerical state are to receive diagnostic evaluation, treatment, and appropriate aftercare, if they wish to be eligible for "a permanent contractual assignment, excluding ministry to minors or others at risk."[131]

5. THE CHICAGO EXPERIENCE, 1991–92

In the fall of 1991, Cardinal Bernardin publicly apologized to parishioners of St. Odilo's parish who had learned that their pastor, the Reverend Robert E. Mayer, who had left the parish for what were initially characterized as "personal reasons," had in fact been removed for allegations of sexual misconduct with a twenty-year-old man.[132] After his removal, a fourteen-year-old girl from the parish alleged that he had molested her.[133] "The congregation also discovered that Father Mayer had been assigned to St. Odilo's, and to other parishes before that, despite a lawsuit for sexual misconduct brought against him in 1982."[134]

The cardinal wrote to all of the parishes in the archdiocese, admitting "mistakes for which I am deeply sorry," in the reassignment of priests with a history of child sexual abuse, and announcing that he was appointing a three-member commission to investigate the archdiocese's handling of complaints of child sexual abuse by priests, to review the files of such priests currently on assignment, and to recommend a policy for the future handling of these complaints.[135] The commission was made up of Julia Quinn Dempsey, a juvenile court judge; John P. Madden, a former adviser to the Illinois Department of Children and Family Services; and Bishop John R. Gorman, auxiliary bishop of Chicago and a clinical psychologist.[136]

The commission issued its report on June 11, 1992. Cardinal Bernardin announced on September 21, 1992, that he had put many of its recommendations into place:

1. The creation of a nine-member review board, made up primarily of laypersons, to consider all allegations of child sexual abuse by clergy, to oversee investigations, and to advise the cardinal about an accused priest's fitness for ministry
2. The establishment of a fitness review officer, a layperson credentialed in dealing with child abuse issues, who would staff

the review board, do intake on complaints regarding priests, and report to civil authorities

3. The appointment of a victims' assistance minister to deal with victims, their families, and the parish community
4. The creation of archdiocesan-wide educational programs on how to prevent child abuse
5. The requirement that all seminarians undergo advanced psychological screening and take courses in sexual development
6. The establishment of a unified personnel record system to keep track of priests throughout their careers
7. Compliance with all civil reporting requirements regarding sexual misconduct and cooperation with official investigations[137]

In its review of the archdiocese's clergy files, the commission determined that "39 priests were...subjects of valid accusations. Some were dead or had left the priesthood. The remaining 21 were removed from the active ministry and will not be assigned to regular parish work."[138] Never before had a diocese allowed a primarily lay board to examine its clergy files. Never before had a diocese removed priests from ministry based on the advice of a primarily lay board. Under the leadership of Cardinal Bernardin, the Chicago Archdiocese had taken steps to combat the sexual abuse of children by its priests that no other diocese had taken. The cardinal also took the step of mailing a copy of his new policy to all diocesan bishops in the United States for their information and consideration.[139]

6. THE CANADIAN EXPERIENCE, 1989–92

In the spring of 1989, allegations of abuse against the Irish Christian Brothers in the province of Newfoundland in Canada became public. A number of brothers were charged with the physical and sexual abuse of the boys entrusted to their care at Mt. Cashel Roman Catholic Orphanage, a boys' home operated by the brothers in Saint John's, Newfoundland.[140] "In this case, allegations had originally surfaced in 1975, and in a widespread state-church cover-up, certain brothers had been permitted to leave the province without facing criminal proceedings. The story remained in the headlines for several years."[141]

The archbishop of Newfoundland Alphonsus Penney reacted to this crisis by empanelling an independent commission to investigate the question of the sexual abuse of minors in the archdiocese. The commission found there to be credible accusations of the sexual abuse of minors against thirteen priests and twenty-three religious brothers in the archdiocese.[142] It also criticized the archbishop for his failure to act once he had knowledge of the abuse. Acknowledging his neglect, the archbishop resigned.[143] The commission's report spurred the Canadian bishops to action.

The result was *From Pain to Hope*, a document issued on June 1, 1992, by the Canadian bishops' conference. Unlike their American counterparts, the Canadian bishops were able to take joint action to deal with the clergy child sexual abuse crisis. *From Pain to Hope* describes the Church culture that helped to create the crisis:

> A contributing factor to child sexual abuse is a church that too readily shelters its ministers from having to account for their conduct; that is too often tempted to settle moral problems behind a veil of secrecy, which only encourages their growth; that has not yet fully developed a process of internal reform in which the values of familial communion would predominate. Challenges for personal conversion and institutional change are far from lacking. We would like to see our church take firm steps which would leave no doubt as to its genuine desire to eradicate the phenomenon of child sexual abuse.[144]

The report concludes with fifty recommendations for action that the bishops agreed to follow, and it asks Canadian Catholics to "study the recommendations [the bishops] have made and decide for themselves whether or not we have been true to it."[145]

Among the fifty recommendations are the establishment in every diocese of a bishop's delegate to handle accusations of child sexual abuse by clergy. The delegate is to act immediately and where the delegate finds reasonable cause, the delegate is to ensure that all applicable civil law reporting requirements are met.[146] A finding of reasonable cause also triggers the removal of the accused priest from ministry and his placement on administrative leave.[147] Every diocese is to create an advisory committee consisting of the bishop's delegate, a canon lawyer, a civil lawyer, and professionals who have treated sexual abuse and parents.[148] This committee is to advise the bishop on the establishment of "a basic protocol regarding situations of sexual abuse."[149]

The report does envision the return to ministry of priests who are sexual abusers of children after their treatment.[150] While there are conditions on such a return (for example, it has to be recommended by the treatment center, it has to be in a low-profile assignment, it has to be monitored, and it cannot be near children), there is no doubt that the Canadian bishops do endorse both the treatment model and a return to ministry after treatment. There is no equivalent recommendation in *From Pain to Hope* that the canonical penal process is to be used against priest-perpetrators. While therapy is required,[151] the canonical penal process is simply a "whether or not" proposition.[152]

From Pain to Hope can also be properly criticized for its stingy attitude toward victims. As did their American counterparts three years earlier in the general counsel's statement,[153] the Canadian bishops speak in parallel text, including both abuser and victim in their circle of concern. While *From Pain to Hope* speaks of "compassion towards victims of abuse," the document also says that "same compassion should also affect the response of the church to those who are accused."[154] Bishops are advised to "provide a sympathetic and attentive hearing within the church to each victim of sexual abuse committed by a priest,"[155] but strangely, no counseling is to be offered to a victim until "after sentence has been pronounced against a priest."[156] Unless the Canadian justice system is the quickest on earth, that leaves victims hanging for a very long time before they receive any real solicitude from the Canadian bishops.

Still in 1992, much to their credit, the Canadian bishops did, as a group, adopt the fifty recommendations of *From Pain to Hope* and they did ask to be held publicly accountable to its standards. As the document states, "We will let our readers study the recommendations we have made and decide for themselves whether or not we have been true to it."[157]

7. ARCHBISHOP PILARCZYK'S STATEMENT, JUNE 1992

At the June 1992 meeting of the bishops, there was a "day long executive session on aspects of clergy sexual misconduct."[158] As reported by Thomas Reese:

> The major topic of the executive session was sexual abuse of children by priests. The bishops heard from a panel of experts and bishops. In a statement at the conclusion of the meeting, Archbishop Pilarczyk as NCCB president addressed the problem with more directness and candor than had ever been done on a national level. He called sexual abuse of a child "reprehensible conduct directed at a most vulnerable member of our society....
>
> He admitted that mistakes had been made in the past when people treated sexual abuse as a moral fault for which repentance and a change of scene would result in a change of behavior. Far more aggressive steps are needed to protect the innocent, treat the perpetrator, and safeguard our children. Where a lack of understanding and mistakes have added to the pain and hurt of victims and their families, they deserve an apology and we do apologize.[159]

At this same meeting, Archbishop Pilarczyk amazingly "revealed that in 1987 the conference had recommended a five-step program for dealing with sexual abuse by clergy or church employees."[160]

These five steps were:

1. Respond promptly to all allegations where there is reasonable belief that the incident has occurred.

2. If the allegation is supported by sufficient evidence, promptly relieve the alleged offender of his ministerial duties and refer him for appropriate medical evaluation and intervention.
3. Comply with all obligations of civil law on reporting the incident and cooperating with the investigation.
4. Reach out to the victims and their families and communicate a sincere commitment to their spiritual and emotional well-being.
5. Within the confines of respect for the privacy of the individuals involved, deal as openly as possible with members of the community about the incident.[161]

In announcing these five steps as the uniform recommendations of the conference from 1987 onward, Archbishop Pilarczyk also reminded his audience that "our national episcopal conference is not a governing body and it cannot pass rules and regulations which bind the actions of its members outside of a limited number of areas delegated to it by the universal law of the Church."[162]

8. THE NATIONAL CONFERENCE OF CATHOLIC BISHOPS' ADOPTION OF THE PILARCZYK STATEMENT, NOVEMBER 1992

At their fall 1992 meeting, the American bishops were confronted with victims' groups picketing the Washington, D.C., hotel where the meeting was being held. "At the November 1992 gathering of U.S. bishops in Washington, D.C., a dozen SNAP [Survivors' Network of Those Abused by Priests] members staged a protest."[163] The conference president Archbishop Daniel Pilarczyk of Cincinnati asked Cardinal Roger Mahony of Los Angeles, Bishop Harry Flynn of Lafayette, Louisiana, and Auxiliary Bishop A. James Quinn of Cleveland to meet with the leaders of the victims' groups.[164] In his report to the bishops at the November 1992 meeting, Cardinal Mahony said that "we spent a little over an hour listening to their outpouring of anger, hurt and pleading....This period of time was one of the most moving experiences in my 17 years as a bishop."[165] The victims asked that the Church be "a living, caring and healing church, not as a legal obstacle which stifles our pastoral outreach and projects an image of protecting errant priests at all costs and a minimal concern for the victims."[166] One of the particular concerns of the victims' groups, Cardinal Mahony said, was "that the apparent unevenness in ways dioceses deal with such victims be equalized and harmonized, and that we all project the same pastoral concern that is swift, full and complete."[167]

The meeting of the three bishops with the victims' groups and their subsequent report back to the assembled bishops was evidently what it took to move the bishops off the dime. As reported in *Origins*:

> A resolution on clergy sex abuse was approved Nov. 19 [1992] during the U.S. bishops fall meeting. The resolution was prompted by remarks of Los Angeles' Cardinal Roger Mahony after he and two other bishops met Nov. 16 with some abuse victims....Archbishop Daniel Pilarczyk of Cincinnati, outgoing bishops' conference president, said it was the first time the full body of bishops had spoken on the topic.[168]

Following Cardinal Mahony's report, it was moved from the floor that the bishops' conference adopt as the policy of the conference the five steps announced by Archbishop Pilarczyk the previous June. The bishops' discussion that followed this motion was not without some rancor. It was reported by the National Review Board for the Protection of Children and Young People that, during the floor debate on whether to adopt Archbishop Pilarczyk's five points as the policy of the bishops' conference, one bishop, speaking against the conference's adoption of a uniform policy, told his fellow bishops, "No one is going to tell me how to run my diocese."[169] It has also been reported that "many bishops, Cardinal Bernard Law reportedly a leader among them, resisted any national action that might infringe on the independence of bishops in their own diocese."[170] At the end of the discussion, however, "a resolution endorsing Archbishop Pilarczyk's statement as the view of the entire NCCB was adopted without dissent."[171]

Since, Archbishop Pilarczyk said, this was "the first time the full body of bishops has spoken on the topic," it is important to quote exactly what they said. The resolution, as adopted, reads:

Gathered in general assembly, we the members of the National Conference of Catholic Bishops express our profound concern for those who have been victims of sexual abuse, particularly when that abuse has been committed by a member of the clergy.

The president of our conference, at the close of our assembly last June, spoke clearly and eloquently to this subject with our assent. We reaffirm that statement here and recognize that policies to address the grave issues presented by this problem are in place throughout the country.

In the course of our assembly this week, we have reflected—once again and more deeply—upon the pain, anguish and sense of alienation felt by victims.

At the same time, we affirm the thousands of good, holy and dedicated priests who minister faithfully to God's people.

We pledge ourselves to one another to return to our dioceses and there to examine carefully and prayerfully our response to sexual abuse; to assure ourselves that our response is appropriate and effective; and to be certain that our people are aware of and confident in that response.

Among the elements to be considered for ongoing response, we continue to recommend the following:

- Respond promptly to all allegations of abuse where there is reasonable belief that abuse has occurred.
- If such an allegation is supported by sufficient evidence, relieve the alleged offender promptly of his ministerial duties and refer him for appropriate medical evaluation and intervention.
- Comply with the obligations of civil law as regards reporting of the incident and cooperating with the investigation.

- Reach out to the victims and their families and communicate our sincere commitment to their spiritual and emotional well-being.
- Within the confines of respect for the privacy of the individuals involved, deal as openly as possible with members of the community.

In these days of our assembly, we are reminded again that all our actions should show our church as a living, caring and healing church. We pledge again our care and concern for all victims of abuse wherever and however it occurs. We commit ourselves anew to bring the healing ministry of our church to our people, to dialogue and pray with all who have suffered and to foster opportunities for reconciliation.

It is of value, in the canonical history of the bishops' reaction to the clergy child sexual abuses crisis, to understand just what it meant for the National Conference of Catholic Bishops to endorse Archbishop Pilarczyk's five-point program. The bishops' endorsement, even though unanimous, had absolutely no canonical effect. No bishop, no diocese was bound to follow the plan established in the five steps for dealing with priests who had sexually abused children. Bishops' conferences, such as the National Conference of Catholic Bishops, do not have legislative authority for their territory except in very limited circumstances. Under Canon 455, §1 of the 1983 Code of Canon Law, "A conference of bishops can only issue general decrees in cases where universal law has prescribed it or a special mandate of the Apostolic See has established it either *moto proprio* or at the request of the conference itself."

Neither of these was the case with the five-point program for dealing with clerical sexual abuse of children. Universal law did not establish this as one of the areas in which bishops' conferences could legislate, nor was there a grant of authority from the Apostolic See that would have allowed the bishops to legislate in this area. Indeed, the bishops had not asked for such a mandate.

As a result, the bishops' unanimous endorsement in November 1992 of the five-point program for dealing with clergy child sexual abuse had no legal effect. It did not bind the territory represented by the conference, that is, the United States. It did not even bind the bishops who voted for it in their own dioceses. Its only value was moral suasion. Once the bishops as a group publicly endorsed the five-point program, it was possible for individual bishops to say to their fellows, "This is what you ought to be doing." But nothing could make them do so. As the one bishop said in the floor debate, "Nobody is going to tell me what to do in my diocese." Nonetheless, most bishops did in fact follow the guidelines for their dioceses.

9. THE THINK TANK, 1992–93

Also at the November 1992 meeting of the bishops, a subcommittee of the National Conference of Catholic Bishops' Priestly Life and Ministry Committee was formed. As reported by the Ad Hoc Committee: "In the discussion of the [Pilarczyk] resolution, Bishop Robert Brom announced that the NCCB Committee on Priestly Life and Ministry formed a subcommittee on clergy sexual abuse. That subcommittee was to meet during early 1993 and develop recommendations for the June 1993 meeting."[172] And as reported by Thomas Reese, in their November 1992 meeting, "The bishops also discussed behind closed doors in executive session their request that Rome allow them to dismiss priests involved in sexual misconduct through an administrative procedure." That request, as discussed earlier, was turned down, but it does indicate that by November 1992, the bishops' conference was proceeding on more than one front to deal with the problem of clergy sexual abuse of children. The difficulty in creating a canonical history of those times, and of giving the bishops any credit for the steps they were taking in the early 1990s, is that so much of it was happening in executive session or "behind closed doors."[173] This did not inure to the bishops' benefit. As Stephen J. Rossetti has written: "The media has consistently accused the Church of a cover-up. Church officials, on the other hand, felt unjustly accused and distrusted. They could not understand why Americans could not see how concerned the bishops were and [did not appreciate] all that the Church hierarchy had done. But they had done it all behind closed doors."[174]

The subcommittee on clergy sexual abuse was chaired by Father Canice Connors, president of St. Luke Institute, perhaps the major treatment center used by bishops for sexually abusive clergy. Father Connors put together a two-day meeting, February 21–23, 1993, in St. Louis, Missouri, where a panel of experts on the topic of sexual abuse, including "victims, abusers, physicians, lawyers, seminary rectors, educators, bishops and others"[175] was convened. "It was called a 'think tank' and was designed to offer these experts the chance to reflect honestly and off the record about various dimensions of the problem, especially pastoral care of victims, reassignment after treatment, and research and education."[176]

Father Connors presented the report of the subcommittee at the June 1993 meeting of the American bishops. In a talk that he gave before he presented the subcommittee's recommendations, Connors said that the bishops had already received a bound booklet of the subcommittee's report in a version "tamed by the editors."[177] The implication was that the bishops could not have borne the direct "passion" of the subcommittee's feelings on the matter. Connors "acknowledged that the findings were not precisely worded or nuanced and would probably need refinement before becoming church policy at the local or national level."[178]

"The allegations of sexual misconduct against Catholic priests and the perceived inability of some authorities to respond with decisive pastoral leadership has resulted in a sustained crisis in the Church," the Think Tank's report said.[179] The Think Tank's recommendations had three parts:

Part I: Care of Victims
1. Pastoral care for victims should include concrete and direct offers of assistance.
2. We recommend that while respecting the need for confidentiality, bishops deal with the problem of child sexual abuse in the church in a more open manner.

3. A broad program of child sexual abuse education needs to be undertaken within the church community.
4. Bishops should institute additional local structures to make available professional assistance.
5. The bishops in the United States should set up a task force on child sexual abuse.

Part II: Prevention

6. The NCCB recommend standardized and improved methods of screening candidates for the priesthood and religious life.
7. Take more aggressive steps to address the psychological and spiritual health of the clergy.
8. Perpetrators of sexual abuse should receive in-depth psychological assessment and, if indicated, a quality treatment program that has been shown to be effective.
9. Some church ministers should be trained in recognizing and responding to child sexual abuse.
10. The church should actively support a research center(s) on child sexual abuse.

Part III: Reassignment to Ministry

11. Priests or other ministers who have offended against children should never return to any ministry that includes minors.
12. Priests in recovery should be supervised as long as they remain the responsibility of church authorities.
13. Support for priests in recovery should be considered to prevent relapse.
14. The NCCB should support research on defining risk factors for reoffending after treatment and recommend guidelines for the reassignment of priests in recovery.
15. The church should foster, through its teaching office, an understanding of recovery as a dimension of the redemptive ministry and see in the priest in recovery a witness to this redemption.[180]

In a certain sense, the bishops determined what advice they would get from their Think Tank when they chose the head of St. Luke

Institute to chair it. The Think Tank's recommendations are a complete and utter endorsement of the treatment model to deal with the problem of clerical sexual abuse of children. And note the continued use of euphemisms, even by these highly qualified experts: "priests and other ministers who have offended against children."[181] The offense of these priests and ministers was the sexual exploitation of children. The victims were not simply insulted, they were sexually violated.

Connors had a history of downplaying the harm of clerical sexual abuse of minors. The year before, in *America* magazine, he had written, "Still in speaking forthrightly on behalf of victims, it would be wise to avoid the exaggerations of the victimologists. It is so rare as to be unreported that a priest has ever used violence in abusing a child. We are not involved in the dynamics of a rape but with the far subtler dynamics of persuasion by a friend. As we speak to and about the victims we must be aware that the child sometimes retains a loving memory of the offender."[182]

In the bishops' discussions following the Think Tank's report, it was reported that "Bishop Joseph L. Imesch of Joliet complained that bishops are often prevented by diocesan attorneys and by the attorneys for plaintiffs from contacting victims, even when they want to reach out pastorally."[183]

"On and off the floor, bishops expressed much anguish over the harm that had been done by abusive priests and the errors bishops made in the past of simply assigning these priests to another parish after their crime. The bishops assert that this is no longer happening, but victims' groups complain that some perpetrators are still in active ministry."[184]

In particular response to the Think Tank's endorsement of a return to ministry for sexually abusive priests, "Cardinal Bevilacqua of Philadelphia responded that the presumption must be against return to any ministry because of the danger to future victims."[185] "And while the panel rejected the idea that molesters must automatically be barred from all forms of ministry, regardless of their success in undergoing treatment and supervision, Cardinal Bevilacqua said that, 'we're running out of old age homes where recovering priests could be assigned. It should be that once a priest is found guilty, he is out,' the Cardinal said."[186]

10. THE NATIONAL CONFERENCE OF CATHOLIC BISHOPS' AD HOC COMMITTEE ON SEXUAL ABUSE, JUNE 1993

While choosing not to act on any of the specific recommendations of the Think Tank, what the bishops did do at their June 1993 national meeting as a general response was to establish their own Ad Hoc Committee on Sexual Abuse. As then-conference president Archbishop William Keeler of Baltimore explained it:

> As a result of continuing discussion within our conference, I have appointed an Ad Hoc Committee on Sexual Abuse.
>
> The purpose of this committee is to consolidate and build on the steps already taken to confront specifically the issue of sexual abuse by clergy, and, in a more general way, the broader issue of child sexual abuse in our society. The conference cannot legislate for dioceses in a matter like this. Nor is it necessary that it do so, since virtually every diocese has developed a policy for dealing with such abuse.[187]

The chair of the new Ad Hoc Committee on Sexual Abuse was Bishop John Kinney of Bismarck, North Dakota. Its original members were Cardinal Roger Mahony of Los Angeles, Archbishop John Roach of St. Paul–Minneapolis, Bishop John Favalora of Tampa–St. Petersburg, Florida, Bishop David Fellhauer of Victoria, Texas, Bishop Harry Flynn of Lafayette, Louisiana, and Bishop Terry Steib of Memphis, Tennessee.[188]

The Ad Hoc Committee was mandated "1) to look at assisting the [conference] membership in effectively dealing with priests who sexually abuse minors and others; 2) to examine what the NCCB can do pastorally nationwide to assist in the healing of victims and their families; 3) to address the issue of morale of bishops and priests burdened with the terrible offenses of a few; 4) to assist bishops in screening candidates for ministry and assessing the possibility of reassignment of clergy found guilty of sexual abuse of minors; 5) to recommend steps to safeguard against sexual abuse of minors by employees or volunteers of the Church; and 6) to address the national problem of sexual abuse of children, coming from many directions, especially from within families."[189]

As reported in the *New York Times:*

> Bishop Kinney later gave the conference's reason for establishing a committee rather than adopting the recommendations of the [Think Tank]. "This group is very careful and anytime we put something down in writing, we want to hone it," he said.

> But he said he was determined that the committee would strive to establish a climate in which the emphasis would be on taking bold measures, not perfecting every detail. Emphasizing the need for swift action, he said: "maybe everyone is going to have to sit down with a group of victims and perhaps, abusers, too. That sets up a different dynamic.

> "Establishing a committee may seem neither a daring nor an original thing to do," he said. "The significance of this committee is that it provides the conference with a group accountable to offer it recommendations for decisive action."[190]

It had taken almost nine years since Father Gauthe's arrest in Lafayette, Louisiana, but the American bishops finally had a plan in place to deal with the sexual abuse of children by clergy. With the endorsement by the conference of Archbishop Pilarczyk's five points at their November 1992 meeting and the establishment of the Ad Hoc Committee on Sexual Abuse at their June 1993 meeting, the American bishops had moved to confront the problem of the sexual abuse of children by priests. While there was much to be said about where the five points failed (the reliance on treatment model, for instance, which was repeated in the charge to the Ad Hoc Committee), there was much that they got right.

The Ad Hoc Committee got off to a running start. As Bishop Kinney told the assembled bishops after his appointment:

> There is one goal that I want to see happen. By the time our committee sunsets, I want to make sure that all of us bishops understand the depth and the seriousness, the pain and the agony of this problem and why it strikes at the very heart of the church's trust level and credibility level.
>
> The shock and outrage felt by people over issues of sexual abuse in the church is not, I believe, primarily because of violations of our moral teachings on sexuality by those in authority, as serious as that is. By now, I believe our people understand clearly the clay feet of the ministers of the church. It is not the sexuality of it all. It is rather the dynamic of the misuse of power, domination and the violation of trust between pastor and parishioner, priest and child, teacher and student, counselor and counselee. Victims, their families and friends have felt betrayed by those they trusted and who were given to them in authority. And then once abused and betrayed, some in authority did not listen to their cries for help or were perceived as not hearing them.
>
> If some say of us, even today, "The bishops just don't understand the problem"; if they don't agree that "We bishops get it," then our goal as your committee is to help all of us understand and "get it" both intellectually and in our hearts for the sake of the victims, for our priests, our people—and even ourselves.[191]

11. PROPOSED GUIDELINES ON THE ASSESSMENT OF CLERGY AND RELIGIOUS FOR ASSIGNMENT, NOVEMBER 1993

Prior to the bishops' next national meeting, in November 1993, Bishop Kinney, the chair of the Ad Hoc Committee, met with the leaders of the victims' groups.[192] He described this moment in the history of the Church in the United States as one of "painful grace."[193] At the November 1993 meeting of the bishops' conference, Bishop John Kinney gave the report of his new committee, at that point only six months in existence. He told his fellow bishops that his committee was beginning to assemble information on the topic of the sexual abuse of children, and that he wanted "the information and the data his committee will amass to help the long-term analysis of sexual abuse, not just in the church but in society at large."[194] Another agenda item for the bishops' November 1993 meeting was the adoption of "Proposed Guidelines on the Assessment of Clergy and Religious for Assignment."

The Think Tank had recommended to the bishops at their meeting the previous June that there be standardized and improved methods of screening candidates for the priesthood and religious life and that priests or other ministers who had offended against children should never return to any ministry that includes minors. The "Proposed Guidelines" were the result of collaboration between the bishops and the heads of religious orders in order to address those very issues.[195] It says in an "Explanatory Statement":

> The bishops and major superiors in the United States have been working together to safeguard the Church and society at large against instances of harmful and scandalous behavior committed by clergy or religious. Although often stated in the context of child abuse, our concerns deal with a broader range of seriously improper behavior, such as untreated addictions to alcohol and other substances, abusive behavior or misconduct (especially that of a sexual nature), and financial improprieties. Although relatively

rare, such conduct is still cause for grave concern and is especially odious when minors may suffer harm. It is our goal to prevent insofar as possible this kind of behavior by clergy and religious and to hold them accountable for their conduct. No cleric or religious will be given an assignment where there is any reasonable probability that he or she may bring harm to the Church or to individual persons, particularly minors.

It is not possible to anticipate every instance of misconduct. In some cases, the disorders which cause the misconduct make them extremely difficult to detect until they become manifest. As we know through painful experience, sometimes this behavior is only discovered because it has already caused grave harm to members of our Church and to the community. However, by investigating and evaluating thoroughly the background of all candidates for positions in ministry and by communicating fully with one another, we major superiors and bishops substantially reduce the risk that anyone who has an untreated addiction or who is inclined to engage in any kind of seriously inappropriate behavior will be assigned to ministry.[196]

The guidelines only deal with that situation in which a priest or member of a religious order is being sent for assignment outside the diocese or province of a religious order. In such situations the sending bishop or major superior is to "assess the fitness of the person proposed as a candidate for assignment....This assessment will reflect whether the candidate has exhibited seriously improper behavior, such as an untreated problem with substance abuse, violations of celibacy, sexual impropriety, physical abuse, or financial impropriety."[197] The guidelines also specify that "the major superior or bishop of the candidate is to provide the receiving major superior or bishop a written statement about the suitability of a candidate for the proposed assignment. The statement will indicate whether anything in the history or background of the candidate should in any manner limit his...service in that assignment."[198]

Assuming that the bishops and the religious orders kept to it, this policy effectively put an end to the possibility that a priest with a history of child sexual abuse could be simply transferred to another assignment outside the diocese or province in order to get him away from a troublesome situation. Note, however, that the policy does seem to permit the reassignment of a priest with a history of child abuse who, after treatment, is not perceived to be a risk to children, and nothing in the policy prevented bishops or major superiors from reassigning priests who had sexually abused children within the same diocese or province of a religious order. Still, the policy is to be commended for its frank description of clergy sexual abuse as "harmful," "scandalous," and "especially odious when minors may suffer harm," and its clear declaration as the national policy of the bishops that "no cleric or religious will be given an assignment where there is any reasonable probability that he or she may bring harm to the Church or to individual persons, particularly minors."

12. THE BERNARDIN ACCUSATION AND ITS AFTERMATH

At this same November 1993 national meeting, the bishops had to deal with yet another media circus. There were protesters there again from the victims' groups, but the media was focused on charges of sexual abuse against Cardinal Joseph Bernardin of Chicago. These charges, made as part of a $10 million lawsuit by a former seminarian based on his "recovered" memories, were released to the public days before the bishops' national meeting in an obvious attempt to get national publicity for the charges. As reported in *America* magazine:

> Three days before the meeting—some say the timing was too exquisite not to have been planned—a man claimed Chicago's Cardinal Joseph Bernardin had sodomized him when he was a 17-year-old. He had just recovered this

memory last month, he alleged, though the abuse is sup-
posed to have occurred some 15–18 years ago when the
Cardinal was the archbishop of Cincinnati. The Cardinal
immediately went before television cameras to deny the
charges. His forthrightness was more than matched, of
course, by that of reporters who inquired of him on camera
if he had ever been sexually active. No, he said. O tempora,
o mores—especially mores.[199]

The charges against the cardinal were more than ironic, in that
the Chicago archdiocese under Cardinal Bernardin had taken the lead
in dealing with sexually abusive priests. Chicago, alone among the
American dioceses, had taken the step of creating a lay review board
that actually read and vetted the files of all diocesan priests then serving, and that recommended the removal from ministry, which the cardinal followed up on, of all priests who had had credible allegations of
sexual abuse of a minor made against them. At the end of his keynote
address in the November 1993 bishops' meeting, Archbishop Keeler,
then-conference president, who had not mentioned the topic of child
abuse at all in his talk, "turned to Chicago's besieged archbishop, calling him 'dear Cardinal Bernardin' and assuring him the full support of
the bishops, who gave the Cardinal a standing ovation."[200]

The charges against Cardinal Bernardin were eventually withdrawn.[201] His accuser, Steven Cook, explained to a February 28, 1994
press conference in Cincinnati that he no longer believed that his
memories of abuse by Cardinal Bernardin, which had been recovered
through hypnosis, were reliable, and, as a result, he was filing a motion
for voluntary dismissal of his charges against the cardinal. U.S. District
Judge S. Arthur Spiegel dismissed all individual claims against
Cardinal Bernardin, with prejudice, which meant that they could not
be refiled.[202]

There is no doubt that the accusations against Cardinal
Bernardin, based on the questionable science of "recovered" memories,
once they were known to be false, acted to put a brake on the media's
coverage of the clergy child sexual abuse issue. The media had been

burned in their unquestioning acceptance of Cook's accusations, and once burned they were now both weary and shy. As Canice Connors commented on the media fiasco, "Since the media had to confess to its hyped and false accusations against Cardinal Bernardin there has been no significant national coverage of 'abuse cases.' With investigative reporters busy in other places, many have welcomed the intermission as an opportunity to move on, relying on the notoriously short American memory cycle."[203] Connors was writing in 1999, taking note of, at that point, a six-year hiatus in the public spotlight, from the end of 1993 onward, on the issue of Catholic priests sexually abusing youngsters.

In turn, this lack of a media spotlight in the years immediately after the Bernardin accusation slowed down, some would say even halted, the need that the bishops felt to continue addressing the problem of the sexual abuses of children by clergy. As Peter Steinfels has noted:

> After 1993 the momentum that had finally built up was lost. The biggest single factor was probably Steven Cook's false accusation made in November 1993 (and withdrawn 108 days later) against Cardinal Bernardin himself. Cook's lawyer...orchestrated the accusation with CNN to gain massive news coverage. Some critics of the bishops' previous inaction badly injured their credibility by precipitously hailing Cook's charges. Embarrassment at CNN's and [the lawyer's] manipulations undoubtedly sobered the media.

> Although the story of predatory priests was demoted from nightly news to occasional revivals during a sweeps week or following extraordinarily large settlements, church officials were aware that a tremendous backlog of cases remained from earlier decades. Unfortunately, with the pressure off, there was little thought about an overall approach to handling them.[204]

The lack of urgency in the bishops' handling of the clergy child sex abuse crisis after 1993 was also noted by Bishop Kinney, chair of the Ad Hoc Committee. As he admitted to a reporter in an interview about that time in the Church's history, "The climate was different."[205]

13. THE AD HOC COMMITTEE, 1994–96

From its inception, Bishop Kinney's Ad Hoc Committee on Sexual Abuse was very active. Before the end of 1994, it had published its first report, *Restoring Trust: A Pastoral Response to Sexual Abuse.*[206] This report, which was presented to the bishops at their November 1994 meeting, contained a review of the sexual abuse prevention policies of 157 dioceses, with commentary, a report on ten treatment centers for clergy, and related articles on the topic of the sexual abuse of minors by clergy.[207]

The fact that, by the end of 1994, 157 dioceses had followed the lead of Washington, D.C., Seattle, Salt Lake City, Davenport, St. Cloud, and Chicago was itself a clear indication that now, ten years after the crisis began in Lafayette, Louisiana, most dioceses were prepared to deal with it in serious fashion. Many of these dioceses had, in imitation of Salt Lake City, Davenport, and Chicago, established review boards, outside the normal diocesan structures, to advise bishops on child sexual abuse charges against priests, including, for example, whether or not the priest should remain in ministry.[208] As Bishop Kinney, chair of the Ad Hoc Committee on Sexual Abuse, has explained,

> The Ad Hoc Committee gathered and studied diocesan policies and offered additional recommendations in a 1994 report, "Restoring Trust." The Committee found that some dioceses were already on their second generation of policies, refining those established several years before. Many had also developed a variety of mechanisms both for handling allegations and for offering support to victims. The report made clear that Catholic dioceses have been as quick as most other religious and professional groups in developing guidelines and taking action to deal with sexual abuse.[209]

The 1994 report contained an important section on "Policies" that proposed twenty-eight concrete "guidelines" to the bishops on how they should handle allegations of the sexual abuse of a minor by a priest. These policies provided a complete plan for every diocese to use in combating the problem of the sexual abuse of children by clergy. They provide:

General Guidelines
1. That all dioceses consider having a written policy on the sexual abuse of minors.
2. That the tone of the diocesan policy, particularly in its introduction, be clearly pastoral while appropriately dealing with the legal (civil and canonical) and financial obligations of the diocese.
3. That the policy be a public document, thereby indicating that the local church is open to the accountability implied in it.
4. That any qualifying statements required in a policy be appropriately presented so that the pastoral tone is not diminished.
5. That a glossary be provided of the technical terms used in the policy.

Prevention—Education
6. That the policies make a special reference to prevention and education measures in place.
7. That the policies include a reference to appropriate screening procedures for seminarians, employees and volunteers with responsibilities for dealing with young people.
8. That the policy be communicated to priests and religious, and to employees if applicable, and that all acknowledge acceptance in a formal manner.
9. That in education sessions priests be provided with regular opportunities for updating their knowledge on child sexual abuse from viewpoints such as new scientific knowledge, church policy and canon law, civil laws and of moral theology, professional ethics, the theology of sexuality, the pastoral care of victims and coping with the disclosure of misconduct by a colleague.
10. That consideration be given to setting up a diocesan advisory board to evaluate periodically the effectiveness of the policy in place and to propose revisions as indicated.

Administrative Guidelines In General

11. That consideration be given to having the diocesan policy apply to clergy, religious and employees in the context of sexual abuse, misconduct, exploitation and harassment.

12. That in the principal diocesan policy dealing with sexual abuse there be mainly general references to the manner of dealing with clergy and religious, and there be developed a subpolicy to cover the intricacies of canon law in their regard.

13. That each diocese examine its history in this regard and, based on the risk to innocent and the vulnerable, consider having a risk track and a non-risk track approach to implementing the procedures.

14. That because of the special skills required to do a proper and expeditious investigation, individuals with the primary responsibility for this role be given appropriate training before assuming this position.

15. That there be identified in each diocese experts from the many disciplines involved in the serious study of issues connected with sexual abuse in order to approach the problem in its pastoral, legal, psychological, sociological, medical and educational dimensions.

Civil Law

16. That policies be reviewed to assure that this principle of honoring civil law obligations is articulated in a practical manner.

17. That policies clearly state a willingness to cooperate with government authorities (civil and criminal proceedings) to the extent possible in the circumstances.

18. That there be an explicit reference in the policy regarding coverage of the accused's legal expenses.

19. That, while maintaining a pastoral tone, the policy be clear that there could be occasions when the church may in justice defend itself.

Insurance

20. That to the extent possible the pastoral and educational tone of the policy be maintained with reference to the insurance aspects that must be included in it.

21. That dioceses seek insurance contracts to provide optimum pastoral and clinical support to those in need.

Victims

22. That every policy recognize that primary attention be given to the person alleged to have been offended, to the family and to the parish community.

23. That the policy indicate there is some kind of multidisciplinary body available to provide concrete, direct and individualized assistance to victims, their families and the affected parish community.

24. That the diocese seek ways to involve the people in general in the whole process of healing the often serious and long-lasting aftereffects of child sexual abuse.

25. That the diocese promote sessions to affirm and encourage the body of priests, whose morale can be adversely affected by the actions of relatively few of their colleagues.

Accused

26. That, given the complexity inherent in the reassignment question, the diocesan policy make provision for some type of advisory body to assist the bishop in this regard.

27. That the policy of the diocese be as detailed as feasible on the possibilities and types of assignment that may or may not be open to a priest guilty of sexual abuse.

Media

28. That the diocesan policy make reference to an approach for consistently relating with the media and to a designated, well-informed and experienced spokesperson (with substitute) for all inquiries and news conferences.[210]

These guidelines run from the very basic (that every diocese have a written policy, that investigations be done by those trained to do so, and that civil law reporting requirements be met) to the very pastoral (that "every policy recognize that primary attention be given to the person alleged to have been offended, to the family and to the parish community").[211] The guidelines also endorse a Chicago-type review process, using an "advisory body," before any priest with a history of sexual abuse is reassigned, and in fact contemplates that reassignment may not be open to such a priest.[212]

These twenty-eight guidelines were an attempt to elaborate on the five principles endorsed by the entire conference at their meeting one year back, in November 1993. By November 1994, however, these twenty-eight guidelines never made it to the floor of the bishops' meeting for a vote. They remained only the recommendations of the Ad Hoc Committee. As reported in the *New York Times:*

> The ad hoc committee's task was to put meat on the bare bones of the five principles that the bishops' conference had endorsed the year before as guidelines for dioceses in sexual abuse cases. Bishop Kinney recalled the "high intensity" with which the committee worked from 1993 to 1995. It heard the testimonies of victims of abuse, and more than once, Bishop Kinney said, he would return to his room after a meeting and weep. Although the committee's recommendations were more specific than the five principles they were still less stringent than the policy the bishops approved in Dallas [2002]. Even so, the earlier recommendations never made it to the floor of the bishops' conference for debate and a vote.[213]

That was unfortunate, because a floor discussion and vote on these twenty-eight recommendations might have moved the bishops farther along the path to a coherent national policy that they could all agree to implement, much as the Canadian bishops had done. But in the "different climate" that prevailed after the national press debacle in reporting unsubstantiated charges of sexual abuse against Cardinal Bernardin, the heat was off the bishops. And with the heat off, they evidently found no need for further joint action on the child sexual abuse crisis.

Although not perfect, the recommendations of Bishop Kinney's Ad Hoc Committee were a step forward and were worth discussing, despite their apparent endorsement of the treatment model. There is an entire section in the 1994 report on "Treatment Centers," listing ten of them and explaining how the bishops should deal with them. In the section labeled "Treatment," which consists of one article, "Expectations of Treatment for Child Molesters," by Frank Valcour, MD, of St. Luke Institute, reassignment after treatment is strongly recommended for all except the worst cases:

> Some child molesters are seriously damaged individuals with limited internal resources to bring to the task of treatment. Such individuals, with great support, may be able to maintain a fragile recovery. Little remains, however, for them to spend outside themselves either in a restricted ministry or some type of meaningful employment. At the other end of a very broad spectrum is a priest whose recovery is so solid that much is left over after basic recovery commitments are met. For some such people their recovery itself may represent an enhancement of the resources they bring to the service of others including ministerial service.[214]

One year later, in November 1995, the Bishops' Ad Hoc Committee on Sexual Abuse issued volume II of *Restoring Trust: A Pastoral Response to Sexual Abuse.* Volume II followed the format of volume I. It contained excellent, sensitive material on the care of victims, but still included material endorsing the treatment model. There were reports on eight additional treatment facilities for priest-abusers in addition to the ten facilities listed in volume I. In "Will Priests Sexually Abuse After Treatment?" James J. Gill, SJ, MD, reported anecdotal evidence from a number of treatment centers of relatively low levels of recidivism by priest-abusers who had successfully completed a long-term residential program and who had returned to a highly structured and monitored ministry with appropriate aftercare activities. Gill advised the bishops, "Bishops could help to inform the laity that many professionals in the field of mental health care are agreed that the majority of priests who have abused minors sexually are able to be treated successfully, and that most are able to be assigned to some form of ministry again—as long as there is close supervision, together with provisions that will keep them apart from children and teenagers."[215]

Gill also mentions that "statistics related to the recidivism rate of priests treated professionally as sexual abusers are not readily available. This fact was discovered with some surprise and disappointment when the bishops' Ad Hoc Committee on Sexual Abuse began its fact-finding work this past year." The Ad Hoc Committee, in an attempt to address the lack of critical information on this and other matters relating to the sexual abuse of children by priests, proposed to the Administrative Committee of the bishops' conference that a study be undertaken by the bishops:

> Nor were Bishop Kinney and his committee more successful with other ideas proposed to the Administrative Committee of the bishops' conference, a body of more than 50 members that serves, among other things, as a kind of steering committee for the whole conference. One proposal, he said, was to collect data from dioceses about the extent of the problem, the numbers of perpetrators and victims, the disposition of these cases and the amount of money expended. Although some of that information is supposed to be gathered by the new national review board authorized in Dallas and headed by Gov. Frank Keating of Oklahoma, its absence up to now created a void that has been filled by speculation and guesswork.[216]

Important studies that could have helped the bishops and that were proposed by their own Ad Hoc Committee were not done. Having created the Ad Hoc Committee, it appears that the bishops lost enthusiasm for the task of dealing with the sexual abuse of children by clergy. As reported at the time:

Recently, while discussing priestly sexual misconduct, a normally very knowledgeable bishop who spoke on condition of anonymity touched on the attitude of his fellow bishops, and the work of Bishop Kinney's committee in particular. Although the bishops' intentions in setting up the committee were good, the bishop said, the hierarchy is now reluctant to cooperate. He went on to say that the bishops' Administrative Committee had received a request from Bishop Kinney's committee to survey all the dioceses on the extent of the problem and the amount of money paid out in legal settlements and therapy for offenders and victims. But the majority of bishops on the Administrative Committee would not even approve this collection of data, he said.[217]

Another proposal for a healing session of the bishops was also batted aside by the Administrative Committee. As Bishop Kinney explained:

These ideas "were discussed in the administrative committee," he recalled, but they "never saw the light of day, they just didn't fly." Why not? "The climate was different," he said again. Some bishops, he said, were even uncomfortable about any committee explicitly named "on Sexual Abuse." In addition, many bishops had suspicions about the conference's infringing on the authority of each bishop.[218]

Despite this lack of encouragement from the Administrative Committee in the post-Bernardin years, Bishop Kinney and his Ad Hoc Committee on Sexual Abuse soldiered on. In November 1996, they produced volume III of *Restoring Trust*. This work is appreciably shorter than the two prior volumes. It takes the form of a report on how they met the original mandate of the committee given to it by then-Archbishop Keeler in November 1993, and effectively summarizes the activities of the committee already described above in this history. Volume III in 1996 was the last publication of the Ad Hoc Committee on Sexual Abuse. Until the Dallas Charter and Norms were adopted by the bishops in their June 2002 and November 2002 meetings, this report of the Ad Hoc Committee was the last significant document of the National Conference of Catholic Bishops on the issue of clergy sexual abuse of children.[219]

D. SUMMARY

The bishops had turned the corner in the 1992–93 timeframe. By that point they all knew, without a doubt, that sexually abusive priests could not be returned to ministry. The horrendous examples of Father Gilbert Gauthe in Lafayette, Louisiana, Father James Porter in Fall River, and the Servants of the Paraclete in Jemez Springs, New Mexico, were all behind them. Each of these situations involved known priest-child sexual abusers being returned to ministry after some kind of attempt at treatment, who then went on to injure yet other children. Andrew Greeley has written of this period that "mistakes were perhaps understandable before 1986, when at their meeting at St. John's Abbey the bishops heard for the first time a systematic presentation about child abuse. They became less understandable after 1993, when the hierarchy put together a perfectly reasonable set of guidelines (which were systematically ignored) and when Cardinal Joseph Bernardin distributed copies of his policies in Chicago to every bishop in the country."[220] In concluding, Greeley wrote, "As far as I am concerned, the statute of limitations on knavish imbecility ended in 1992. That bishops could reassign abusive priests after the early 90's was, I'm sorry to have to say it, sinful."[221]

The year 1992 was indeed a "watershed year" for the bishops' conference.[222] As noted, their public relations arm, in February 1992, issued a statement regarding the national "policy on priests and sexual abuse of children," which involved quick investigation of claims, removal of the priest where the evidence warranted it, reporting where the law required it, and pastoral care to victims and their families. Then, in June 1992, conference president Archbishop Daniel Pilarczyk of Cincinnati confirmed that the conference had uniformly advised dioceses, from 1987 onward, that five steps were necessary to deal with the clergy child abuse crisis, namely respond promptly to allegations, remove the priest and refer him for treatment when there was sufficient evidence, comply with civil law reporting requirements, reach out to victims and their families, and be as open and transparent as possible. In November 1992, after some of the bishops met with the victims' groups, the entire conference advised that every diocese adopt these five steps.

When the five steps were overwhelmingly recommended by the conference in November 1992, the bishops were on the public record for the first time with a uniform policy, albeit only advisory, to deal with the sexual abuse of children by Catholic priests. By that time, they had the joint action of their Canadian colleagues as an example, as well as the policies of several dioceses and archdioceses to guide them. The pieces of the solution were in their hands to be put together if they could. If the American bishops had combined the joint action of the Canadian Conference of Catholic Bishops with its demand for public accountability together with the Archdiocese of Chicago's policy of a predominantly lay review board to enforce the promise that no priest with a history of the sexual abuse of a child would remain in ministry, the problem would have been over in 1992. These were, in fact, the two weaknesses in the bishops' 1992 program: that their action was not binding on every bishop and that an offending priest's return to ministry was still contemplated as a possibility under the five steps.[223]

But, as the bishops' media arm admitted, there could be no real national policy because "the Conference has no jurisdictional authority in such matters as a governing board."[224] On the reassignment issue, as will be discussed in the following chapter, some bishops were so committed to the treatment model that they could not, as a group, rule out the reassignment of abusive priests, although by this same time period many—if not most—individual bishops were, in fact, refusing reassignment to such priests.[225]

It was well understood by the end of 1992 that the Catholic Church in the United States had an extremely serious problem with sexually abusive priests in ministry. The fact that abusive priests had been sent back to parishes after treatment and had abused more youngsters was in the national knowledge bank, primarily due to litigation against the Church that had focused public attention on these priests. Yet, in the court of public opinion, the Church, with the actions that the bishops took in 1992, was seen as having learned its lesson. With the false allegations of Cardinal Bernardin the following year, the public spotlight was finally off. It was almost as if American public opinion was saying, "Okay, bishops, you have made some serious mistakes, but you have also promised to change. You are on probation. Don't let it happen again."

But it did happen again. As Andrew Greeley noted, some bishops did keep sexually abusive priests in ministry well after 1992. Greeley was not the only public commentator to make this observation. Bishop John Kinney, the first chair of the bishops' Ad Hoc Committee on Sexual Abuse, himself noted publicly in 2002, "I thought we'd learned our lessons—that we bishops had agreed how to deal effectively with priests who abuse children. Some bishops clearly were not listening....When I heard about the problem in Boston, I was shocked. How could this happen? How could they send bad priests off to new parishes? Weren't they listening to us?"[226]

When the reassignment of sexually abusive priests after 1992 became public knowledge in 2002, the terms of the Church's public probation were off, and the Church was penalized for its infractions as far back as memory ran. It was the failure of only a few bishops to realize that sexually abusive priests, even after treatment, could not be reassigned that allowed the clergy child sexual abuse crisis to fester in the United States after 1992 and then to erupt with such violence ten years later. Those bishops, and their names are well known, are the reason why the clergy child sexual abuse crisis did not end in 1992.

In 2002, Father Richard McBrien, a theologian at Notre Dame University, was quoted as saying "The [American Catholic] bishops have done little or nothing to address this problem. The proof of that is in the scope and intensity of the current crisis. If they had done something significant, we would not be in the mess we're in today."[227] But the American bishops, in fact, did not do nothing. As described in this chapter, the bishops actually did quite a lot. The problem was that they did not do it as a group, with the same conditions prevailing in every diocese, and with the same insight as to the nonassignability of abusive priests, even after treatment. The canonical inability of the conference to mandate joint action and their inability, not as individuals, but as a group to grasp the seriousness of the reassignment issue are the major reasons why the problem of the sexual abuse of children by priests in the United States grew to crisis proportions in 2002 before it was adequately dealt with at Dallas in a much more drastic fashion than would have been the case had they been more uniform and more insightful in 1992.

5

THE TREATMENT OPTION

A. INTRODUCTION

In the early years of the clergy sexual abuse of children crisis that hit the Catholic Church in the United States in the mid-1980s, before there were changes in the law to make the canonical prosecution of these crimes more likely, the canonical penal process was not utilized in cases regarding sexually abusive priests. Even after 1994, once the American bishops had asked for and received from the Apostolic See changes in the law that were thought to make canonical prosecutions easier, the canonical penal process was still rarely used before the Dallas Norms were approved in 2002. What did the bishops do with these abusive priests in the meantime if they did not subject them to canonical trials and removal from ministry? What was the original response of the bishops to priests who had sexually abused young people?

John Beal explains: "It has become the new conventional wisdom that the first response to a founded complaint of sexual abuse is to remove the accused priest from active ministry, and, with his free and informed consent, of course, to refer him for psychological evaluation and, if indicated, treatment."[1] In fact many canonists had endorsed this approach from the crisis's earliest days. Finding all the difficulties they did with the canonical penal process, canonists had to turn elsewhere. They turned to therapy. As Thomas Green wrote in the first Canon Law Society of America's commentary on the Code of Canon Law in 1984, when the crisis was just breaking in the diocese of Lafayette, Louisiana, "Frequently the most beneficial approach is a therapeutic one rather than a penal one, especially if there is diminished imputability on the part of the cleric."[2] He was seconded in this opinion by James

115

Proctor, writing three years later in 1987: "However, the case of misconduct stemming from mental or psychological factors probably will not be resolved by the imposition of penalties. Once again we must defer to the therapeutic model."[3] Proctor actually envisaged therapy as part of a larger scheme:

> Sadly, some accusations of clerical misconduct are true. Having arrived at this conclusion in an honest and fair manner (i.e., having respected the integrity of the penal and/or procedural law), it is the responsibility of the bishop or of the court to take the appropriate steps with the guilty cleric.
>
> There can be no doubt that simple transfer or removal of the offender is no longer an adequate response to these situations, either in terms of civil law, nor [sic] in terms of ecclesiastical concern. On the other hand, simply abandoning a guilty cleric cannot be countenanced either in canonical practice nor [sic] in simple human charity.
>
> In the therapeutic model, there is much less difficulty in deciding the cleric's disposition. Psychiatric intervention combined with a rehabilitative atmosphere and a proven regimen of counseling seems to be the common approach.[4]

Therapy also was preferred to the penal process by some canonists because it allowed the diocesan bishop to meet his other duties toward his clergy. As James Provost said, "There may be a need to distance the diocese as much as possible from the sexual misconduct of a cleric, but the bishop cannot distance himself from the person of the cleric himself without violating a grave responsibility of his office."[5] In this sentiment he is backed up by Francis Morrisey: "Thankfully, most bishops and superiors have avoided the penalty approach, possibly because it appears vindictive, possibly also because the processes are unwieldy, or possibly because the priest has already suffered enough harm and shame."[6]

B. CANON 1722 AND ADMINISTRATIVE LEAVE

The first part of the treatment option was to remove the accused priest from his parish assignment and to mandate that he attend a treatment center. As Canice Connors described it:

> Today there is no question about how to deal with an accusation of child sexual abuse in a church setting. Any priest accused of sexual misconduct with children is immediately placed on administrative leave by the bishop or his religious superior. If, after a careful and thorough investigation, it is clear that the accusation has merit, the priest is then sent to a recognized mental health institution for an evaluation. If the evaluation shows a psychological or psychiatric problem, he is given whatever treatment is necessary.[7]

Note the sequence in Connors's description. The priest is placed on administrative leave as soon as an accusation is made. An investigation into the charges only follows the removal of the priest from his assignment and his placement on administrative leave. As described, and as in fact implemented, administrative leave was an extrajudicial process, inasmuch as, until an investigation was completed, no canonical penal process could begin.[8]

The use of administrative leave has been severely criticized. As John Beal wrote, "Clerics accused of alcoholism, sexual misconduct, or a variety of merely 'goofy' behaviors are, in a way chillingly reminiscent of Stalin's use of mental institutions, routinely assigned involuntarily to treatment centers where they may or may not continue to enjoy remuneration and coverage by medical insurance. Although these 'assignments' have all the earmarks of expiatory penalties, they are not meant as penalties and so no process is due."[9]

Francis Morrisey believed that more was required than just an accusation, such as an admission or a finding of cause for additional action, before a priest could be placed on administrative leave. He wrote:

If the priest admits to the allegations, or if the delegate finds that indeed there is matter for further action, the priest is to be given an administrative leave within twenty-four hours or as soon thereafter as possible, and an appropriate place chosen for him to reside pending the outcome of the inquiry. At no time, though, should he return to the parish or to the pastoral work where he is assigned (if such is the case) or approach the persons involved. If appropriate, a penal precept (cf. c. 1319) could even be issued to this effect.

Furthermore, the priest's faculties to preach (c. 764) and to hear confessions (c. 974, §1) should be removed. He would also be asked not to celebrate Mass publicly. While such measures could be painful, they are necessary to protect the good of the community.[10]

Administrative leave is not a concept found in canon law, and so is not defined in the law. It is based on a reading of Canon 1722 that allows a bishop to "exclude the accused from the sacred ministry or from some office and ecclesiastical function, [to] impose or forbid residence in some place or territory, or even [to] prohibit public participation in the Most Holy Eucharist." "Currently, canonical 'administrative leave' is usually understood to entail the prohibition of an accused cleric from exercising his ministry, from continuing to reside in the parish to which he had hitherto been assigned and from contacts with his former place of residence and often the order to reside in a place designated by his Ordinary."[11] As one of its earliest defenders, Bertram Griffin, explained:

Canon 1722 permits an administrative prohibition at any stage in the process to preclude scandal, to protect the freedom of witnesses (or victims), and to safeguard the course of justice. The accused may be removed from ministry or office, can be required to reside in or avoid a given place or territory, and may even be prohibited from public participation in the Eucharist. The ordinary must hear the promoter of justice and cite the accused before taking such actions. The prohibitions must be revoked if the reason ceases, and they are automatically revoked when the penal process ceases.

[However,] for pastoral reasons, the bishop may wish to confront the cleric immediately after the accusation is made and before the investigation is complete. In such cases, it may be argued that canon 1722 may also be used during the investigation phase provided the accused is heard and the promoter of justice is consulted. Administrative leave is usual in many professions during internal investigations of alleged offenses. The bishop may at least impose a penal precept requiring the accused to reside in or refrain from residing or ministering in a certain place or territory during the investigation. He may also require the accused to avoid contact with certain persons during the investigation.[12]

As did Connors, Griffin contemplated the use of administrative leave under Canon 1722 once a charge was made against a priest, and before the preliminary investigation into the charge, to determine its truth or falsity, is complete. Griffin was an excellent canonist, and he well understood that his interpretation that administrative leave could be imposed at any time once an accusation was received was not supported by the text or context of Canon 1722. As to its text, Canon 1722 states explicitly that a priest can be removed from his assignment only after he is cited (formally accused) in regard to the crime, which can happen only after the preliminary investigation has been completed and has established some basis to believe that the accused priest has committed the crime and should be prosecuted for it. As to context, Canon 1722 comes after the canon on the requirement of a preliminary investigation (1717) and after the canons that describe the initiation of a formal process (1718–21). Griffin's argument, rather, was from the purpose of the law. Since Canon 1722 says that the removal of the priest from his assignment is meant to preclude scandal, to protect the witnesses, and to safeguard justice, Griffin wrote that implementing these purposes can justify the immediate removal of the priest from his assignment prior to the completion of a preliminary investigation.[13] As he explained:

> It is precisely during the investigative phase when such purposes can be met by "administrative leave." Witnesses are heard during the investigative phase and their evidence presented to the accused after citation to join issue and respond to the bill of complaint of the promoter of justice. It is precisely during this investigative phase when their freedom must be protected.[14]

John Beal disputed this interpretation of the Code of Canon Law. Relying on the legislative history of Canon 1722, its text and context, Beal wrote that an accused priest cannot be removed from his assignment until after the preliminary investigation of Canon 1717 has been completed:

> Canonical tradition, the text and context of c. 1722, the mind of the legislator and parallel passages in the Oriental Code all lead to the same conclusion. "Administrative leave" may be imposed only after the completion of a preliminary investigation. The accused must be cited and given an opportunity to respond, at least extrajudicially, to the allegation and to the proposal to impose "administrative leave." This initial citation and hearing can occur before the penal process is formally inaugurated, either in conjunction with the Ordinary's decree initiating the penal process or subsequently. However, "administrative leave" can only be imposed in connection with a penal process, whether actual or imminent. It cannot be imposed on the basis of an accusation alone. This conclusion is settled law, inconvenient perhaps, but still the law.[15]

Interestingly, although Beal did not believe that the universal law of the Church permitted the use of administrative leave until after the preliminary investigation had been completed and the priest had been formally charged or cited with having committed a canonical crime, he admitted, but did not think it wise or fair, that a diocese may, as a matter of particular law, impose administrative leave "as soon as an accusation of misconduct is received."[16] And, of course, there was nothing canonically improper for the bishop to suggest to the accused priest that, for his own benefit, he needed some distance from the accuser, which meant that, at least for the time being, he should leave the assignment. Accused priests who willingly left their assignments did not raise canonical issues of the propriety of administrative leave. As John Beal put it: "If diocesan officials approach the accused cleric not as adversaries but as concerned brothers, if they assure him that administrative leave connotes no admission of guilt and that he will be returned to his position should the charges prove baseless, if they emphasize that such a leave is in his own best interests as well as that of the Church, and if they assure him that he will be provided for in the interim, the accused cleric may well accept administrative leave voluntarily."[17]

C. CANON 1044 AND PSYCHIC ILLNESS

Once a priest was sent on administrative leave, usually to a treatment center, there quickly followed a psychological evaluation, preliminary to a course of treatment. If this evaluation found that the priest was in fact suffering from one of a number of sexual paraphilia,[18] such as pedophilia or ephebophilia,[19] the next step was for the bishop to declare him impeded from the exercises of orders, under Canon 1044, §2, 2o: "The following are impeded from the exercise of orders—a person who is affected by amentia or some other psychic illness described in Canon 1044, 1o, until the ordinary, after consulting an expert, permits the exercise of the order."

As Craig A. Cox has described it:

If the allegations of such behavior are found to be true, then there is clearly a psychological infirmity that would prevent the cleric involved from ministering responsibly and effectively. Thus, it may be much more appropriate to employ a procedure to investigate whether an impediment is present in cases regarding allegations of aberrant sexual behavior. Should the inquiry verify that such behavior has occurred then with the intervention of the expert required by canon 1044, §2, 2º, the existence of the impediment can be declared and the law itself prevents the exercise of orders.[20]

Whether or not a priest who had sexually abused a child was suffering from a psychic illness as specified in Canon 1044, §2, 2º became a matter of some contention.

William Woestman criticized the use of Canon 1044, §2, 2º to remove sexually abusive priests from ministry.[21] He took the position that the language of Canon 1041, 1º, which had been incorporated by reference into the text of Canon 1044, §2, 2º, required the type of amentia or psychic illness that rendered the priest *"inhabilis...ad ministerium rite implemendum,"* incapable of properly performing his ministry, before he could be declared impeded in the exercise of his orders. He then went on to give a narrow definition to this phrase, limiting it to mean those "who cannot perform the ceremonies or sacred rites for the celebration of the Eucharist or other sacraments."[22] Under Woestman's interpretation of Canons 1041, 1º and 1044, §2, 2º, it would almost never be the case that a priest with a sexual paraphilia was incapable of properly administering the sacraments and therefore impeded in his ministry.[23]

John Beal disputed Woestman's interpretation of *"inhabilis...ad ministerium rite implemendum"* as used in Canon 1041, 1º. In Beal's view, the word *ministerium* had to be looked at as more than simply sacramental. "Ordained ministry," he states, "cannot be limited to a narrow cultic sense of confecting the eucharist, however priestly this act may be."[24] Such a limited view of the priesthood, Beal says, is post-Tridentine, but pre–Vatican II. "Although Professor Woestman's narrow understanding of the *ministerium* proper to the ordained has strong resonances with traditional post-Tridentine attempts at a theology of the priesthood, it is irreconcilable with the teachings of the Second Vatican Council on the ministry and life of presbyters and bishops. In *Lumen gentium* and more profusely in *Presbyterorum ordinis,* the Council parted company with the post-Tridentine tendency to identify the ministry of priests with a narrow cultic role and articulated the ministry of bishops and presbyters in terms of their respective participations in the teaching, sanctifying and governing mission of Christ himself."[25]

As a result, Beal supported the proposition that Canons 1041, 1º and 1044, §2, 2º can be used in certain circumstances by a diocesan bishop to declare a sexually abusive priest impeded. In this regard, he cited a decision by the Signatura that stated:

> The priestly state or condition requires a capacity in the subject of exercising orders, that is, of performing the ministry properly, which capacity requires qualities suitable to orders. The qualities of this type which must be possessed are those which allow the fulfillment of the munera (offices or mission) of the priesthood, on the one hand, without harm to anyone, and on the other hand effectively and fruitfully. If these qualities are absent so that the good of souls is not provided for, not only because of amentia (insanity) but in addition because of a mental disorder of some type, this can constitute an impediment to the proper exercise of priestly ministry.[26]

Beal would require proof from experts in psychology or psychiatry that the sexually abusive priest was affected by a psychic infirmity, which is almost always the case with men so disordered that they seek sexual pleasure from children, before a bishop could declare the priest impeded.[27]

Patrick Lagges, writing at the same time as Beal,[28] also gave a wider interpretation to *"inhabilis...ad ministerium rite implemendum"* as used in Canon 1041, 1º. Lagges started his analysis with Canon 124, §1 and its requirements for the placement of a juridical act, which he said amounted to a determination of whether the person is "able to exercise the external elements that are required for juridical acts."[29] This was basically Woestman's position. But Lagges went on to say that, "however, there is also another meaning of the term 'rite,' which goes beyond the mere formalities and requisites of external acts."[30] He then looked at parallel uses of "rite" in the 1983 Code and concluded:

> Finally, it should be pointed out that clerics carry out their ministry in a particular way. That is, there are certain rights and obligations which are specified in the law itself, which oblige a cleric to act in a certain way or to avoid acting in a certain way (citing canons 273–289). It also would be necessary to take these canons into account when deciding whether a cleric is capable of rightly exercising ministry in the Church. For example, a man who characterologically is not able to live out his obligation "to observe perfect and perpetual continence for the sake of the kingdom of heaven" (c. 277, §1) is not able to exercise clerical ministry in the manner prescribed by the Church. Therefore, he might be able to be judged incapable of rightly carrying out the ministry.[31]

D. THE TREATMENT CENTERS

Enter the treatment centers. It was to these institutions that the bishops turned for a determination of a priest's fitness for ministry after he was found to have sexually abused a child. The bishops used these centers in the role of the "experts" required by Canon 1044, §2, 2° for a determination of psychic illness, but also to treat their impaired priests. The use of treatment centers as the first response to a priest's sexually abusive conduct with a child also had the important canonical effect of making a penal process, with the penalty of laicization, an almost impossible alternative. Once a priest was sent to a treatment center, it was rare that he emerged with a clean bill of mental health, thus laying the groundwork for a defense of an impaired mental state that, under Canon 1324, prevented the imposition of the ultimate penalty in the canonical penal process.

There remained the thorny canonical question as to whether a bishop could order a priest to have a psychiatric or psychological evaluation. In 1998, the Congregation for the Clergy, in an administrative recourse brought by a pastor who had been ordered by his bishop to undergo psychological examination at a center named by the bishop, ruled:

> It is the consistent teaching of the Magisterium that investigation of the intimate psychological and moral status of the interior life of any member of the Christian faithful can not be carried on except with the consent of the one to undergo such evaluation, as it is clearly written about in the instruction of the Secretariat of State in their 6 August 1976 letter to pontifical representatives.

> Therefore this Congregation concludes that your Excellency can not, in this case, under pain of obedience, oblige your priest...to undergo psychiatric evaluation.[32]

Writing in *Civilta Cattolica* in May 2002, Gianfranco Ghirlanda, SJ, dean of the canon law faculty at the Pontifical Gregorian University, supported the proposition that priests accused of child sexual abuse could not be required to undergo psychological evaluation by their bishops.[33] This protection of priests' rights was almost always honored in the breach. Priests accused of child sexual abuse were "asked" to submit to psychological evaluation at named treatment centers, but the price of refusing was removal from their assignment, the loss of their faculties, and sometimes the financial support of the diocese.[34]

A lack of freedom on the part of the priest in consenting to psychological evaluation was not the only problem that the Apostolic See had with the treatment centers. In its notorious 1993 decision regarding Father Anthony Cipolla of the Diocese of Pittsburgh, the Apostolic Signatura seriously criticized the St. Luke Institute, which had evaluated Father Cipolla, and which many bishops at the time were using. The Signatura wrote:

> In the first place, we must take note of the fact that Conte a Coronata expressly says that *"in hoc autem iudicio ferendo multum deferendum est iudicio peritorum, qui RECTIS PRIN-*

CIPIIS instructi sint." [In making this judgment, however, great deference should be given to the judgment of experts who are guided by CORRECT PRINCIPLES.] This point is extremely important today, when there are so many psychological and psychiatric systems which assume an anthropology which is simply alien to any Christian anthropology. In the present case, the St. Luke Institute, a clinic founded by a priest who is openly homosexual and based on a mixed doctrine composed of Freudian pansexualism and behaviorism, is surely not a suitable institution apt to judge rightly about the beliefs and lifestyle of a Catholic priest. We should note further that behaviorism, with a "direction rigidly anchored in scientific positivism...makes use of the principles of learning and conditioning in order to interpret and modify behavioral abnormalities." (Psychiatria, op. cit., p. 59) This behavioristic tendency becomes all the more sinister when linked to the reigning myths of our totally secularized society and to a pansexualism which could only consider "abnormal" the traditional behavior of a Catholic priest.[35]

The difficult canonical issues on a priest's "consent" to psychological evaluation and the Signatura's language regarding St. Luke's,[36] did not noticeably affect the American bishops' use of St. Luke's or the other treatment centers, however.

As noted in the previous chapter, the bishops' Ad Hoc Committee had surveyed and recommended eighteen treatment centers[37] for priests who had sexually abused youngsters:

In 1994, the Ad Hoc Committee on Sexual Abuse issued guidelines to the nation's then 191 dioceses to help them develop policies to deal with the problem of sexual abuse of minors. Almost all dioceses responded and developed their own policies (USCCB document: Guidelines for Dealing with Child Sexual Abuse, 1993–1994). By this time, pedophilia was recognized as a disorder that could not be cured, and a problem that was becoming more prevalent due to the increase of pornography. Before 1994, bishops took their cue from experts in the psychiatric profession who believed pedophilia could be successfully treated. Priests guilty of sexual abuse were sent to one of several treatment facilities across the United States. Bishops often relied upon the judgments of experts in determining whether priests were fit for ministry. This doesn't mitigate the negligence on the part of some in the hierarchy, but it does offer some insight.[38]

A number of the centers where the bishops sent sexually abusive priests, and certainly those used most frequently such as St. Luke Institute, Southdown, and the Servants of the Paraclete centers, were actually operated in relation with the Church itself. The comments of Father Jay Mullins of Boston, who was sent to St. Luke's for evaluation in 1992 and who has consistently denied the allegations against him, are telling: "I wasn't aware there was any place like that. Seeing all of it, I thought, the bishops know where they're sending all of us. They know the magnitude of the problem."[39] Indeed, although no numbers of cases were collected by the bishops before they pledged to do so in the Dallas Charter in 2002, the very fact that the sexually abusive priests of the United States had access to so many treatment centers, many of them Church-sponsored, should have indicated to the bishops the scope of the problem long before 2002.

E. THE TREATMENT OPTION

In its defense, the treatment option was certainly better than what the bishops had been doing before they turned to therapy. In the days before the bishops' reliance on psychiatry and psychology, priests were most often sent on a spiritual retreat[40] and then simply placed back in a parish, usually far away from the one where they had molested their young victims.[41] The sexual abuse of children was treated as a sin, which of course it was, and the remedy for sin was confession and repentance. Father was sorry. He would not do it again. With the grace of repentance, however, rarely came recovery.

The manner in which the bishops relied on the treatment option is best illustrated by the career of Father John Geoghan of the Boston Archdiocese, best illustrated in the sense that, due to litigation against the Boston Archdiocese, the entire personnel file of Father Geoghan is available to public scrutiny. His own lawyer described him as "a poster boy for the issue of sexual abuse by the clergy."[42] Stephen J. Pope, a theologian at Boston College, says of him, "His was the most flamboyant case of serial sexual molestation by a clergyman, and the way he got passed on from one parish to another became the image of what not to do. The name John Geoghan now stands as a symbol for the sexual abuse of clergy and the hierarchy not taking precautions against sexual abuse."[43]

John Geoghan was also a poster child for the bishops' reliance on psychotherapy and treatment centers to handle the problem of priests who had sexually abused children.[44] From his first referral for psychotherapeutic treatment after an incident reported in 1968, Father Geoghan made a tour of the treatment centers of the United States and Canada for sexually abusive clergy. During his thirty-six-year priestly career, his treatment stops were:

> 1968 - Seton Institute, Baltimore, Maryland
> 1980 - One Year Sick Leave, privately treated by Dr. John H. Brennan (psychoanalysis) and Dr. Robert W. Mullins (psychotherapy)
> 1984 - More Private Treatment by Drs. Brennan and Mullins
> 1989 - St. Luke Institute, suburban Washington, D.C. (April)
> 1989 - Institute of Living, Hartford, Connecticut (August–November)
> 1990 - One Year Check-Up at the Institute (December)
> 1990 - Dr. Brennan (December)
> 1994 - Massachusetts General Hospital, Boston, Massachusetts
> 1995 - St. Luke Institute, suburban Washington, D.C.
> 1996 - Southdown Institute, Aurora, Ontario, Canada[45]

At last, in 1996, it dawned on officials of the Boston Archdiocese that the treatment option might not be working for Father Geoghan. Father Brian Flatley, assistant to the secretary for ministerial personnel in Boston, stated in an April 1996 memo to Cardinal Law that Geoghan "had not been 'totally honest' with his doctors and said that he could not be convinced that Geoghan was 'not lying again' in denying allegations that he had molested four Waltham boys [in 1994]."[46] On June 4, 1996, Father Flatley again wrote Cardinal Law recommending that he take a hard line with Geoghan. "'Father Geoghan is clever,' Flatley added. 'He withheld information from each assessing group, only to admit a little bit more to the next tester. He is a real danger. I think he needs to be in residential care.'"[47] The very next day Cardinal Law wrote to Geoghan "that if he did not seek treatment 'it will be necessary for me to invoke canonical penalties.'"[48]

Twenty-eight years after the first credible complaints of sexual abuse were made against John Geoghan in 1968, an official of the Boston Archdiocese has finally mentioned canonical penalties.[49] This should have been the first, as opposed to one of the last, archdiocesan responses to Geoghan's sexual abuse of youngsters. But note that, even when the canonical warning came, the threatened penalty was not for the sexual abuse of children, but for Geoghan's not following instructions to seek treatment. Obedience appears to have been more important than chastity, and certainly more important than protecting young children.

In July 1996, the first of many lawsuits was filed against Geoghan by a mother alleging that he had sexually abused her three sons whom she had taken to him for counseling.[50] He was also under criminal investigation at this time for accusations of child sexual abuse in Waltham, Massachusetts.[51] Sticking to the treatment option, the archdiocese gave Geoghan two choices: either treatment at St. Luke Institute again or at the Southdown Institute in Canada.[52] Geoghan chose Southdown over St. Luke's. He spent almost half a year there in residential treatment. This was Geoghan's final treatment stop.

Aside from his 1996 stay at Southdown, Geoghan was returned to an assignment by the Archdiocese of Boston after each of his treatment stays, where he went on to abuse more children.[53] When questioned about the 1984 reassignment in one of the many lawsuits against the Boston Archdiocese, Cardinal Law said:

> But I also viewed this as a pathology, as an illness, and so consequently, I, not being an expert in this pathology, not being a psychiatrist, not being a psychologist, my modus operandi was to rely upon those whom I considered and would have reason to consider to have an expertise that I lacked in assessing this pathology, in assessing what it is that this person could safely do or not do.[54]

A former auxiliary bishop of Boston, Alfred C. Hughes, has explained the Boston Archdiocese's approach to Geoghan:

> My predecessors and I thought we were addressing the issues at hand and providing for the appropriate protection of any potential victims. We had no knowledge of the extent of his abuse of children. Each of my predecessors who had received reports of actual molestation had returned him to ministry only after professional evaluation, treatment and positive recommendation for return to ministry.[55]

Again, one has to wonder at which point the Boston Archdiocese ought to have figured out that the treatment option was not working for John Geoghan's pathology. But the Boston Archdiocese was hardly alone in its reliance on the treatment option. As the report of the Philadelphia Grand Jury explains, "When asked by the Grand Jury why he placed obviously dangerous men in positions where they could abuse children, Cardinal Bevilacqua repeatedly testified that he relied on the advice of therapists."[56] In New York, when questioned about some cases in his former diocese of Bridgeport, Connecticut, Cardinal Egan said:

> The policy and practice that I established for the Diocese and followed in every instance required that any clergy

accused of sexual misconduct with a minor was, after pre-liminary diocesan investigation, to be sent immediately to one of the most prominent psychiatric institutions in the nation for evaluation. If the conclusions were favorable, he was returned to ministry, in some cases with restrictions, so as to be doubly careful. If they were not favorable, he was not allowed to function as a priest.[57]

In a deposition in a lawsuit against the Diocese of Joliet, Illinois, when asked why he allowed abusive priests to remain in ministry, Bishop Joseph Imesch admitted "that there were several priests he allowed to continue in the ministry even though he had concluded there were credible allegations of sexual abuse against them. But he said he allowed them to keep their jobs because they went through therapy."[58]

These were not the only bishops who allowed abusive priests to return to ministry after treatment. In 2002, the *Dallas Morning News* claimed that it had statistics indicating that at least 111 of the then-serving bishops of the United States had retained priests in ministry "after admissions of wrongdoing, diagnoses of sexual disorders, legal settlements, even criminal convictions."[59] When asked about these numbers, the bishops' spokesperson Monsignor Frank Maniscalco "expressed no surprise."[60] He explained, "The bishops made what they thought were prudent decisions at the time. The decisions were made on the best advice available."[61] This "best advice" came from the treatment centers to which the bishops had sent their troubled priests.

F. THE RELATIONSHIP BETWEEN DIOCESES AND TREATMENT CENTERS

The *Boston Globe* relates a revealing anecdote about how dioceses related to treatment centers:

Seven years ago [in 1995], Minneapolis psychologist Gary Schoener got a call from a rattled John Roach, Archbishop of Minneapolis and St. Paul. Roach asked Schoener to review the records the Archdiocese had received from the centers that had been treating priests: the St. Luke Institute, the now-defunct House of Affirmation, and the Servants of the Paraclete in New Mexico.

"The archbishop said, 'For God's sake, are we getting bad advice?'" Schoener recalled. "Are they using the wrong tests? Are they misinterpreting them? Is one of the centers better than the others?"

Schoener reported back a few weeks later. He had been impressed by the psychiatric reports, which he said would pass muster in secular hospitals. But he faulted the centers for accepting the church's investigations at face value, for failing to contact victims, and for leaving responsibility for follow-up to the priest's diocese. In short, the psychiatrists were working for the church. They "wanted to be liked," Schoener said.

"The mindset of these folks was to get him back there, that somehow the guy was fixable," said Schoener. "They are a key part of the mistake."

"It's not that I don't blame the church. I blame them both."[62]

There is no doubt that the treatment centers were telling the dioceses that their broken priests were fixable. The literature of the time is full of such assurances.[63] Speaking to the National Diocesan Attorneys Meeting in Williamsburg, Virginia, on April 30, 1990, Dr. Leslie M. Lothstein of the Institute of Living in Hartford, Connecticut, assured the assembled lawyers that "the fact is that many priests who are labeled as child molesters are treatable and can return to ministry."[64] In *Slayer of the Soul*, Stephen J. Rossetti of the House of Affirmation, collaborating with Lothstein, wrote, "The experience among the residential treatment centers is that these child sexual abusers can be treated effectively."[65] In the same volume, Frank Valcour, MD, of the St. Luke Institute, wrote, "Pedophilia and ephebophilia, as well as other sexual behavior disorders, are quite treatable and successful treatment programs have flourished in church-affiliated institutions."[66] Canice Connors, who at different times headed both Southdown and St. Luke Institute, wrote that "priests who are in recovery from the disease that caused them to molest children can be, in their recovery, good and thoughtful ministers of Christ as well as caring and holy men."[67]

In this respect, the treatment centers were in league with the bishops who wanted these priests back, healthy and able to serve in the diocese again. Leslie Lothstein has written of the relationships of Church-run treatment centers with the bishops:

> There were Church-owned and operated institutions (St. Luke's Institute, Servants of the Paracletes *[sic]*, St. John Vianney) that directly reported to the Church hierarchy and whose existence depended on Church monies and whose medical records were sometimes shared with the referring bishop or superior.
>
> Dual agency is a particular problem for Church-sponsored treatment centers. Dual agency exists when a person has obligations to two parties that may interfere with one's ethics, objectivity, and professionalism.[68]

The Philadelphia Grand Jury report, noting that the treatment center where the Archdiocese of Philadelphia sent its sexually abusive priests for treatment, St. John Vianney, was sponsored by the archdiocese, says:

> The therapists, however, more often than not worked for [the archdiocese]. That they understood their role as protecting the Archdiocese from legal liability was evident in many of the files we reviewed.

The therapists at Saint John Vianney, for example, warned in their "psychological evaluation" that returning Fr. John Gillespie to his parish, where he had abused two current parishioners, could present a risk. The risk, however, was not that the priest might further harm the victims—it was that he might apologize to them. Archdiocesan therapists warned: "If he pursues making amends with others, he could bring forth…legal jeopardy."[69]

In an especially egregious example cited by the Grand Jury, the archdiocese allegedly asked for and got a diagnosis on a priest-child sexual abuser changed by a therapist at St. John Viannney.[70]

Dual agency might explain why the Church-run treatment centers deferred to episcopal needs in their treatment of sexually abusive priests, but there was more at work here. For example, when Auxiliary Bishop Robert Banks of Boston did not like John Geoghan's 1989 discharge report from the Institute of Living, he asked for and got a written clarification that provided a basis for returning Geoghan to St. Julia's parish.[71] Lothstein's criticism implies that bishops preferred to use Church-run treatment centers because they could control events there. But the Institute of Living, where Lothstein is employed and where Geoghan was a patient, is not Church-run. What could explain the deference?

Barry Werth, writing in the *New Yorker* magazine takes up the story:

For the Institute of Living, the bishops' need for clinical cover in the face of these costly lawsuits came at an opportune time. "The eighties were a decade of ruin for the institute," a former senior staff psychiatrist told me. In 1981, he said, the institute had three hundred and eighty beds, drew patients from around the country, kept them for months, and had a six-month waiting list. By 1990, after H.M.Os had rewritten the rules for private in-patient care throughout the Northeast and elsewhere, the institute had become a cash-strapped regional facility with a hundred and twenty beds, many of them available. Amid fears that the institute might go out of business, the board of directors aggressively expanded its programs for priests and other professionals—doctors, lawyers, judges, executives—whose care could be provided for by generous third party payments. "With priests, of course, the pocket was bottomless," this psychiatrist recalls. "The Church would pay what it took, for as long as was necessary." He added that the treatment of troubled priests, some of whom had been accused of pedophilia, soon became one of the institute's most lucrative services, in a program called the Impaired Professional and Clergy Program of the Retreat.[72]

Stays at psychiatric centers for sexually abusive priests lasted five and six months.[73] Monthly charges ran from $5,000 to $9,000, all paid for, not by quibbling insurers, but by the dioceses themselves. In difficult economic times, it must have been hard for any treatment center, Church-related or otherwise, to give their paying customers news that they did not want to hear.[74] One psychiatrist who had worked at the Institute of Living told the *Hartford Courant* that "in the 1980's, when the institute was struggling financially, it viewed the treatment of clergy as a profitable niche. Speaking on condition of anonymity, the psychiatrist said there were conversations, formally and informally, about worries that the church could take its business elsewhere. 'These were good patients for the institute,' the psychiatrist said. 'The diocese paid cash.'"[75]

James Gill, a Jesuit priest who worked as a psychiatrist in the Institute of Living's clergy treatment program, described the problem of the bishops' trying to slant the diagnosis. He told the *Hartford Courant,* "Bishops frequently fail to share information."[76] Gill attributed this, not to a desire to mislead, but to the fact that "the church is simply a secretive organization that is unaccustomed to the full disclosure required in treatment centers."[77]

But withholding facts was not the only way to influence a diagnosis. Sometimes the attempt to influence the treatment center was much more direct. "Gill acknowledged there have been times when he believed a bishop was sending a priest for treatment with a specific outcome in mind—namely to get a green light to send him back to work. One of those times happened early in his own career, he said, when a cardinal personally appealed to him to pronounce a priest fit for duty. 'I thought this guy was going to need months of therapy,' Gill said. 'But the cardinal showed up and told me he needed the guy back in his parish.'"[78] And, of course, there is the example of Bishop Banks and the Institute of Living's rewrite of John Geoghan's 1989 discharge report.

When it was revealed that, in a deposition in a lawsuit involving the time he was bishop of Bridgeport, Connecticut, Cardinal Egan had "pointed to the institute's psychiatric reports as the justification to return priests to ministry,"[79] some of whom "swiftly reoffended,"[80] the Institute of Living shot back. The institute's staff went public with a very strong criticism of the bishops who had used their services:

> A nationally renowned psychiatric hospital that for years has treated clergy accused of sexual misconduct now says it was deceived by the Roman Catholic Church into providing reports that the church used to keep abusive priests in ministry.
>
> The church sometimes concealed information about past complaints against clergy sent for treatment, and disregarded warnings that the hospital's evaluations should not determine a priest's fitness for parish work, doctors at Hartford's Institute of Living said in interviews.
>
> As a result, the institute may have unwittingly provided the clinical cover cited by New York Cardinal Edward M. Egan and other church officials as their reason for not suspending some accused priests, including such now-notorious figures as the defrocked John Geoghan in Boston, accused of molesting more than 130 people.

"In some cases, necessary and pertinent information related to prior sexual misconduct has been withheld from us," said Dr. Harold I. Schwartz, the institute's chief of psychiatry. "In some cases, it would appear that our evaluations have been misconstrued in order to return priests to ministry."

Schwartz spoke of the "surprise we have experienced, to learn only recently as these scandals were emerging in the press, that in so many instances we have been providing treatment to individuals while being so inadequately informed."[81]

The Philadelphia Grand Jury found this same pattern at work in the Philadelphia Archdiocese. In a part of their report entitled "Church officials interfered with evaluations," the Grand Jury said:

[This] policy afforded easy opportunities for Archdiocese managers to manipulate treatment and diagnoses to keep abusive priests in the ministry. Secretary for Clergy Lynn often failed to provide incriminating information to therapists about priests he sent for evaluation. No Church-affiliated therapists spoke to victims or witnesses. The Cardinal allowed priests to shop for diagnoses, granting requests for second opinions when the priest was dissatisfied with the first.[82]

There is no doubt that a certain symbiosis developed between the treatment centers and the dioceses that made use of them for their sexually abusive priests. But under the glare of publicity, once it became known that some treatment centers had helped some bishops recycle their abusive priests, the relationship degenerated into one of finger pointing.[83] The bishops could take the position, "We re-assigned these priests because the treatment centers said it was safe to." The treatment centers could counter, "The bishops did not disclose material facts to us. They slanted the diagnosis."[84] Unfortunately, they were both right.

G. REASSIGNMENT AFTER TREATMENT

No one could argue that it was wrong or improper on the part of the bishops to send sexually abusive priests away for treatment. Any adult who seeks his sexual pleasure from a child is sick. Priests with this mental disease needed psychotherapeutic help, and so the treatment option was, in fact, the correct option for them.

The problem with the treatment option is what happened after treatment, namely the bishops' reassignment of these priests to active duty based on assurances from the treatment centers that they could safely perform in ministry.

As Leslie Lothstein explained in 1990:

> Most sexually addicted priests can be returned to a success-ful ministry after treatment. Deciding which priests are low risks for such assignments is not an easy matter. Part of the process involves permitting the priest to become engaged in intensive psychological treatment over a long period of time, and then establishing an aftercare program which not only addresses the individual priest's problems but also models a program of care and healthy lifestyle.[85]

The aftercare program often involved what was thought to be a "safe assignment" for the priest, one without any regular contact with young people. As Cardinal Bevilacqua famously said in 1993, "We're running out of old age homes."

But there were problems with so-called safe assignments for priests with a history of sexual abuse. As I pointed out in 1993:

> Such "safe assignments" are also thought to lessen the risks of the priest pedophile or ephebophile repeating his previ-ous sexual abuse of children. Assignments to hospital chap-laincies or convent chaplaincies or diocesan chanceries are suggested for this purpose. The difficulty with this is that children can be patients in hospitals. They can certainly visit hospitals as they can convents. The same is true of chancery

buildings. Perhaps the priest pedophile or ephebophile will not abuse a youngster *at* these assignments, but what if on his time off he contacts and abuses a child whom he met on this assignment? Unless such men are locked in their rooms when they are not actually working, it is certainly possible if not probable that they may use their free time to molest youngsters....Quite simply, an assignment operates as a badge of trust. It is an implicit statement that this priest has been tried and found trustworthy.[86]

In effect, there is no such thing as a safe assignment. When John Geoghan was finally pulled from parish ministry in 1993 and assigned to work at Regina Cleri, the retired priests' home in Boston, that was meant to be a safe assignment, yet in his free time he still haunted the swimming pool at the Boys and Girls Club in Waltham.

What, then, was to be done with sexually abusive priests after they had completed a course of treatment for their illness? Could they ever be returned to ministry, any form of ministry? In Catholic belief, a priest is an icon of Christ. The Congregation for the Doctrine of the Faith, in *Inter Insigniores*, a declaration approved by Pope Paul VI, said:

The Church's constant teaching, repeated and clarified by the Second Vatican Council and again recalled by the 1971 Synod of Bishops and by the Sacred Congregation for the Doctrine of the Faith in its Declaration of 24 June 1973, declares that the bishop or priest, in the exercise of his ministry, does not act in his own name, "in persona propria"; he represents Christ, who acts through him: "the priest truly acts in the place of Christ," as Saint Cyprian already wrote in the third century. It is this ability to represent Christ that Saint Paul considered as characteristic of his apostolic function (cf. 2 Cor 5:20, Gal 4:14). The supreme expression of this representation is found in the altogether special form it assumes in the celebration of the Eucharist, which is the source and center of the Church's unity, the sacrificial meal in which the People of God are associated in the sacrifice of

Christ: the priest, who alone has the power to perform it, then acts not only through the effective power conferred on him by Christ, but *"in persona Christi,"* taking the role of Christ to the point of being his very image, when he pronounces the words of consecration.

The Christian priesthood is therefore of a sacramental nature: the priest is a sign, the supernatural effectiveness of which comes from the ordination received, but a sign that must be perceptible and which the faithful must be able to recognize with ease. The whole sacramental economy is in fact based upon natural signs, on symbols imprinted upon the human psychology: "Sacramental signs," says Saint Thomas, "represent what they signify by natural resemblance." The same natural resemblance is required for persons as for things: when Christ's role in the Eucharist is to be expressed sacramentally, there would not be this "natural resemblance" which must exist between Christ and his minister if the role of Christ were not taken by a man: in such a case it would be difficult to see in the minister the image of Christ. For Christ himself was and remains a man.[87]

In his apostolic letter, *Ordinatio sacerdotalis* of May 22, 1994, Pope John Paul II declared this to be the infallible teaching of the Church, as was confirmed by a subsequent letter of the Congregation for the Doctrine of the Faith signed by its then-prefect Cardinal Joseph Ratzinger.[88]

Based on this very clear teaching of the Church, the theologian/author George Weigel has written:

A priest who sexually abuses the young has so disfigured himself as an icon of the eternal priesthood of Christ that he cannot function any longer as a priest. Period. Therefore, both clerical sexual pedophiles in the strict sense of the term (those who sexually abuse prepubescent children) and those who habitually seduce and abuse minors, heterosexually, or, as has been far more prevalent, homosexually, must be dismissed from the clerical state and permanently barred from any future ecclesiastical office. Such sanctions must apply to priests past, present, and future.[89]

The syllogism is compelling: A priest is an icon of Christ. When he sexually abuses a child, a priest permanently disfigures himself as an icon of Christ. Since he, by his own actions, has destroyed his ability to iconize Christ, a sexually abusive priest can no longer function as a priest. Period. Sadly, it was the inability of some bishops to make these rather clear connections that allowed them to seek the reassurance of the treatment centers to place sexually abusive priests back in ministry. Pope John Paul II had no difficulty seeing the syllogism, however. In his address to the U.S. Cardinals on April 22, 2002, he said unequivocally, "there is no place in the priesthood and religious life for those who would harm the young."[90]

H. SUMMARY

Why did the bishops fall so easily into the use of the treatment option as a major response to the clergy sexual abuse of children crisis? There are a number of reasons.

First of all, the treatment option allowed the bishops to quickly defuse an otherwise explosive situation and to give assurances to concerned parents that they were handling the situation. As described in chapter 3, when parents brought claims of child sexual abuses by a priest to the Church, their primary goal was to see that no other children would be hurt. Lawsuits and publicity were rarely the first thought of aggrieved parents and children. The treatment option allowed the bishop to tell angry and concerned parents that "Father is sick. He is being sent away from the parish to a hospital for treatment. He will not hurt another youngster." Unfortunately, such assurances were sometimes insincere. As reported by the Philadelphia Grand Jury:

When confronted with allegations that they could not easily ignore, Church officials sometimes sent priests for psychological evaluations. A true determination of a priest's fitness to minister was not, however, their main purpose. Cardinal Krol's use of these evaluations for public-relations purposes was blatant. He often transferred child molesters to new parishes before evaluations finding them mentally fit—usually with no convincing evidence—were completed or received by the Archdiocese. We saw this in the cases of Frs. Trauger and Leneweaver.

Father Leneweaver was transferred to his last assignment even when the evaluation did not declare him fit. Cardinal Krol found the evaluation useful nonetheless, as his Chancellor explained in a memo, so that "the faithful of West Chester," the priest's old parish, would be reassured "that the case of Father Leneweaver is being carefully studied and that he was not being reassigned routinely." On another occasion, when the mother of one of Fr. Leneweaver's victims complained that her son's molester had merely been recycled to a new parish, Chancellor Statkus wrote that he "assured her that truly Father Leneweaver was appointed in accord with medical advice, and that he [had] undergone therapy and medical attention."[91]

Second, in situations where the police were involved, the promise to put the abusive priest in a treatment center was seen as a way to convince the state not to proceed criminally against the priest. In effect the guardians of public order were asked to let the Church handle the problem internally by referring the priest for treatment, again, because he was sick. This approach worked in a number of cases, although less so as the crisis became more and more public. Recall that one of lawyer F. Ray Mouton's proposals to the prosecuting authorities in Louisiana was to allow his client, Father Gilbert Gauthe, to serve his sentence in a treatment facility. That was the original reason for his visit to St. Luke Institute in suburban Washington, D.C. Unfortunately, when a number of similar cases of child abuse involving other priests in the Lafayette Diocese came to light, such a proposal was no longer marketable to the public prosecutors. And once the extent of clergy child sexual abuse became clear to prosecutors across the nation, together with the fact that some bishops had reassigned sexually abusive priests after treatment, the alternative of treatment instead of jail time was no longer an option.

Third, the treatment option gave the bishops a way to handle the problem of sexually abusive priests and at the same time to avoid scandal. Scandal is a major concern in the Church's law. Scandal, its avoidance or repair, is mentioned twenty-eight times in the Code of Canon Law and most of the references are in the penal law.[92] The treatment option avoided scandal by keeping the matter secret. Father was sent away because he was sick. "It's an illness. We can't talk about it. Father has a right to his privacy."

Many bishops were genuinely concerned that, if the sexually abusive conduct of priests with minors became public knowledge, grave damage would be done to the Church's image and scandal would be given to the faithful. There was a genuine fear that public knowledge of a priest's sexual abuse of a child would cause confusion among the faithful as to what the Church taught and believed. There is nothing worse that a church can do than to be perceived as being hypocritical—teaching one thing and doing another. That is the true meaning of scandal: to cause confusion among the faithful as to what the Church teaches and believes.

But in their attempt to avoid scandalizing the faithful, the bishops made the problem worse. The faithful were not told why a sexually abusive priest was pulled from a parish. It was as if they had no right to know. The faithful were not told a sexually abusive priest's past when he was returned to ministry after treatment. Again, it was as if they had no right to know. The treatment centers were not even told the priest's entire prior sexual history. Why should the doctors be burdened with inconvenient knowledge that could lead to a worse diagnosis? Avoiding scandal became an excuse for an excessive secrecy that characterized the entire crisis of priests sexually abusing children.

Eventually the secrecy required to avoid scandal was broken as more and more priests' files and bishops' depositions became public in litigation against the bishops. But for decades the treatment option kept the problem of sexually abusive priests out of the public eye. One incident cited by the Philadelphia Grand Jury is emblematic of this approach:

> Monsignor Kelly also recounted to the Chancellor a phone call he had received following Fr. Leneweaver's departure from Saint Agnes from a parishioner inquiring about the priest's health and praising his work with the youth. The pastor then boasted: "We have been able, certainly with your help, to keep suspicion from entering people's minds."[93]

Avoiding scandal was a major concern of the bishops and the treatment option seemed tailor-made for such an approach.

Fourth, the treatment option gave the bishops a means to deal with a problem that they did not understand and did not know how to handle. The bishops understood that, if they referred these priests to the psychotherapists, the problem was out of their hands. This may best be described as the Pontius Pilate syndrome, but it is a very human response when people are confronted with a problem that they do not fully comprehend and that, in fact, frightens them. And that is where the bishops were in the middle of the clergy child sexual abuse crisis. Recall Francis Morrisey's comment when the crisis broke, "What was to be done?" It is a very human response, when confronted with a problem that is incomprehensible and frightening, to turn to the experts. People take their lingering illnesses to their doctors, their insoluble legal problems to their lawyers, and the bishops took their sexually abusive priest problems to the psychotherapists.

Fifth, the treatment option provided the possibility that these priests could continue to function in ministry, once they were "successfully treated." There is no doubt that the bishops wanted these men back, healed of their problems, no longer a danger to young people and able to function in ministry again. Recall that the problem of priests who sexually abused children was coming to light just after a time when a reported 23,000 men had left the Catholic priesthood in the United States and the seminary population had plummeted.[94] As explained in the *Hartford Courant*, "That jibes with an institute doctor's suggestion during a 1987 newspaper interview that the church, concerned about a clergy shortage, was anxious to get priests back into circulation after treatment. 'The bishops and vicars of priests, and leaders of religious communities, want everyone back,' Dr. Thomas J. Conklin said."[95]

Sixth, the treatment option was theologically attractive. George Weigel has written that the bishops' reliance on the treatment option was a triumph of the therapeutic over the theological.[96] In fact, the treatment option was a melding of theology and therapy. As Canice Connors wrote:

> We must recognize as a Church that forgiveness is a part of the warp and woof of who we are as Christians. For us to say that the one unforgivable sin for a priest is to molest children is to fly in the face of the redemptive message of the Lord Jesus. It will be important to continue to search for situations in which priests in recovery can minister in our Church in ways that are self-fulfilling and of benefit to the Church. Church leaders cannot throw priest child molesters aside, urge them to leave the priesthood, even seek ways to make leaving the priesthood easy, and continue to honor the gift of priesthood as it was given to us by Jesus Christ.[97]

There was nothing wrong with forgiving sexually abusive priests, but absolving them of their sins did not absolve them of the consequences of their sins.

The therapeutic community was, of course, high on forgiveness, but when therapy became the preferred option of the bishops to deal with sexually abusive clergy, disorder entered the Church. The Church's own law was ignored and the consequences were disastrous. As John J. Coughlin has eloquently written, "When the psychological model replaced the canonical order, the conditions were set for great harm to individuals and to the common good."[98]

6

CANONICAL LESSONS TO BE LEARNED

How could it happen? How could so many bishops get it so wrong? How could the crisis of sexual abuse of children by clergy so spin out of control to the point of doing irreparable damage to the Church in the United States? There are a number of ecclesiological reasons for the crisis, and others have written extensively about them. This is not meant to be a restatement of those reasons. Rather, based on the preceding five chapters, this is a summary of nine proposed canonical lessons to be learned from this tragedy.

A. THE BISHOP'S DUTY TO INVESTIGATE CRIMES

The first canonical lesson is that a bishop cannot shirk his duty under the Code of Canon Law to investigate canonical crimes. Canon 1717, §1 says that "whenever an ordinary [a bishop] has knowledge which seems true that a canonical crime has been committed, he is to carefully inquire personally, or through a delegate, about the facts, the circumstances and the culpability." The Latin verb used in Canon 1717, *inquirat,* which is a subjunctive, leaves no wiggle room. It means that the bishop "must inquire" whenever he has reason to suspect that a canonical crime has been committed in his diocese. The sexual abuse of children by a priest is considered a canonical crime by the canon law, and has been so considered for almost two millennia. When a bishop had reason to suspect that a priest had sexually abused a child, the canon law obliged him to investigate, either personally or through another, because this was knowledge of a canonical crime.

Yet too often there never was an investigation by the diocesan bishop when a complaint of sexual abuse of a child by a priest was received. All that usually happened was that the priest delegated by the bishop to look into such charges asked the accused priest if the charges were true. If the priest said no, that apparently sufficed. That, however, is not what the Code means by an investigation. Asking an accused priest whether or not he is guilty of sexual abuse and settling for the answer he gives is a conversation, not an investigation.

By not performing these investigations once he has knowledge of a crime, in addition to not complying with the Church's own law, the bishop is stepping on the rights of the victim. Canon 1341's disfavor of a canonical penal process is not applicable here. Canon 1341 only comes into play once a crime is determined to have been committed, and it cannot be used to justify not performing a Canon 1717 investigation. A person who has been the victim of a canonical crime, who brings that canonical crime to the attention of the bishop, has a right to have those charges pursued in accordance with the law. Canon 1717, §1, by imposing on the bishop the obligation to investigate, creates in the victim a concurrent right to have the investigation carried out. For every duty imposed by the Code, there is a concurrent right.

B. A MEANS TO VINDICATE RIGHTS

The second canonical lesson is that the Church's legal system must develop effective methods for vindicating the rights of the faithful. Canon 221, §1 says that "the Christian faithful can legitimately vindicate and defend the rights which they possess in the Church in the competent ecclesiastical forum in accord with the norm of law." But no norm of law has been clearly established for vindicating rights stepped on by a diocesan bishop, and there is no easily accessible ecclesiastical forum where those people whose rights have been trampled on can go.

Clearly, a victim who brings an accusation of sexual abuse to the bishop has a right under the Code to have the bishop investigate the charge, and, if it is credible, to proceed with a canonical criminal process against the priest. But if the bishop fails in this duty, there is very little that the victim can do. Bishops do not have to explain their decisions and there is no way to make them. The Code does not require bishops to offer the faithful reasons that might justify their decisions and actions, even when they substantially affect the faithful in such situations as whether or not to investigate charges of child sexual abuse against a priest or whether or not to reassign, after treatment, a priest who is a child sexual abuser.

In the Code of Canon Law, diocesan bishops are answerable only to the Apostolic See. When a bishop fails in a duty that the law imposes on him, individual Catholics who are injured by this failure can lodge charges against the bishop with the Apostolic See, namely the Congregation for Bishops. But action by the Apostolic See against a bishop is very rare. A bishop has to espouse outright heresy for the Apostolic See to act, and not one diocesan bishop in the United States—and there are unfortunately a good many who would qualify—has even been called on the carpet in Rome for ignoring his duty to properly investigate charges of child sexual abuse made against one of his priests. Regardless of Canon 221, there really is no effective way for a person whose rights a bishop has ignored to do much about it.

This is the case despite what Canon 1389, §2 says. That canon reads, "A person who through culpable negligence illegitimately places or omits an act of ecclesiastical power, ministry, or function with harm to another is to be punished with a just penalty." Has a bishop who has failed to perform an investigation of charges of sexual abuse by one of his priests "omitted an act of ecclesiastical power with harm to another"? A very strong argument could be made that this is the case. Certainly by not investigating such a charge, which then leads to leaving the priest in his current assignment or simply moving him to another assignment, a bishop has exposed many more youngsters to harm. But the prosecution of a bishop for such a failure would have to be done by the Apostolic

See itself, since only the Apostolic See is competent to do so, and that has never happened.

C. TRIBUNALS FOR THE PENAL PROCESS

The third canonical lesson is that the Church must develop professional tribunals, regional or national, if necessary, that can handle the penal process. Diocesan tribunals failed to prosecute Canon 1395, §2 crimes, the sexual abuse of a minor by a cleric, when such prosecutions may have stopped the problem in its tracks. Admittedly, the reforms of the 1983 Code made it more difficult to proceed penally against sexually abusive priests. But the canonical tools were there. They were not tried and found wanting, they were simply not tried. This means that, to a large extent, all the canonical criticism about the difficulty of the penal system remained theoretical. And this led to greater difficulties.

Priests who were sexual abusers of children surmised that they would not suffer any canonical penalties because the penal system was not being used. What could have been a major deterrent to their sexually abusive behavior was dropped from the Church's legal arsenal by the same bishops charged with maintaining the integrity of the Church's laws. Voltaire's comment in *Candide* is not inapposite here. There should have been canonical prosecutions *"pour encourager les autres."* Although canonical penal proceedings are not public, the clergy does know about them. They are discussed through the clerical grapevine. A number of canonical trials across the country as the crisis was breaking in the mid-1980s might have had a salutary effect in preventing future crimes.

The failure to use the Church's legal system to prosecute sexually abusive priests also had the effect of delaying Rome's understanding of the seriousness of this issue. If there had been canonical trials, there surely would have been canonical appeals. If Rome had seen, not a scattering of child abuse cases among priests in the United States (usually presenting as administrative recourse cases), but had rather been confronted with a large number of appeals by priests from penal determinations of guilt (with full acts of the case to examine) the Roman authorities may have understood much earlier the seriousness of the problem.

Instead of allowing the Church's own canonical system to reveal the extent of this crisis, however, the bishops' default allowed the American civil law system to become the vehicle for the revelation of priestly sexual abuse. Of course, there is nothing wrong with priests who have sexually abused youngsters being prosecuted civilly for such crimes. They should be. In fact, the existence of a canonical penal process should never be seen as an alternative to public prosecution, and perhaps the canonical penal process should encourage this by reference to the applicability of civil law in penal matters, as it does in a number of other sections of the Code. Just as the canonical prosecution of sexually abusive priests might have stopped the crisis in its tracks, so too public prosecution of priests who had sexually abused children, especially if recommended by the Code, would have had the same effect. Lengthy jail terms can be highly instructive to those of a similar criminal bent. But it was a tragedy that competent American tribunals did not exist to handle these crimes canonically, which by default then fell to the American civil law system.

D. THE BISHOP'S AUTHORITY IN THE DIOCESE

The fourth canonical lesson is that bishops need to exercise their ordinary, proper, and immediate authority in their own dioceses, without looking over their shoulders for instructions from Rome. During the clergy child sexual abuse crisis, the bishops dithered while expecting some canonical *"solutio ex machina"* from Rome. They spent their time (the first full ten years of the crisis, from 1984 to 1994) waiting for Rome to tell them what to do, to allow them certain modifications in the penal process, some of which may not even have been necessary. Then, when they received the changes in Canons 1395, §2 and 1362, §1, 2º that they sought, they rarely, if ever, made use of these tools. This was a decade lost while the crisis was building. Shifting the burden to Rome allowed the bishops to temporize, all the while saying, "We can't do anything. We are waiting for Rome." The effect of the squandered opportunity of those ten years on the eventual dimensions of the crisis was immense. It allowed its negative consequences to propagate exponentially.

The inability of diocesan bishops to deal with the devastating issue of clergy sexual abuse of children without instructions from Rome is also a frightening commentary on the self-image of the American bishops. Why did they feel a need for Roman direction on a question where their own canonical obligations to investigate crimes and to prosecute them where warranted were so clear? Rome may appoint the bishops, but their people sustain them. And their people were suffering. The fact that firm action by the bishops on this issue had to await clarification from headquarters is sad.

E. THE NATIONAL BISHOPS' CONFERENCES

The fifth canonical lesson is that, in certain areas, national bishops' conferences must be empowered to act promptly and on their own initiative. The U.S. national conference is not a governing body. Neither is the Canadian national conference. Yet the Canadian bishops had no trouble binding themselves in 1992 to joint action, albeit not perfect, on the issue of the clergy's sexual abuse of children. In the United States, on the other hand, bishops overly concerned with their prerogatives in their own dioceses prevented the conference from taking significant joint action until they were forced to do so under the glare of enormous public pressure in Dallas in 2002. Until then, the most the American national conference could do was to issue advisories.

The day is gone when what happens in one diocese has no impact on the other dioceses in the United States. Around the clock, instantaneous journalism on cable and Internet allows no problem to remain local in the United States. In the final analysis, the consequences of the Boston Archdiocese's reassignment of sexually abusive priests reverberated through every other diocese in the United States. To Boston can be traced the Grand Juries and attorney generals' reports in New York, Pennsylvania, New Hampshire, and Maine. To Boston can be traced changes in the statute of limitations on child sexual abuse in Connecticut, Illinois, Ohio, Kansas, and California and its proposal in other states. That is a lot of damage to lay at the feet of one archdiocese, but the chain of events is indisputable. Without the almost incomprehensible negligence of the Boston Archdiocese, there is no *Boston Globe* exposé. Without the *Boston Globe* exposé, there is no national spotlight. Without the national spotlight, there is no rehash of cases from the 1970s and 1980s that exploded into the national crisis of 2002.

To a certain extent, this is also a failure in the Church's legal system. Despite the promise of the Second Vatican Council, when the canon law on bishops' conferences finally came to be written, Rome's fear of potentially centrifugal forces won the day. Bishops' conferences are not governing bodies. Their ability to legislate for their territory under Canon 455, and thus bind their colleagues to joint action, is minuscule. This fact made the clergy child abuse crisis worse in the United States.

No serious canonist wants to see the universal Church divide into a number of national churches, but on the other hand, national conferences need to be able to move quickly to deal with national crises. If anything called for aggressive national action, the clergy child abuse crisis in the United States did. Yet the conference was not capable of this.

F. THE BISHOP'S DUTY TO FOSTER THE COMMON GOOD

The sixth canonical lesson is that diocesan bishops need to be conscious of their responsibility to foster the common good and to balance the rights of priests and laity. A diocesan bishop is bound by Canon 383, §1 to show concern for all the Christian faithful committed to his care, regardless of age, condition, or nationality, and in Canon 223, §2, when rights conflict, he is to foster the common good.

But some bishops were so concerned with their own image and the image of the hierarchical Church that they forgot the welfare of the least among us. They were so concerned with the rights of individual priests that they forgot the rights of the young victims. These bishops so feared the lesser scandal involved in upsetting the faithful with the knowledge that a priest had committed terrible sexual crimes that they failed to avoid a greater scandal, revealing the fact that many in the hierarchy had little or no interest in protecting children from priest predators. They exalted clerical rights over the rights of all others. They failed in the critical duty of balance, which is what is required by those charged with seeing to the common good.

G. SECRECY AS A LEGAL VALUE

The seventh canonical lesson is that no legal system or system of governance can be effective when its highest value is secrecy. *Crimen sollicitationis*, which gave jurisdiction over the crime of the sexual abuse of minors by clergy to the Holy Office in 1962, was never officially published. Instead, it was sent, in secret, to the world's bishops, with the instruction to keep it secret by placing it in the secret archives of the diocese. Twenty-two years later, when the crisis of clergy sexual abuse began in the United States, the existence of this document and the jurisdiction of the Congregation for the Doctrine of the Faith, which was not subject to prescription, had been forgotten. Saddled with a short five-year statute of prescription, American bishops did not prosecute this crime. The effect of the consistent application of the norms of *Crimen sollicitationis* on the clergy child sexual abuse crisis in the United States will never be known because secret norms are not enforceable norms.

In yet another bow to secrecy, in order to avoid scandal the bishops adopted their own highly secretive way of dealing with sexually abusive priests. They were shipped off to treatment centers because they were sick. Parishioners were told little or nothing of the real problem. This secrecy in turn led to a complete lack of accountability from the bishops. Since no one knew what they were doing, no one could ask any questions. It was a perfect world, but one that eventually came crashing down around their feet, as such worlds always do.

If the bishops do not hold themselves accountable to each other and to their people, and harm results, then the larger civil society will find ways to make the bishops accountable. Avoiding scandal is simply not a valid excuse for secrecy and a lack of accountability. Televised depositions of bishops in the dock are not pleasant for Catholics to watch and they certainly could not have been pleasant for the bishops under scrutiny, but that is the choice: openness and accountability to their own people, within their own Church, or the forced openness and scrutiny of civil society.

The idea that secrecy should be a value, let alone a foundational one, in Christ's Church, its legal system, or its system of governance should be abhorrent. Secrecy is the enemy of openness and truth. Jesus said, "For all who do evil hate the light and do not come to the light, so that their deeds may not be exposed. But those who do what is true come to the light, so that it may be clearly seen that their deeds have been done in God" (John 3:20–21). How can his body on earth exalt secrecy and not see it as betraying him all over again, especially when that secrecy has done substantial harm to his little ones and to his Church?

H. THE BISHOP'S DUTY TO DETERMINE ASSIGNMENTS

The eighth canonical lesson is that diocesan bishops cannot delegate the question of the assignment or reassignment of their priests to others, not even psychiatric professionals, under any circumstances. A bishop must know the strengths; he must know the weaknesses of the men with whom he shares a common priesthood. The assignment of priests is the bishop's duty, which he must exercise and take responsibility for. Many bishops abdicated their canonical authority to the psychiatrists and psychologists, all the while trying to manipulate the result. As it was actually used, the treatment option was disastrous for the Catholic community. Priests were treated and many were helped, help that they should not be begrudged. But the assurances of the treatment centers that these men could be safely returned to ministry failed to comprehend or factor in the communitarian nature of their ministry. Priesthood in a vacuum is meaningless. Priests must have a community to minister to. It was clear from the start, and the bishops would have known it if they were paying attention, that Catholic parents did not want sexually abusive priests serving in their community. As noted in chapter 3, the first response of parents typically was, "Get him out of here and don't bring him back." But too many bishops did bring them back, after a stint at therapy, and the second condition was worse than the first.

I. A NECESSARY CHANGE IN THE LAW

The ninth canonical lesson is perhaps the most important. The canonical penal process had difficulty, and eventually failed, to deal with the sexually abusive behavior of certain priests with minors. Perhaps the canonical penal process is not the best tool to handle priests who sexually abuse youngsters. The law of the Church has a long history of treating certain acts as rendering a man irregular for ministry. Canon 1044, §2, 2° was tried by some bishops as a way to remove sexually abusive priests from ministry by declaring them impeded in the exercise of their ministry due to a psychic illness. There are difficulties with this canon because it requires the substantiation, not simply of the sexual abuse, but also of an underlying psychic illness.

It has recently been suggested that the Code of Canon Law could be modified to declare a priest guilty of violating Canon 1395, §2 to be impeded from the exercise of ministry. This alternative would require proof of the elements of the crime, including imputability, although a penal process would not itself be necessary since an irregularity is not a penalty. But this alternative still shoots us back into the Church's penal process, which has not been very effective in this crisis. It should also be noted that Canon 1395, §2 only applies to clerics, so child sexual abuse that occurred prior to a man's diaconal ordination would not be disqualifying.

The Code of Canon Law recognizes certain acts as impediments to the receipt of orders, such as voluntary homicide, procured abortions, self-mutilation, or attempted suicide. While some canonists persist in referring to these impediments as *ex delicto,* the 1983 Code eschewed such distinctions. Perhaps the Code should also include on that list of impeding acts the act of sexual contact by an adult with a person below the age of eighteen, with no reference to Canon 1395, §2 and no references to a crime.

The Code also lists certain acts that make a person irregular for the exercise of orders already received. Here too the list should include the act of sexual contact by an adult with a person below the age of eighteen. Once the commission of such an act had been proven, that would be enough. There would be no need to refer to Canon 1395, §2; no need for proof of psychic illness; no need for a penal process; no need to worry about whether the act met a technical definition of sexual abuse, which canonists seem to have a difficult time arriving at; no need to worry about imputability or prescription; no need to worry about an *ex post facto* penalty since irregularities are not penalties. Simply state in Canon 1041 that adult men who have had sexual contact with a minor are irregular for receiving orders, and in Canon 1044, §1 that they are irregular for the exercise of orders already received. As has been noted many times, Pope John Paul II in his final address to the assembled American cardinals in April 2002 said very unequivocally, "People need to know that there is no place in the priesthood for those who would harm the young." The time is long past for saying one thing and doing another. If the Church stands behind the successor of Peter, these words must have a meaning beyond the rhetorical. They must become a part of the Church's legal system.

NOTES

CHAPTER ONE

1. Matthew 18:6–7.
2. 1 Corinthians 6:9–10.
3. Ephesians 5:5–7.
4. "The Didache or the Teaching of the Twelve Apostles," trans. James A. Kleist, in *Ancient Christian Writers*, no. 6, ed. Johannes Quasten and Joseph C. Plumpe (Washington, D.C.: Catholic University of America, republished by New York: Paulist Press, 1948), at 16. See also John S. Grabowski, "Clerical Sexual Misconduct and Early Traditions Regarding the Sixth Commandment," *The Jurist* 55 (1995): 527–91, at 556. An even earlier reference can be found in the Epistle of Barnabas, which says, "You shall not eat the hare....Why? Do not...be a pederast or like such people, because the hare grows a new anus every year." "The Epistle of Barnabas," trans. James A. Kleist, in *Ancient Christian Writers*, no. 6, at 51. The Epistle of Barnabas is apocryphal, but it appears in the *Codex Siniaticus*, which is one of the oldest complete copies of the New Testament. *Ancient Christian Writers* No. 6, *supra*, in introductory note to the Epistle of Barnabas, at 36.
5. Polycarp, "Letter to the Philippians," in *The Apostolic Fathers*, vol. I, I Clement. II Clement. Ignatius. Polycarp, trans. Kirsopp Lake (London, 1975), 288–91, quoted in Charles J. Scicluna, "Sexual Abuse of Children and Young People by Catholic Priests and Religious: Description of the Problem from a Church Perspective," in *Sexual Abuse in the Catholic Church: Scientific and Legal Perspectives*, ed. R. Karl Hanson, Friedemann Pfafflin, and Manfred Lutz (Vatican City: Libreria Editrice Vaticana, 2004), 13–22, at 14. Greek terms omitted.
6. Athenagoras of Athens, "A Plea for Christians," chapter XXXIV, "The Vast Differences in Morals between Christians and Their

Accusers," trans. B. P. Pratten, http://www.earlychristianwritings.com/
athenagoras.html, February 22, 2006.

7. Carl Joseph von Hefele, *Histoire des Conciles d'apres Les
Documents Originaux* (Paris: Letouzey et Ane, 1907), tome I, Premiere
Partie, 259.

8. Ibid., 317–20; see also "Council of Ancyra," New Advent
website, http://www.newadvent.org/fathers/3802.htm, February 22,
2006.

9. Roman M. T. Choli, "The *lex continentiae* and the
Impediment of Orders," *Studia canonica* 21 (1987): 391–418, at 395.

10. James A. Brundage, *Law, Sex and Society in Medieval Europe*
(Chicago: University of Chicago Press, 1987), 169.

11. John T. McNeil and Helena M. Gamer, *Medieval Handbooks
of Penance: A Translation of the Principal "Libri Poenitentiales" and
Selections from Related Documents* (New York: Columbia University
Press, 1990), 172–73 (David); 103, 113 (Cummean); 185, 190
(Theodore); 226 (Bede). But see Peter Payer, *Sex and the Penitentials*
(Toronto: Toronto University Press, 1984), 40: "Unfortunately, it is
often impossible to distinguish between canons addressed to religious
individuals and those meant for males generally." The text of these
Penitentials also does not clearly describe children as the objects of
these sins, although they would certainly be understood to be possible
victims. Thus, Doyle is overstating the case when he writes that "several of the more prominent Penitential Books refer to sexual crimes by
clerics against young boys and girls." The Penitential Books certainly
refer to sexual crimes, and the references are almost certainly (but not
always) to clerics or monks, but "young boys and girls" are not specified as the sole or even the particular victims of these sins. See Thomas
P. Doyle, "Roman Catholic Clericalism, Religious Duress, and Clergy
Sexual Abuse," *Pastoral Psychology* 51 (2003): 189–231, at 194.

12. McNeil and Gamer, *Medieval Handbooks*, 226.

13. Brundage, *Law, Sex and Society*, 174.

14. Ibid., 152.

15. The Latin reads: "Cap. 35—De clericis vel monachis, si
fuerint masculorum insectatores. Clericus vel monachus adolescentium
vel parvulorum insectator, qui vel osculo, vel aliqua occassione turpi
deprehensus fuerit, publice verberetur, et coronam amittat, decalva-
tusque turpiter, sputamentis obliniatur in facie, vinculisque artatus fer-

reis, carcerali sex mensibus angustia maceretur, et triduo per hebdomadas singulas ex pane hordaceo ad vesperam reficiatur. Post haec aliis sex mensibus sub senioris spiritalis custodia segregata in curticula degens, operi manuum et orationi sit intentus, vigiliis et fletibus subjectus, et sub custodia semper duorum fratrum spiritualium ambulet, nulla privata locutione, vel consilio, deinceps iuvenibus conjungendus." Burchard of Worms, *Decretum. Liber Decimus Septimus,* cap. 35, in *Patrologiae,* ed. J. P. Migne (Paris: Migne, 1853), 140:925.

16. Paul J. Isely, "Child Sexual Abuse and the Catholic Church: An Historical and Contemporary Review," *Pastoral Psychology* 45 (1997): 277–99, at 281.

17. Peter Damian, *Letters 31–60, Fathers of the Church—Mediaeval Continuation Series,* trans. Owen P. Blum (Washington, D.C.: Catholic University of America Press, 1990), 8 (letter 31, chapter 10).

18. Ibid., 6–7 (letter 31, chapter 8).

19. Ibid., 29 (letter 31, chapter 38).

20. The Latin reads: "Adulterii malum vincit fornicationem, vincitur autem ab incestu. Peius est enim cum matre, quam cum aliena uxore concumbere. Sed omnium horum pessimum est quod contra naturam fit, ut si vir membro mulieris non ad hoc concesso voluerit uti. Usus enim naturalis si ultra modum prolabitur, in uxore quidem veniale est, in meretrice damnabile. Iste, qui est contra naturam, execrabiliter fit in meretrice, sed execrabilius in uxore. Tantum valet ordinatio creatoris et ordo creaturae, ut in rebus ad utendum concessis, etiam cum modus exceditur, longe sit tollerabilius, quam in eis, que concessa non sunt, vel unus vel rarus excessus." Pars II C. 32 q. 7 c. 11, in *Concordia Discordantium Canonum ac Primum de Iure Naturae et Constitutionis, Corpus Iuris Canonici,* ed. Aemilius Friedberg, 2nd Leipzig ed. (Tauchnitz, 1879). All cites to the *Corpus* are from this edition.

21. The Latin reads: "Sollicitatores alienarum nuptiarum, itemque matrimoniorum interpellatores, etsi effectu sceleris potiri non possunt, propter uoluntatem perniciosae libidinis extra ordinem puniuntur.

§. 1. Qui stuprum puero (abducto vel corrupto comite), persuaserit, aut mulierem aut puellam interpellaverit, quidue inpudicitiae gratia fecerit, domum prebuerit pretiumue, quo is persuadeat, dederit, perfecto flagicio punitur capite, imperfecto in insulam deportatur. Corrupti comites summo supplicio afficiuntur." Pars II D. 1 de pen. c. 15.

22. The Latin reads: "Ad sacros ordines non accedat, nisi virgo, aut probatae castitatis. Nemo ad sacrum ordinem permittatur accedere, nisi aut virgo, aut probatae castitatis, et qui usque ad subdiaconatum unicam et virginem uxorem habuerit." Pars I D. 32 c. 12.

"Sacerdotibus semper castitatis observanda precipitur. Sacerdotibus, ut semper valeant altari assistere semper ab uxoribus continendum, semper castitatis observanda precipitur." Pars I D. 31 c. 2.

"Qui divinis sacramentis deserviunt, continentes esse oportet. Item in Concilio Cartaginensi II. [cap. 2.] Episcopos, presbiteros, diacones ita ut placuit, et decet sacrosanctos antistites aut sacerdotes, aut Levitas, vel qui sacramentis divinis inserviunt, continentes esse decet in omnibus." Pars I D. 31 c. 3.

23. Lateran III, c. 11: COD 217: "Quicumque incontinentia illa, quae contra naturam est, propter quam *venit ira Dei in filios diffidentiae*"; translated from *Decrees of the Ecumenical Councils,* ed. Norman Tanner (London and Washington, D.C.: Sheed and Ward and Georgetown University Press, 1990), 217; cited in James H. Provost, "Offenses Against the Sixth Commandment: Towards a Canonical Analysis of Canon 1395," *The Jurist* 55 (1995): 632–63, at 635; see also Brundage, *Law, Sex and Society,* 399: "The Third Lateran Council thought it necessary to adopt a canon specifically prohibiting 'that incontinence which is against nature' and decreed that clerics guilty of unnatural vice must either forfeit clerical status or be confined indefinitely in a monastery."

24. *Decretales Gregorii IX* (Extravagantium Liber), X.5.31.4.

25. Lateran IV, c. 14, in *Decretalium Collectiones,* ed. Aemilius Friedberg, 2nd Leipzig ed. (Tauchnitz, 1879), 452; cited in Scicluna, and translation in part based on Scicluna.

26. *Decretales Gregorii IX* (Extravagantium Liber), X.3.1.13.

27. "Si quis vero, tam laicus quam clericus, de crimine propter quod venit ira Dei in filios diffidentiae, convictus fuerit, poenis per sacros canones, aut ius civile respective impositis puniatur." Translated from *Decrees of the Ecumenical Councils,* ed. Norman Tanner, I:622–23; also cited in *Codicis Iuris Canonici Fontes,* ed. Petrus Card. Gasparri, *Concilia Generalia—Romani Pontifices usque ad annum 1745* (Romae: Typis Polyglottis Vaticanis, 1947), I:108. Hereinafter Gasparri, *Fontes.*

28. Council of Trent, Thirteenth Session, Decree on Reformation, chapter IV, in *The Canons and Decrees of the Sacred and Ecumenical*

Council of Trent, ed. and trans. J. Waterworth (London: Dolman, 1848), 84.

29. "Si quis crimen nefandum contra naturam, propter quod ira Dei venit in filios diffidentiae, perpetravit, Curiae saeculari puniendus tradatur, et si clericus fuerit, omnibus ordinibus degredatus simili poenae subiiciatur." Gasparri, *Fontes,* I:200.

30. Ibid., I:229.

31. Sacred Congregation for the Council, *Lavellana seu Romanum,* June 8 and July 6, 1726, Gasparri, *Fontes,* V:763–64. I am indebted for this reference to James Provost, "Offenses Against the Sixth Commandment," 632–63.

32. "Delicta carnis universim spectata intelligentur illa gravia et externa peccata contra *sextum decalogi praeceptum* aut cum aliis aut cum publico scandalo commissa" (emphasis in original). Franz X. Wernz, *Ius Decretalium* (Prato: Giachetti, Filii et Soc., rev. ed., 1913), 6:383; cited and translated in Provost, "Offenses Against the Sixth Commandment," 641.

33. The *Catechismus Romanus* promulgated by Pope Pius V in 1566, at Pars 3, caput 7, no. 2, states that the sixth commandment forbids adultery and other sins against the purity of the mind and the body: "Eius igitur duplex vis est: altera, qua disertis verbis adulterium vetatur; altera quae eam sententiam inclusam habet, ut animi corporisque castitatem colamus." Cited in John Tuohey, "The Correct Interpretation of Canon 1395: A Study of the Sixth Commandment in the Moral Tradition from Trent to the Present Day," *The Jurist* 55 (1995): 592–631, at 597. "Alphonsus Ligouri, whose own writings may be said to lay the foundation for the manuals [theology textbooks for the use of priests and seminarians], saw both an explicit and an implicit condemnation of acts against chastity [in the sixth commandment]" (600, n. 18).

34. Wernz, *Ius Decretalium,* 6:384.

35. The phrase is used in Canon 2357, §1, prohibiting laypersons from committing crimes *contra sextum* with minors; Canon 2357, §2, prohibiting adultery, concubinage, or other crimes *contra sextum* by laypersons; Canon 2358, prohibiting clerics in minor orders from committing crimes *contra sextum;* Canon 2359, §2, prohibiting clerics in major orders from committing crimes *contra sextum* with minors;

Canon 2359, §3, prohibiting clerics in major orders from generic crimes *contra sextum* not otherwise dealt with in Canon 2359, §1, §2.

36. The Latin reads: "Si delictum admiserint contra sextum decalogi praeceptum cum minoribus infra aetatem sexdecim annorum,…suspendantur, infames declarentur, quolibet officio, beneficio, dignitate, munere, si quod habeant, priventur, et in casibus gravioribus deponantur."

37. Provost, "Offenses Against the Sixth Commandment," 644.

38. Canon Law Society of America, *Revised Guide to the Implementation of the U.S. Bishops' Essential Norms for Diocesan/ Eparchial Policies Dealing with Allegations of Sexual Abuse of Minors by Priests or Deacons* (Washington, D.C.: Canon Law Society of America, 2004), 11, citing Pio Cipriotti, "De consumatione delictorum attento eorum elementum obiectivo: Caput IV," *Appolinaris* 9 (1936): 404–12; Domenicus M. Prummer, *Manualis Iuris Canonici* (Freiburg-i-Br: Herder, 1922), 667.

39. John P. Beal, "Doing What One Can: Canon Law and Clerical Sexual Misconduct," *The Jurist* 52 (1992): 642–83, at 679; citing Bertram F. Griffin, "The Reassignment of a Cleric Who Has Been Professionally Evaluated and Treated for Sexual Misconduct with Minors: Canonical Considerations," *The Jurist* 51 (1991): 326–39, at 338.

40. Thomas J. Green, "Clerical Sexual Abuse of Minors: Some Canonical Reflections," *The Jurist* 63 (2003): 366–425, at 373. Unfortunately, euphemisms have become ingrained in the Church's response to sexual abuse. See the *Report of the Grand Jury, of September 17, 2003,* misc. no. 03-00-239, Court of Common Pleas, First Judicial District [Philadelphia] of Pennsylvania, Criminal Trial Division, describing the files of the Archdiocese of Philadelphia, at 43: "Written records of allegations often left out the names of potential victims, while euphemisms obscured the actual nature of offenses. An attempted anal rape of a 12-year-old boy, for example, was recorded in Archdiocesan files as 'touches.' The Grand Jury often could not tell from memos reporting 'boundary violations' and 'unnatural involvements' exactly what Church officials had been told."

41. Pope John Paul II, apostolic letter *motu proprio, "Sacramentorum sanctitatis tutela,"* April 30, 2001, *Acta Apostolicae Sedis* 93 (2001): 737–39.

42. English translations of the 1983 Code are taken from Canon Law Society of America, *Code of Canon Law: Latin-English Edition* (Washington, D.C.: Canon Law Society of America, 1998). The corresponding canon in the Code of Canons for the Oriental Churches, Canon 1453, §1, does not mention either the sixth commandment or transgressions with minors. The Latin reads: "Clericus concubinarius vel aliter in peccato externo contra castitatem cum scandalo permanens suspensione puniatur, cui persistente delicto aliae poenae gradatim addi possunt usque ad depositionem." "A cleric who lives in concubinage or otherwise persists in an external sin against chastity causing scandal is to be punished with a suspension. If he persists in the delict, other penalties can gradually be added, including deposition." *Codex Canonum Ecclesiarum Orientalium Auctoritate Ioannis Pauli Promulgatus* (Vatican City: Libreria Editrice Vaticana, 1995), Canon 1453, §1. All English translations of the 1990 Code of Canons of the Eastern Churches are from Canon Law Society of America, *Code of Canons of the Eastern Churches, Latin-English Edition* (Washington, D.C.: Canon Law Society of America, 1992).

43. E. Miragoli, "Il confessore e il 'de sexto,'" *Quaderni di diritto ecclesiale* 4 (1991): 238–58; Thomas J. Doyle, "The Canonical Rights of Priests Accused of Sexual Abuse," *Studia canonica* 24 (1990): 335–56, at 348; Thomas J. Green, "Sanctions in the Church," in *The Code of Canon Law: A Text and Commentary*, ed. James A. Coriden, Thomas J. Green, and Donald E. Heintschel (New York: Paulist Press, 1985), 893–931, at 929.

44. This definition is the one that the USCCB used in the Dallas Norms of 2002. As those norms went on to say, "the norm to be considered in assessing an allegation of sexual abuse of a minor is whether conduct or interaction with a minor qualifies as an external, objectively grave violation of the sixth commandment," citing the USCCB's *Canonical Delicts Involving Sexual Misconduct and Dismissal from the Clerical State*, 1995, 6.

45. *Codex Iuris Canonici auctoritate Ioannis Pauli PP. II promulgatus* (Vatican City: Typis Polyglottis Vaticanis, 1983), Canon 277, §1; hereinafter CIC, 1983.

46. James H. Provost, "Some Canonical Considerations Relative to Clerical Sexual Misconduct," *The Jurist* 52 (1992): 615–41, at 630.

47. Ibid., 630.

48. Ibid.

49. Canon Law Society of America, *Code of Canon Law: Latin-English Edition* (Washington, D.C.: Canon Law Society of America, 1998), Canon 277, §2.

50. John E. Lynch, "The Obligations and Rights of Clerics (cc. 273–289)," in *New Commentary on the Code of Canon Law*, ed. John P. Beal, James A. Coriden, and Thomas J. Green (New York: Paulist Press, 2000), 343–81, at 359.

51. Provost, "Some Canonical Considerations," 636.

52. Ibid., 637.

CHAPTER TWO

1. Jason Berry, *Lead Us Not into Temptation* (New York: Doubleday, 1992), 50.

2. AP Wire, "Pedophile Ex-Priest Goes Free, Heads for Texas," *Detroit News*, February 4, 2000, Religion Section, http://www.detnews.com/2000/religion/0002/05/02050012.htm, September 9, 2005.

3. Gauthe only served ten years of the sentence. He was released in 1995, and the district attorney had him returned to jail to face charges in a 1982 child rape. A judge ruled, however, that the rape charge was covered by the earlier plea bargain and ordered Gauthe released from prison. AP Wire, "Pedophile Ex-Priest."

4. CBS News, "The Church on Trial, Part 1," *Sixty Minutes*, June 12, 2003. Transcript available at http://www.cbsnews.com/stories/2002/06/11/60II/printable511845.shtml.

5. Ibid.

6. *Boston Globe* investigative staff, *Betrayal: The Crisis in the Catholic Church* (Boston: Little, Brown, 2002), 173; hereinafter *Betrayal*.

7. Berry, *Lead Us Not*, 372.

8. Reverend John B. Feit pleaded no contest to a charge of "aggravated assault in the attempted rape of…a 20-year-old college student" in 1962. He was also questioned in the murder of another young woman. He served at Jemez Springs from 1967 to 1972. See Reese Dunklin, "Convicted Priest Helped Abusers Stay in Ministry," *Dallas Morning News*, January 19, 2004, http://www.dallasnews.com/

spe/2002/bishops/stories/071302dnpriest.d1a3.html, September 9, 2005.

9. Leslie M Lothstein, "The Relationship Between the Treatment Facilities and the Church Hierarchy: Forensic Issues and Future Considerations," in *Sins Against the Innocents,* ed. Thomas G. Plante (Westport: Praeger, 2004), 123–37, at 133: "In the case of the Servants of the Paracletes *[sic]* in Jemez Springs, New Mexico, a Church-sponsored treatment facility, working with a diocese, used poor judgment by allowing errant sexual priests under their care to continue to minister to vulnerable populations of children whom they eventually sexually exploited."

10. Ellen Barry, "Priest Treatment Unfolds in Costly, Secretive World," *Boston Globe,* April 3, 2002, A1+.

11. *Boston Globe* website, "Sexual Scandals Strike at Highest Level of US Catholic Church," http://www.boston.com/globe/spotlight/abuse/extrasbishops-map.htm, September 9, 2005. See also "Archbishop Sanchez Submits Resignation," *Origins* 22:42 (April 1, 1993): 722–24, at 722. According to this report, "Archbishop Robert Sanchez of Santa Fe, N.M., said in a March 19 letter to the archdiocese that he had 'written to the Holy Father, humbly asking him for permission to resign from my position as archbishop....' The letter came two days before CBS-TV aired a segment of its '60 Minutes' program in which three women said that a number of years ago, when they were in their late teens, they were involved in relationships of sexual nature with the archbishop; the program suggested that as a result Sanchez might have been lenient toward sexual improprieties by other priests."

12. Archbishop Michael Sheehan, "Archbishop's Letter Explains Bankruptcy Risk," *Origins* 23:30 (January 13, 1994): 529–30. See also Demetria Martinez, "Lawyers' Strategies Vie in Bankruptcy Case—Santa Fe, New Mexico Archdiocese Priest Sexual Misconduct Suits," *National Catholic Reporter,* January 14, 1994. *Find Articles* website, http://www.findarticles.com/p/articles/mi_m1141/is_n11_v30/ai_14760028, September 9, 2005. See also Lothstein, "Treatment Facilities," 133: "The Jemez Springs case led to the ouster of the bishop who was also accused of sexual misconduct. Eventually the treatment facility for priests in Jemez Springs, New Mexico, closed and moved to Saint Louis, Missouri."

13. *Boston Globe* staff, "James Porter—Key Dates," *Boston Globe,* July 16, 1992, A14+.

14. Linda Matchan, "Porter Guilty of Molesting Baby Sitter," *Boston Globe,* December 12, 1992, A1+ (National News).

15. *Boston Globe* staff, "James Porter—Key Dates," A14+.

16. Linda Matchan and Stephen Kurjian, "Porter's Treatment Questioned," *Boston Globe,* July 16, 1992, A1+; see also *Court TV Crime Library,* "Father James Porter: Pedophile Priest," chapter 4, "Cured Again," http://www.crimelibrary.com/serialkillers/predators/porter/index_1.html, September 9, 2005.

17. Linda Matachan, "Ex-Priest Accused in Minnesota," *Boston Globe,* July 14, 1992, A1+. Father John B. Feit, head of the center, wrote "glowing letters of recommendation on Porter's behalf, and was instrumental in placing him in a Minnesota diocese at the end of his 'treatment.'" Ron Russell, "Camp Ped," *Los Angeles New Times,* August 15, 2002, http://www.bishop-accountability.org/ca-la/mahony-2002-08-a.htm, September 20, 2005. This is the same Father Feit who had himself pleaded no contest to a charge of aggravated assault on a young woman prior to his work at Jemez Springs. See text at n. 8, *supra.*

18. James L. Franklin, "Porter Says Church to Blame," *Boston Globe,* December 8, 1993, A33.

19. Ed Housewright, "Trial Opens Against Ex-Priest, Diocese," *Dallas Morning News,* May 16, 1997, http://nl.newsbank.com/nl-search/we/Archives?, September 22, 2005.

20. "Rudy Kos was married in the Catholic Church in 1966 and received a civil divorce in 1971. In 1975 he expressed an interest in becoming a priest of the Dallas Diocese but his initial application for admission to the seminary was denied. On February 17, 1976 he received a Church annulment from the Dallas Tribunal for his marriage. This annulment was necessary for Kos ever to be ordained as a Catholic priest." Thomas J. Doyle, *Memorandum to Sylvia Demarest,* May 16, 1996, In re: Does v. Diocese of Dallas, 50; hereinafter Doyle Memo, http://www.bishop-accountability.org/tx-dallas/resources-files/doyle-memo, September 21, 2005.

21. Both of his brothers testified against him at the civil trial; "former Catholic priest Rudolph 'Rudy' Kos repeatedly sexually abused two younger brothers when he was a teenager and spent a year in a juvenile detention facility for abusing a neighbor, his brothers testified

Friday." Ed Housewright, "Ex-priest's Siblings Tell of Sex Abuse; Diocese Denies It Knew of Molestation Charges," *Dallas Morning News,* May 17, 1997, http://nl.newsbank.com/nl-search/we/Archives?, September 21, 2005. "As part of the annulment process the diocese was obliged to contact Kos' former wife which they did by phone on Dec. 19, 1975. Although the diocesan representative, Fr. Duesman, was asked to send questionnaires to the ex-wife so that she could respond in writing, no questionnaires were ever sent. The documentation contains references to the ex-wife, Kathy's, deposition in which she states that she advised the priest that Kos should not become a priest because he had a problem with sexual attraction to boys." Doyle Memo, 50; see also Pamela Schaeffer, "Reporter's Trial Notes," *National Catholic Reporter,* August 15, 1997, "[Kos's] ex-wife in testimony to have the marriage annulled in 1975 so Kos could enter seminary, said he was gay and 'has problems with boys.'" http://natcath.org?NCR-Online/ archives2/1997c/081597/081597f.htm, October 3, 2005.

22. Ed Housewright, "Victim Says Kos Phoned From Center," *Dallas Morning News,* May 29, 1997, http://nl.newsbank.com/nl-search/we/Archives?, September 21, 2005.

23. Ibid.

24. Michael Saul, "Kos Gets Life Term for Molesting Boys," *Dallas Morning News,* April 2, 1998, http://www.bishop-accountability. org.tx-dallas/Dallas-1998-04-05.htm, September 9, 2005.

25. Ed Housewright, "Dallas Bishop Testifies He Warned Kos," *Dallas Morning News,* July 2, 1997, 1-A. After the trial, Monsignor Robert Rehkemper of Dallas was quoted as saying, "No one ever says anything about what the role of the parents was in all this. They more properly should have known because they're close to the kids....I am sure some kids were damaged, but I think the damage might have happened even without Father Kos, you see." Thomas Keneally, "Cold Sanctuary," *New Yorker* (June 17-24, 2002): 58–66, at 60.

26. *Betrayal,* 43.

27. According to Shanley's archdiocesan personnel file, he was on assignment at "330 East 39th Street, New York, New York, 10016," as late as February 27, 1995. This is the address of Leo House, a Church-sponsored guest house, frequented by young persons. As the *Boston Globe* reported, "When Shanley was finally sent for treatment in late 1993 to the Institute of Living in Hartford, he admitted that he had

molested boys and had also had sexual relationships with men and women. The handwritten notes of the Rev. William F. Murphy, an archdiocesan official, pointed out that Shanley admitted to substantial complaints. The record cited his admissions to nine sexual encounters, four involving boys. It was after those admissions that the cardinal endorsed Shanley's application to run a guest house in New York City frequented by youths." Michael Rezendes, "Critics Blast Law for Comment on Archdiocese Files, "*Boston Globe,* April 13, 2002, A1. Shanley's personnel records are available at http://www.bishop-accountability.org/assign. Shanley-Paul-Richard.htm, September 9, 2005.

Geoghan was removed from his last parish assignment in January 1993, after which he was assigned to Regina Cleri, a residence for retired priests, from which assignment he went on to molest other youngsters, including the molestation for which he was convicted. *Boston Globe* staff, "Geoghan Preferred Preying on Poorer Children," *Boston Globe,* January 7, 2002, A1; *Boston Globe* staff, "Geoghan's Troubled History," *Boston Globe,* January 7, 2002, A1+; available at http://www.bishop-accountability.org/service-records/service-archive/ supportingdocs/Geoghan-John-J-History.htm, September 9, 2005. Cardinal Law's contemporaneous response to the *Boston Globe*'s publication of stories about Porter's sexual abuse of minors in 1992–93 was, "By all means we call down God's power on the media, particularly the *Globe.*" Peter Steinfels, "Bishops Assail Press on Sex Charges," *New York Times,* November 16, 1993, A24.

28. Steinfels, "Bishops Assail," A24.

29. *Betrayal,* 234. See also *America* staff, "Signs of the Times, Boston Priest Advocated Sex with Boys," *America* (April 22, 2002): 3, as follows:

"At a press conference on April 8, [2002] lawyers for an alleged victim of sexual abuse by the Rev. Paul R. Shanley released documents indicating that church authorities allowed the priest to continue in ministry despite receiving allegations that he molested minors and evidence that he supported sexual relations between men and boys. Famed in the 1960s and 1970s for his work with Boston street kids, Father Shanley is now becoming notorious for the numerous allegations that he sexually molested dozens of boys over the years.

"At a meeting in Milwaukee in 1978, he said the church's call for homosexuals to live celibate lives is unrealistic. In 1979 Cardinal

Humberto Medeiros, then archbishop of Boston, transferred Father Shanley to parish ministry after receiving complaints about the priest's appearance as a speaker at a Boston conference on man-boy love that has been described as the founding conference of the North American Man-Boy Love Association (Nambla). In that talk Father Shanley reportedly spoke approvingly of a sexual relationship between a man and a boy and criticized society for treating such relationships as crimes. 'We have our convictions upside down if we are truly concerned with boys,' a local gay newspaper quoted him as saying.

"Among the letters released was a 1990 letter from Bishop Robert J. Banks, then Cardinal Bernard Law's archdiocesan vicar for administration, informing Msgr. Philip A. Behan, then vicar general of San Bernardino, that Father Shanley was planning to stay in the California diocese for a year on medical leave and hoped to find housing there 'in a religious house or parish rectory.' The letter called Father Shanley 'a priest in good standing' and said, 'I can assure you that Father Shanley has no problem that would be a concern to your diocese.' Bishop Banks, now bishop of Green Bay, Wis., said on April 8, 'Obviously, I was not aware of any allegations against Father Shanley before I sent the letter.'

"Shanley's presence in the San Bernardino diocese led to a lawsuit against the San Bernardino diocese alleging that he had also sexually abused a minor there, which in turn led to the extremely rare occurrence of one diocese suing [actually cross-claiming against] another diocese."

See *America* staff, "Signs of the Times, Diocese Sues Archdiocese Over Priest Accused of Sexual Abuse," *America* (April 14, 2003): 5, as follows:

"Facing a lawsuit related to sexual abuse by a Boston priest, the Diocese of San Bernardino in California has sued the Archdiocese of Boston to recover any damages it may incur. In 1990 the Boston Archdiocese attested to the good standing of the Rev. Paul Shanley when the priest moved to the San Bernardino area on medical leave and wanted to engage in priestly ministry there. Kevin English, now 30, sued the San Bernardino Diocese in January, alleging that Father Shanley sexually abused him while the priest was living and working in the diocese.

"In its cross-complaint, filed on April 1, the Diocese of San Bernardino accuses Boston archdiocesan officials of 'misrepresentations and suppression of information' in a letter of January 1990 that described Father Shanley as a 'priest in good standing' who 'has no problem that would be a concern to your diocese.' The San Bernardino Diocese said since it was given no warning of Father Shanley's problems 'the diocese has no responsibility in the actions that caused this lawsuit and should not bear its financial burden.'"

30. *Betrayal,* 219.

31. Robert O'Neill, "Former Priest John Geoghan Killed in Prison; Was Center of Church Abuse Scandal," *Associated Press Boston.com News,* August 23, 2003, http://www.boston.com/news/daily/23/mass-geoghan.htm, September 12, 2005.

32. Denise Lavoie, "Defrocked Priest Sentenced to 12 to 15 Years for Child Rape," *Associated Press Boston.com News,* February 15, 2005, http://boston.com/Boston.com/news/local/massachusetts/articles/2005/02/15, September 12, 2005.

33. Jonathan Finer and Alan Cooperman, "Catholic Church Settles in Boston: Alleged Victims to Share $85 Million," *Washington Post,* September 10, 2003, A1+.

34. John C. Gonsiorek, "Barriers to Responding to the Clergy Sexual Abuse Crisis within the Roman Catholic Church," in *Sins Against the Innocents,* ed. Thomas G. Plante (Westport: Praeger, 2004), 139–53, at 152.

35. John Jay College of Criminal Justice, *The Nature and Scope of Sexual Abuse of Minors by Catholic Priests and Deacons in the United States 1950–2002, A Research Study Conducted by the John Jay College of Criminal Justice* (Washington, D.C.: United States Conference of Catholic Bishops, February 2004), hereinafter referred to as John Jay Report.

36. Ibid., Table 3.5.4.

37. Ibid.

38. Ibid.

39. Ibid.

40. Ibid., Table 4.3.1.

41. This is an extrapolation from Table 3.5.4 of the John Jay Report; 3,629 of a total of 8,419 allegations grouped by gender and age were boys in this age group.

42. Thomas J. Green, "Clerical Sexual Abuse of Minors: Some Canonical Reflections," *The Jurist* 63 (2003): 366–25, at 370.

CHAPTER THREE

1. Francis G. Morrisey, "The Pastoral and Juridical Dimensions of Dismissal from the Clerical State and of Other Penalties for Sexual Misconduct," *CLSA Proceedings* 53 (1991): 221–39, at 223.

2. *Acta Apostolicae Sedis* 93 (2001): 737–39.

3. CIC, 1983, c. 1717, §1. The Code actually says "ordinary," not bishop, but in the area of clergy sexual abuse of children, "some authors have suggested that the complexities of such cases virtually preclude anyone but the diocesan bishop from making the key decisions in such cases." Edward N. Peters, *Penal Procedural Law in the 1983 Code of Canon Law* (Washington, D.C.: Catholic University of America, 1991), 245, n. 7. Peters cites Jerome E. Paulson, "The Clinical and Canonical Considerations in Cases of Pedophilia: The Bishop's Role," *Studia canonica* 22 (1988): 77–124, at 105–6 and Bertram F. Griffin, "Canon 1722: Imposition of Administrative Leave Against an Accused," *Roman Replies and CLSA Advisory Opinions 1988*, ed. William Schumacher and J. James Cuneo (Washington, D.C.: Canon Law Society of America, 1988), 103–8, at 104.

4. The language of the Code is in the subjunctive, *inquirat*, which imposes a duty. As Velasio de Paolis has written, "L'Ordinario perciò ha l'obbligo di investigare quando arrivi al suo orécchio la notizia di un qualche delitto, che abbia almeno la nota dello verosimiglianza." Velasio de Paolis, "Processo Penale nel Nuovo Codice," in *Dilexit Justitiam*, ed. Zenon Grocholewski and Vincenzo Carcel Orti (Vatican City: Libreria Editrice Vaticana, 1984), 473–94, at 481. Very few, if any, bishops followed this injunction of the Code, however. As John P. Beal has written, "It seems that at least some of the disasters of recent years have resulted from the failure of church officials to deal responsibly with information about clerical sexual misconduct when it was brought to their attention." John P. Beal, "Doing What One Can: Canon Law and Clerical Sexual Misconduct," *The Jurist* 52 (1992): 642–83, at 644.

5. CIC, 1983, c. 1717, §1. Unfortunately, this obligation to perform an investigation was often ignored. See Office of the Attorney General Commonwealth of Massachusetts, *The Sexual Abuse of Children in the Roman Catholic Archdiocese of Boston* (July 23, 2003): 57–58.

6. CIC, 1983, c. 1341.

7. Ibid., c. 1720, 1°; c. 1723, §1.

8. The Code of Canons for the Oriental Churches does require notification to the accused, not necessarily during the preliminary investigation, but certainly before the hierarch decides to proceed with charges in a penal process. *Codex Canonum Ecclesiarum Orientalium Auctoritate Ioannis Pauli Promulgatus* (Vatican City: Libreria Editrice Vaticana, 1995), Canon 1469.

9. CIC, 1983, cc. 197–99, c. 1362.

10. Ibid., c. 1362, §1, 2°.

11. Ibid., §2.

12. Ibid., c. 1395, §2.

13. Sheila Taub, "The Legal Treatment of Recovered Memories of Child Sexual Abuse," *Journal of Legal Medicine* 17 (1996): 183–214.

14. John Alesandro, "Dismissal from the Clerical State in Cases of Sexual Misconduct," *CLSA Proceedings* (1994): 29–67, at 38. In 2001, the apostolic letter *Sacramentorum sanctitatis tutela* of Pope John Paul II extended these changes in the law to the universal Church.

15. CIC, 1983, c. 221, §1; c. 1342, §3.

16. Ibid., c. 1720, 2°.

17. Ibid., 3°. It should be noted that, in accord with Canon 1347, §1, a censure, for example, suspension, cannot be imposed unless the offender has been warned at least once beforehand. It should also be noted that, once the decree has been issued, the accused can, in accord with Canon 1733, §1, seek to engage the bishop in an equitable solution through common counsel, and, in accord with Canon 1734, §1, seek a revocation or emendation of the decree. And finally, of course, an appeal against the decree is permitted by Canon 1737.

18. CIC, 1983, c. 1342, §1.

19. Ibid., c. 1342, §2; see, however, John P. Beal, "At the Crossroads of Two Laws: Some Reflections on the Influence of Secular Law on the Church's Response to Clergy Sexual Abuse in the United States," *Louvain Studies* 25 (2000): 99–121, at 115, where he writes, "The first sign of this new [administrative laicization] procedure appeared in June of 1998 when the news media reported that three priests, two in Boston and one in Dallas, who had admitted to sexual abuse of minors, had been penally dismissed from the clerical state by

the Roman Pontiff personally. The one rescript I have been able to review reads:

"'The Supreme Pontiff John Paul II, having heard the report of the Most Eminent Cardinal Secretary of State concerning the delicts mentioned in can. 1395, §2 perpetrated by the aforementioned presbyter of the diocese of D. in the United States of America, after having examined the impossibility of proceeding to this dismissal from the clerical state through the judicial penal process according to the norms of cann. 1342, §2 and 1425, §1,2,°,a), after those preliminary formalities mentioned in cann. 1717–1719 have been completed, by a decision that is supreme and unappealable and liable to no recourse, decrees that the previously mentioned penalty of dismissal is to be imposed on the said priest.'

"The decree is printed on the letterhead of the Congregation for Divine Worship and the Discipline of the Sacraments. To it are appended the usual conditions and restrictions imposed by the Congregation in rescripts of 'laicization' (with the addition of the word 'dismissal' at several points) and the signatures of the Congregation's prefect and subsecretary."

See also Gregory Ingels, "Dismissal from the Clerical State: An Examination of the Penal Process," *Studia canonica* 33 (1999): 169–212, at 169, where he writes of "the administrative dismissal from the clerical state of at least four priests in the United States during 1998 effected through a direct intervention by their diocesan bishops to the Holy Father."

See also Francis G. Morrisey, "Addressing the Issue of Clergy Abuse," *Studia canonica* 35 (2001): 403–20, at 412–13: "After much discussion, a policy [on administrative laicizations] was indeed put into effect, although no formal document on this subject has been officially issued. Some of the first cases received much publicity in the secular press. The Congregation for the Clergy has recently developed a procedure to be applied in such cases, and which protects the rights of the priests in question" [citing Congregation for the Clergy, private reply, protocol no. 2169/98, November 11, 1998]. "This Dicastery would like to confirm that there is the possibility of seeking, through these same offices, dismissal from the clerical state *ex officio* and *in poenam* from the Holy Father for priests who refuse to freely request the dispensation. The judgment of the exceptional nature of a particular case is based upon thorough examination of the merits of each one."

As of February 7, 2003, faculty was granted by the Holy Father to the Congregation for the Doctrine of the Faith to dispense from the judicial process and refer directly to the Holy Father "in grave and clear cases" of clergy who had sexually abused minors for administrative dismissal from the clerical state; CDF can also, in such cases, itself impose an administrative dismissal at the request of the diocesan bishop after he has completed the preliminary investigation. William H. Woestman, *Ecclesiastical Sanctions and the Penal Process: A Commentary on the Code of Canon Law,* 2nd ed. revised and updated (Ottawa: Faculty of Canon Law, St. Paul University, 2003), 315.

This is a major change in the law which, previously, pursuant to Canon 1342, §2, was not to allow the imposition of a perpetual penalty through the administrative process. But see also Thomas P. Doyle, "The Canonical Rights of Priests Accused of Sexual Abuse," *Studia canonica* 24 (1990): 335–56, where he writes of laicization imposed "*ex officio* by the Holy See even without the cleric's petition and possibly against his wishes," at 347; and "laicization *ex officio* by the Holy See has been done in isolated instances in the past, although no documentation or hard proof of this is readily available," at 348. Doyle, who worked as a canon lawyer at the Apostolic Nunciature in Washington, D.C., in the mid-1980s, was evidently writing from his personal knowledge.

While I deeply admire Father Doyle's compassion for the victims of sexual abuse by the clergy, and wish that it had been much earlier shared by the bishops, his more recent canonical positions are more difficult for me to accept. In his affidavits and testimony on behalf of victims in the civil courts, he has opined that a diocesan bishop bears legal responsibility for all clergy child sexual abuse that goes on in his diocese, whether he had prior knowledge or not, due to the fact that, according to Doyle, in canon law, diocesan priests are the 24/7/52 agents of the bishop. I do not believe that the canon law supports such a conclusion, and I have often wanted to ask Father Doyle about Canons 533 and 550, which allow pastors and assistants to take holidays.

20. CIC, 1983, c. 1425, §1, 2º.
21. Ibid., c. 1723, §2.

22. Ibid., c. 1721, §1.

23. Ibid., c. 1324, §1, 1º; if there is a complete lack of the use of reason, as opposed to its imperfect use, then no penalty at all can be imposed. c. 1323, 6º.

24. Ibid., c. 1324, §1, 2º.

25. Ibid.

26. Ibid., §1, 3º.

27. Ibid., c. 1324: "The perpetrator of a violation is not exempt from a penalty, but the penalty established by law or precept must be tempered or a penance employed in its place if the delict was committed [in the presence of a mitigating factor]."

28. Ibid., c. 1737, §1.

29. Ibid., c. 1628; c. 1438, 1º and 2º.

30. Ibid., c. 1441, §1, 1º.

31. Ibid., c. 1638.

32. Ibid., c. 1643.

33. Thomas J. Green, "Canon 1342, §2 Involuntary Dismissal from the Clerical State," in *Roman Replies and CLSA Advisory Opinions 1991*, ed. Kevin W. Vann and Lynn Jarrell (Washington, D.C.: Canon Law Society of America, 1991), 118–21, at 120. Penal dismissals by the Apostolic See, however, would not be appealable.

34. Canon 1341 reads: "An ordinary is to take care to initiate a judicial or administrative process to impose or declare penalties only after he has ascertained that fraternal correction or rebuke or other means of pastoral solicitude cannot sufficiently repair the scandal, restore justice, reform the offender."

35. John G. Proctor, "Clerical Misconduct: Canonical and Practical Consequences," *CLSA Proceedings* 49 (1987): 227–44, at 237.

36. James H. Provost, "The Christian Faithful," in *The Code of Canon Law: A Text and Commentary*, ed. James A. Coriden, Thomas J. Green, and Donald E. Heintschel (New York: Paulist Press, 1985), 117–73, at 155.

37. Morrisey, "Pastoral and Juridical Dimensions," 227.

38. Ibid., 239.

39. Elizabeth McDonough, "Sanctions in the 1983 Code: Purpose and Procedures; Progress and Problems." *CLSA Proceedings* 52 (1990): 206–21, at 208.

40. Thomas J. Green, "Clerical Sexual Abuse of Minors: Some Canonical Reflections," *The Jurist* 63 (2003): 366–425, at 369.

41. Adam J. Maida, "The Selection, Training and Removal of Diocesan Clergy," *Catholic Lawyer* 33 (1990): 53–60, at 60.

42. Bertram F. Griffin, "The Reassignment of a Cleric Who Has Been Professionally Evaluated and Treated for Sexual Misconduct with Minors: Canonical Considerations," *The Jurist* 51 (1991): 326–39, at 333. Though Griffin did in the same sentence state that "there are times when penal sanctions may be imposed as a last resort."

43. See also Woestman, *Ecclesiastical Sanctions*, 67: "it is not the victims that should determine the punishment of the offender. The victims must be heard, listened to attentively, but they must not be allowed to dictate Church policy and the application of penalties for offenses committed" (footnote omitted). Under Canon 383, §1, a diocesan bishop is to be concerned for all the Christian faithful entrusted to his care, which would include, of course, the victims of clergy sexual abuse. And since one of the purposes of a penal process under Canon 1341 is to restore justice, the rights of the victim should be taken into account in any fair attempt to restore the equilibrium of the Church.

44. National Review Board for the Protection of Children and Young People, *A Report on the Crisis in the Catholic Church in the United States* (Washington, D.C.: United States Conference of Catholic Bishops, 2004), 97–99; hereinafter NRB *Report*.

45. Proctor, "Clerical Misconduct," 237.

46. Morrisey, "Pastoral and Juridical Dimensions," 224.

47. Morrisey, "Addressing the Issue of Clergy Abuse," 404.

48. Patrick R. Lagges, "The Use of Canon 1044, §2, 2° in the Removal of Parish Priests," *Studia canonica*, 30 (1996): 31–69, at 32; See also Morrisey, "Pastoral and Juridical Dimensions," 229: "It seems quite difficult to be able to hold a canonical trial against an accused cleric unless he has been warned beforehand about the consequences of his actions. For this reason, many dioceses insist today that the priest sign a statement to the effect that he is aware of the diocesan policy relating to sexual misconduct and of its consequences."

49. John P. Beal, "To Good To Be True? A Response to Professor Woestman on the Interpretation of Canons 1041, 1° and 1044, §2, 2°," *Monitor Ecclesiasticus* 121 (1996): 431–63, at 431.

50. Thomas J. Green, "Book VI: Sanctions in the Code," in *New Commentary on the Code of Canon Law,* ed. John P. Beal, James A. Coriden, and Thomas J. Green (New York: Paulist Press, 2000), 1527–1605, at 1600, n. 295; hereinafter *New CLSA Commentary.*

51. McDonough, "Sanctions," 214–21.

52. Morrisey, "Addressing the Issue of Clergy Abuse," 414.

53. Ibid., 420.

54. Lagges, "Use of Canon 1044, §2, 2º," 32, n. 2.

55. Although it is called penal law, it must be remembered that, in the 1983 Code of Canon Law, penal law does not have at its heart punishing the wrongdoer so much as it does restoring the overall well-being of the Church that the wrongdoer has injured. As Dean Angelo Urru points out regarding the Church's penal law, "È stato dato largo spazio alla misericordia cristiana; sono state promosse ragioni pastorali e si è provveduto a che la punizione non recasse danno ne pregiudizio ad esse; si è cercato di salvguadare sempre la dignita della persona umana e i suoi diritti. Per le stesse ragioni le pene *vindicative* hanno preso il nome di pene *espiatorie* e l'uso delle pene nella Chiesa è stato abbondamente ridotto e spesso le pene sono state sostituite da altri strumenti giuridici e pastorali." Angelo G. Urru, "Natura e Finalita della Pena Canonica," in *Il Processo Penale Canonico,* ed. Zbigniew Suchecki (Rome: Lateran University Press, 2003), 61–73, at 64.

56. Morrisey, "Pastoral and Juridical Dimensions," 227.

57. Green, "Book VI: Sanctions in the Code," 1600 (footnote omitted).

58. Beal, "Crossroads of Two Laws," 113; citing Philip Jenkins, *Pedophiles and Priests* (New York: Oxford University Press, 1996), 78–80, and Stephen J. Rossetti, *A Tragic Grace* (Collegeville: Liturgical Press, 1996), 88.

59. Ingels, "Dismissal," 170. Ingels, who is a talented canon lawyer, is no longer in active ministry, due to charges against him involving a fifteen-year-old boy in 1972, prior to his ordination. He was indicted for the sexual abuse of the boy, but the indictment was dismissed after the U.S. Supreme Court overturned California's extension of the criminal statute for child sexual abuse as unconstitutional. Ingels was also the object of a suit against the archdiocese of San Francisco by Jane Parkhurst, who alleged that Ingels had abused her for four years starting when she was a fifteen-year-old high school freshman in 1973.

Parkhurst's lawsuit was reportedly settled for almost $2.7 million. See Beth Fouhy, "US Priest on Abuse Charge," AP Wire, May 25, 2003; Jason Berry, "The Man Who Keeps the Secrets," *San Francisco Magazine* (September 2005), available at http:www.sanfranmag.com/archives/view_story/998; and Ron Russell, "Fast Times at Marin Catholic High," SF Weekly, January 19, 2005, available at http://www.sfweekly.com/Issues/2005-01-19/news/sidebar.html. Russell's work has been severely criticized by the Archdiocese of San Francisco, as was the Berry article for relying on Russell. See Office of Communications, Archdiocese of San Francisco, August 26, 2005, news release, "Archdiocese of San Francisco Strongly Rejects Assertion Made by San Francisco Magazine."

60. Morrisey, "Pastoral and Juridical Dimensions," 221.

61. Ibid., 224.

62. Beal, "Crossroads of Two Laws," 113. American tribunals were not alone in their lack of experience in penal matters. See Jean-Claude Rochet, "Efficacité Du Droit Pénal Canonique," *Année Canonique* 38 (1996): 137–39, at 137: "On a souvent remarqué que 98% des causes traitées par nos Officialités étaient des causes matrimoniales et que 95% étaient des causes de nullité. On ne peut même pas dire, pour plusiers raisons, quel est le pourcentage de causes pénales. Qu'il n'y ait pas de tribunaux spécifiques stables est déjà un indice du peu faveur que le droit pénal recontre dans notre église."

63. Beal, "Doing What One Can," 678.

64. Doyle, "Canonical Rights," 346.

65. John J. Coughlin, "The Clergy Sexual Abuse Crisis and the Spirit of Canon Law," *Boston College Law Review* 44 (2003): 977–97, at 981. In a footnote, Coughlin states, "Unofficial sources suggest that the administrative process of dismissal in exceptional circumstances has been used in about a dozen cases against priests in the United States" (981, at n. 22).

66. McDonough, "Sanctions," 213.

67. Ibid.

68. "From the period of 1917 to 1983 a good portion of the American clergy, including those who became bishops, would have been familiar with this application of Church penal law and would have been practically unaware of the ecclesiastical judicial penal process or of the possibility of a Church trial to punish an offending cleric. Only with the promulgation of the *Code of Canon Law* of 1983, which

had eliminated this institute of *'suspensio ex informata conscientia,'* did many bishops, as a result of various appeals to the Holy See, become aware that a more formal process was to be used in disciplining clerics charged with wrongdoing." Kenneth E. Boccafola, "The Special Penal Norms of the United States and Their Application," in *The Penal Process and the Protection of Rights in Canon Law,* ed. Patricia M. Dugan (Montreal: Wilson & Lafleur, 2005), 257–85, at 282.

69. NRB *Report,* 102. The board adds the obvious suggestion (at 102–3), "In hindsight, the Church would have been better served if a national canonical tribunal or regional tribunals had been established to hear and decide cases involving abuse by priests."

70. CIC, 1983, c. 1362, §1, 2° reads: "Prescription extinguishes a criminal action after three years unless it concerns: an action arising from the delicts mentioned in cann. 1394, 1395, 1397, and 1938, which have a prescription of five years." Canon 1395, §2 is the canon that makes the sexual abuse of a minor by a member of the clergy a canonical crime.

71. CIC, 1983, c. 1362, §2 reads: "Prescription runs from the day on which the delict was committed or, if the delict is continuous or habitual, from the day on which it ceased."

72. Ad Hoc Committee on Sexual Abuse, "Brief History: Handling Child Sex Abuse Claims," *Origins* 23:38 (March 10, 1994): 666–70, at 669.

73. John P. Beal, "To Be or Not To Be, That Is the Question: The Rights of the Accused in the Canonical Penal Process," *CLSA Proceedings* 53 (1991): 77–97, at 82.

74. Morrisey, "Addressing the Issue of Clergy Abuse," 417.

75. Beal, "Doing What One Can," 678 (footnotes omitted). This was a common theme in Beal's writings. See also Beal, "Crossroads of Two Laws," 113: "Third, many of the accusations of sexual abuse brought against clerics involve events that took place many years in the past. However, the penal action for prosecuting offenses mentioned in canon 1395 is extinguished by prescription when five years have elapsed since the date of the delict (c. 1362, §1, 2–§2). Consequently no penal action is available for prosecuting many cases."

76. Beal, "To Good To Be True?" 431.

77. *Crimen sollicitationis* states, in no. 73: "Crimini pessimo, pro effectibus poenalibus, aequiparatur quodvis obscoenum factum externum,

graviter peccaminosum, quomodocumque a clerico patratum vel atten-
tatum cum impuberibus cuiusque sexus vel brutis animantibus *(bestial-
itas)*." "The worst crime, to have penal effects, means any obscene,
external act, gravely sinful, committed by a cleric or attempted by him,
with children of either sex, or with brute animals (bestiality)." Suprema
Sacra Congregatio Sancti Officii, "Crimen Sollicitationis," March 16,
1962, Typis Polyglottis Vaticanis.

According to Dean Brian E. Ferme, "the *crimen pessimum...*was
understood to include paedophilia." See Brian E. Ferme, "*Graviora
delicta:* The Apostolic Letter M.P. sacramentorum sanctitatis tutela," in
Il Processo Penale Canonico, ed. Zbigniew Suchecki (Rome: Lateran
University Press, 2003), 365–82, at 369.

78. CIC, 1917, c. 1555, §1, which reads, "Tribunal Congregationis
S. Officii suo more institutoque procedit sibique propriam consue-
tudinem retinet; et etiam inferiora tribunalia in causis quae ad S.
Officii tribunal spectant, normas ab eodem traditas sequantur
oportet." "The tribunal of the Congregation of the Holy Office acts
according to its own custom and institutes, and it retains for itself its
own proper procedures; and also inferior tribunals, in cases which
belong to the tribunal of the Holy Office, ought to follow the norms
handed down by it."

79. CIC, 1983, c. 1402 reads: "The following canons govern all tribunals of the Church, without prejudice to the norms of the tribunals of
the Apostolic See." Lawrence G. Wrenn, writing in the New CLSA
Commentary, lists the Tribunals of the Apostolic See as the Penitentiary,
the Signatura, the Rota, "and, perhaps, the Congregation for the
Doctrine of the Faith when it deals with more serious offenses."
Lawrence G. Wrenn, "Book VII Processes, Part I," in *New Commentary
on the Code of Canon Law,* ed. John P. Beal, James A. Coriden, and
Thomas J. Green (New York: Paulist Press, 2000), 1607–54, at 1617.
"Perhaps" because *Pastor bonus,* in Part IV, "Tribunals," does not list the
Congregation for the Doctrine of the Faith as a tribunal of the Holy See.
Part IV mentions only the Penitentiary, the Signatura, and the Rota. But
the list could hardly be taxative because in the same *Pastor bonus,* the
jurisdiction of the Congregation for the Doctrine of the Faith over serious crimes against morals *(graviora delicta...contra mores)* was confirmed
by Pope John Paul II in Article 52: "The Congregation examines
offenses against the faith and more serious ones both in behavior or in

celebration of the sacraments which have been reported to it and, if need be, proceeds to the declaration or imposition of canonical sanctions in accordance with the norms or common or proper law." Pope John Paul II, *Pastor bonus*, Apostolic Constitution on the Roman Curia, June 28, 1988, reprinted in Canon Law Society of America, *Code of Canon Law: Latin-English Edition* (Washington, D.C.: Canon Law Society of America, 1998), 681–751, at 709.

80. I realize that "referred" jurisdiction is not the same as "reserved" jurisdiction, but I do think that the better analysis is that, once the crime was "referred," the Congregation's "reserved" jurisdiction kicked in. I do not know how else to construe Cardinal Ratzinger's clear statement made in 2001 that the norms of *Crimen sollicitationis* were in effect until that time. See n. 82, *infra*. I also see the counter argument from Canon 18 that the word *reserved* in Canon 1362, §1, 1º should be strictly interpreted since the effect is to deprive the accused of the benefit of prescription.

81. Beal, "Doing What One Can," at 655: "This instruction…is to be preserved in the secret archives."

82. For a fuller account of the import of *Crimen sollicitationis*, see Ferme, *"Graviora delicta,"* 368–69. The situation is made even more curious by language in the May 18, 2001 letter, *De delictis gravioribus* from Cardinal Joseph Ratzinger, prefect of the Congregation for the Doctrine of the Faith, to the bishops of the entire Catholic Church that accompanied the apostolic *motu proprio, Sacramentorum sanctitatis tutela*. This was "Epistula a Congregatione pro Doctrina Fidei missa ad totius Catholicae Ecclesiae Episcopos aliosque Ordinarios et Hierarchas interesse habentes: *De delictis gravioribus* eidem Congregationi pro Doctrina Fidei reservatis," May 18, 2001. In that letter, then-Cardinal Ratzinger, not an imprecise person, referred to *Crimen sollicitationis* as *"hucusque vigens,"* or as "in force until now," that is, until the issuance of *Sacramentorum sanctitatis tutela* on April 30, 2001. *Origins* 31:32 (January 24, 2002): 528–29, at 529. The Latin is available at Congregation pro Doctrina Fidei, *De delictis gra not vioribus eidem Congregationi pro Doctrina Fidei reservatis, Acta Apostolicae Sedis* 93 (2001): 785–87.

In *Sacramentorum sanctitatis tutela,* the period of prescription for clerical sexual abuse of a minor was set at ten years after the minor turned eighteen. On the other hand, as Ferme points out, with the promulgation of the 1983 Code, "The normative value of the Instruction *[Crimen sollicitationis]* remained but references were to be made to the 1983 Code and not to the 1917 Code which of course had been abrogated (cf. Can. 6 §1,1)." Ferme, *"Graviora delicta,"* 369. The 1983 Code created a five-year period of prescription for the clerical sexual abuse of a minor in Canon 1362, §1, 2°. The same canon, in §1, 1°, leaves undisturbed periods of prescriptions for crimes reserved to the Congregation for the Doctrine of the Faith. Most canonists thought that the five-year statute controlled, and it did for cases heard by diocesan tribunals, but not for those crimes referred to the Congregation for the Doctrine of the Faith.

This is the point of Cardinal Ratzinger's reference in *De delictis gravioribus* to the fact that *Crimen sollicitationis* was in effect until the April 2001 release of *Sacramentorum sanctitatis tutela*—*"hucusque vigens."* If *Crimen sollicitationis,* which gave the Holy Office/Congregation for the Doctrine of the Faith competency to hear the crime of priests who sexually abused minors, was in effect until 2001 (and not until the issuance of the 1983 Code, as some thought), then during the entire period of the clergy sexual abuse of minors crisis in the United States, if these crimes had been referred to the Congregation of the Doctrine of the Faith pursuant to *Crimen sollicitationis,* then they were not prescribable.

As John P. Beal, who wrote in 1992, says: "The ordinary norms governing the prescription of penal actions do not apply to offenses reserved to [the Congregation for the Doctrine of the Faith]" (n. 1362, §1, 1°). Prior to the promulgation of the revised code, competence over certain forms of sexual misconduct by clerics was granted to the Holy Office. The apostolic constitution *Pastor bonus* gives to the Congregation for the Doctrine of the Faith competence to investigate and impose or declare sanctions in "more serious crimes against morals which have been reported to it" [Art. 52]. "[T]he Congregation may be willing to consider a very serious case involving clerical sexual misconduct under its own broader standards for prescription." Beal, "Doing What One Can," 679 (footnotes omitted).

Crimen sollicitationis had a life of its own in the American press when, in July 2003, a plaintiff's attorney sent a copy to the U.S. attorney in Boston, alleging that *Crimen* provided proof that the Vatican had orchestrated a worldwide cover-up of all clergy sexual abuse of children. In paragraph 11, *Crimen* states that the Church's internal legal process regarding crimes reserved to the Holy Office is covered by the Holy Office secret (now pontifical secret), but that is all that it says. It does not say that the civil authorities are not to be notified, it does not say that the existence of the crime is itself to be kept secret or denied. It simply says that the Church's internal legal process is to be kept secret or confidential.

In any event, if the civil lawyers who stumbled onto *Crimen* in 2003 had been able to read Latin, they would have known that then-Cardinal Ratzinger had discussed the existence of *Crimen* two years before their discovery of this "secret Vatican plan" in his widely disseminated *De gravioribus delictis* of May 18, 2001. Maybe it took them two years to do the translation. See Kathleen A. Shaw, "Vatican Document Instructed Secrecy in Abuse Cases," *Worcester Telegram & Gazette,* July 29, 2003, 1. Or perhaps Francis Morrisey's comment is the best. He opined that *Crimen* could not have been used to orchestrate a worldwide cover-up because the document itself was so secret, most bishops were not aware of it! And he was right. See John L. Allen Jr., "1962 Document Orders Secrecy in Sex Cases; Many Bishops Unaware Obscure Missive Was in Their Archives," *National Catholic Reporter,* August 7, 2003, available at http://www.nationalcatholic reporter.org/update/bn080703.htm.

83. Green, "Clerical Sexual Abuse," 371.

84. Doyle, "Canonical Rights," 343.

85. According to the *Diagnostic and Statistical Manual of Mental Disorders,* pedophilia involves "sexual activity with a prepubescent child (generally 13 years or younger)." American Psychiatric Association, *Diagnostic and Statistical Manual of Mental Disorders,* 4th ed (Washington, D.C.: American Psychiatric Association, 1994), 527. "This disorder is characterized by either intense sexually arousing fantasies, urges, or behaviors involving sexual activity with a prepubescent child (typically age 13 or younger). To be considered for this diagnosis, the individual must be at least 16 years old and at least 5 years older than the child." AllPsych Online, The Virtual Psychology Classroom, http://allpsych.com/disorders/paraphilias/pedophilia.html, September 20, 2005.

86. Ephebophilia is not listed as a paraphilia in the *Diagnostic and Statistical Manual of Mental Disorders.* The victim of an ephebophile's

sexual abuse is a postpubescent minor. "There are others who are ephebophiles, i.e., sexually attracted to postpubescent children." Rossetti, *A Tragic Grace,* 67.

87. Proctor, "Clerical Misconduct," 237.

88. Bertram F. Griffin, "Canon 290 Penal Dismissal from the Clerical State," in *Roman Replies and CLSA Advisory Opinions 1988,* ed. William A. Schumacher and J. James Cuneo (Washington, D.C.: Canon Law Society of America, 1988), 66–71, at 67. Griffin was of the opinion that the "grooming" that was a precursor to the actual sexual abuse of a youngster made it impossible to argue that these were crimes of passion for which the full penalty had to be mitigated. He thought that the planning or "grooming" that went into these crimes on the part of the abuser prevented their characterization as spontaneous crimes of passion.

89. Morrisey, "Pastoral and Juridical Dimensions," 232. In a later article, Morrisey emphasized that the presumption of the law was that external acts are imputable to the actor unless otherwise demonstrated, that is, the burden was on the priest to raise the mental illness defense: "If a cleric is involved in sexual misconduct, can he use the defense that he suffers from an illness, so that imputability is lacking (canon 1321)? The Code presumes that if a person carries out a criminal act, he is responsible for his actions. Therefore, the presumption would have to be reversed in each case if such a claim were to be made." Morrisey, "Addressing the Issue of Clergy Abuse," 417.

90. Beal, "Doing What One Can," 679–80.

91. Ibid., 680. Beal voiced the same opinion in a 1996 article: "At still other times, the underlying disorder is so severe that it seems imputability for the delict was, if not extinguished, at least so diminished that the most severe penalty of dismissal from the clerical state either cannot be imposed or seem inappropriate *[sic]*." Beal, "To Good To Be True?" 431.

92. William H. Woestman, "To Good To Be True: A Current Interpretation of Canons 1041, 1º and 1044, §2, 2º," *Monitor Ecclesiasticus* 120 (1995): 619–29, at 619.

93. There was also the consideration that simply defrocking a priest and setting him free in society was not the safest alternative either. See Stephen J. Rossetti, "The Catholic Church and Child Sexual Abuse," *America* (April 22, 2002): 13–16, at 14: "But is this the

safest course of action for children? When priests are dismissed from ministry, they go out into society unsupervised and perhaps even untreated. They are free to do as they please."

94. Thomas J. Reese, "Women's Pastoral Fails," *America* (December 5, 1992): 443–44, at 444.

95. Ad Hoc Committee, "Brief History," 669. See also John J. Coughlin, "The Clergy Sexual Abuse Crisis and the Spirit of Canon Law," *Boston College Law Review* 44 (2003): 977–97, at 987: "Moreover, reliance on the psychological model tended to mitigate the imputability of the offense on the ground that the priest possessed diminished capacity to control his impulses" (footnote omitted).

96. NRB *Report,* 103.

97. Proctor, "Clerical Misconduct," 237.

98. Ibid.

99. CIC, 1983, c. 1727, §1 reads: "The accused can propose an appeal even if the sentence dismissed the accused only because the penalty was facultative or because the judge used the power mentioned in cann. 1344 and 1345." Canons 1344 and 1345 allow a judge to defer or waive a penalty.

100. Canon 1353 reads: "An appeal or recourse from judicial sentences or from decrees, which impose or declare a penalty, has a suspensive effect." See also Proctor, "Clerical Misconduct," 238: "Finally, an appeal or recourse of any penalty (censure or expiatory penalty), administratively or judicially inflicted, automatically suspends the execution of the penalty."

101. Michael O'Reilly, "Recent Developments in the Laicization of Priests," *The Jurist* 52 (1992): 684–96, at 695–96.

102. NRB *Report,* 103.

103. Ann Rodgers-Melnick, "Rare Sanction Imposed on Priest," *Pittsburgh Post-Gazette,* November 16, 2002, A1+.

104. Ibid.

105. Beal, "Too Good To Be True?" 455–56. Karen Ann Ballotta, "Losing Its Soul: How the Cipolla Case Limits the Catholic Church's Ability to Discipline Sexually Abusive Priests," *Emory Law Journal* 43 (1994): 1431–65, at 1449–50; Ann Rodgers-Melnick, "Vatican Clears Priest, Wuerl Rejects Verdict," *Pittsburgh Post-Gazette,* March 21, 1993, A-1+; Apostolic Signatura, definitive sentence, March 9, 1993, P.N. 22571/91 CA.

106. Ballotta, "Losing Its Soul," 1450; Beal, "To Good To Be True?" 456.

107. Beal, "To Good To Be True?" 456.

108. Ibid., 457.

109. Apostolic Signatura, definitive sentence, March 9, 1993, P.N. 22571/91 CA.

110. The Signatura eventually agreed to a *Restitutio in integram* on this case and reversed itself two years later. Apostolic Signatura, definitive sentence, June 24, 1995, P.N. 22571/91 CA. On September 19, 2002, the priest involved was involuntarily dismissed from the clerical state by Pope John Paul II, not for the alleged sexual abuse, but for failure to follow the bishop's decree that he cease any public ministry. Ann Rodgers-Melnick, "Rare Sanction Imposed on Priest," *Pittsburgh Post-Gazette*, November 16, 2002, A-1.

111. Ann Rodgers-Melnick, "Bishops Torn by Cipolla Decision," *Pittsburgh Post-Gazette*, June 21, 1993, A-1.

112. Ibid.

113. In a 1994 case, *coram Colagiovanni*, April 9, 1994, involving a priest who admitted to being a serial pedophile, the Roman Rota did overturn a penal sentence of dismissal from the clerical state imposed by a diocesan tribunal. See Augustine Mendonca, "Justice and Equity: At Whose Expense?" in *The Art of the Good and Equitable*, ed. Frederick C. Easton (Washington, D.C.: Canon Law Society of America, 2002), 189–235, at 232. The same case is referred to by Ronny E. Jenkins, "Jurisprudence in Penal Cases: Select Themes from the Judicial Doctrine of the Tribunal of the Roman Rota," *CLSA Proceedings* 67 (2005): 95–122, at 103. Jenkins notes that the case is reported in *Monitor Ecclesiasticus* 122 (1997): 91–95.

114. Brooks Egerton and Reese Dunklin, "Two-Thirds of Bishops Let Accused Priests Work," *Dallas Morning News*, June 12, 2002, 1A+.

115. See Berry, *Lead Us Not*, 10: "We want Father Gauthe removed from Henry immediately," was the first request of the Robichaux family, whose son was a victim of Gauthe; see also Margaret Gallant, August 16, 1982 letter to Cardinal Medeiros, *Betrayal*, 214: "As you know, our family had a conference with Bishop Daly over two weeks ago. Since that priest [John Geoghan] is still in his parish, it appears that no action has been taken." See also report of the Grand Jury, Philadelphia, Pennsylvania, 109: "Monsignor Kelly warned Msgr.

Statkus that Andy's father 'had not ruled out [going to the police] unless action [was] taken by church authorities.' Monsignor Kelly related that the father 'did not want to see him [Father Raymond O. Leneweaver] again at the Altar or hear him preach.' The father wanted him 'away from here.'"

116. Beal, "Doing What One Can," 647, n. 5.

117. Morrisey, "Pastoral and Juridical Dimensions," 227.

118. CIC, 1983, cc. 1717–19.

119. Ibid., c. 1722; removal from an assignment is only possible once the canonical process has begun, that is, after a preliminary investigation has led to a determination to open the process against the priest. A priest cannot be removed until after the preliminary investigation is over because, by its nature, the preliminary investigation will determine whether there is a process or not. But see Doyle, "Canonical Rights," 335–56: "The leave may be imposed as soon as the ordinary has reason to believe that it is needed. Since it is rare that formal judicial proceedings are held, c. 1722 would be useless to bishops if the narrow interpretation is followed." He then cites Bertram F. Griffin, "Canon 1722: Imposition of Administrative Leave Against an Accused," *The Jurist* 48 (1988): 107 for the proposition that, "in any event, the *dubium juris* raised by canonists on this issue leaves the ordinary free to impose 'administrative leave' whenever necessary during any stage of the penal process."

120. This is no longer the case. The penalty of dismissal from the clerical state has been available administratively since February 7, 2003. See "Decisions, Pope John Paul II, Subsequent to the Promulgation of *Sacramentorum sanctitatis tutela*," in Woestman, *Ecclesiastical Sanctions*, 315.

121. CIC, 1983, c. 1526; c. 1721, §1.

122. Ibid., c. 1547.

123. Ibid., c. 1550, §1.

124. Ibid., c. 1558, §1.

125. Ibid., c. 1425, §1, 2°.

126. Ibid., c. 1567, §1; c. 483, §2.

127. Ibid., c. 1559.

128. Ibid., c. 1561.

129. Ibid., c. 1558, §1; c. 1561.

130. Beal, "Doing What One Can," 655.

131. James H. Provost, "Some Canonical Considerations Relative to Clerical Sexual Misconduct," *The Jurist* 52 (1992): 615–41, at 616.

132. CIC, 1983, c. 391, §1, §2.

133. Stradley, Ronon, Stevens & Young, LLP., *Response of the Archdiocese of Philadelphia to the Report of the Investigating Grand Jury Pursuant to 42 PA. C.S. § 4552(e)* 53 (Philadelphia, 2005).

134. NRB *Report*, 120; the lawyers more often than not were insurance company lawyers. See Adam Liptak, "Religion and the Law," *New York Times*, April 14, 2002, A30: "insurance companies, not church officials chose the lawyers in most of the cases, and the officials are often reluctant to question the lawyers' tactical judgments, legal experts say. Mark E. Chopko, the general counsel of the United States Conference of Catholic Bishops, said that only about 30 of the nation's 194 Roman Catholic dioceses have legal departments."

135. Julia Quinn Dempsey, John R. Gorman, and John P. Madden, *Report to Joseph Cardinal Bernardin, Archbishop of Chicago, The Cardinal's Commission on Clerical Sexual Misconduct with Minors* (Chicago, Ill., June 1992), 20.

136. Morrisey, "Pastoral and Juridical Dimensions," 223.

137. CIC, 1983, c. 1472, §1.

138. Ibid., c. 1598, §1; the second sentence of c. 1598, §1 does allow a judge to sequester specific acts (e.g., individual testimony) "to avoid a most grave danger." This sequestration, however, cannot impede the right of defense.

139. See Ron Russell, "Blind Eye Unto the Holy See," *SF Weekly* July 13, 2005: "Shortly after [the Promoter of Justice] suggested it, however, church officials halted efforts to defrock O'Grady. Recently disclosed church documents suggest the officials were concerned that information [the Promoter] was developing as part of the canon law case might, if discovered, be used by [the plaintiffs] in their civil suit against the church. Such a finding would have been explosive, plaintiff's lawyers say, because it would have given victims ammunition to argue that the church was derelict for having ordained O'Grady." http://www.sfweekly.com/Issues/2005-07-13/news/feature.html, February 16, 2006.

140. Francis G. Morrisey, "Procedures to be Applied in Cases of Alleged Sexual Misconduct by a Priest," *Studia canonica* 26 (1992): 39–73, at 48.

141. McDonough, "Sanctions," 212.

142. Ibid., 213.

143. Reese, "Women's Pastoral," 444.

144. Gregory Ingels, "Examination of the Rights of Priests Accused of Misconduct," presentation to National Federation of Priests' Councils, April 17, 2002, unpublished manuscript, 1.

145. NRB *Report,* 120.

146. Beal, "Doing What One Can," 644.

147. *America* staff, "Signs of the Times: Vatican Official Says Church Has Legal Tools to Address Sex Abuse," *America* (May 20, 2002): 4–5, at 4.

CHAPTER FOUR

1. "The conference's earliest recorded involvement in instances of child molestation occurred in and about 1982, concerning cases in two dioceses. Staff assisted personnel from these dioceses in appreciating the civil liability risks presented by those cases. Although there were occasional inquiries about specific complaints in the next 12 to 18 months, it was not until 1984 that the conference became more heavily involved in assisting resolution of child molestation claims. During that year, public attention was focused on the claims involving the misconduct of Father Gilbert Gauthe." NCCB Ad Hoc Committee on Sexual Abuse, "Brief History: Handling Child Sex Abuse Claims," *Origins* 23:38 (March 10, 1994): 666–70, at 666. Hereinafter referred to as Ad Hoc Committee, "Brief History."

2. In addition to Gilbert Gauthe, the priests were Lane Fontenot and Robert Limoges. See Jason Berry, *Lead Us Not Into Temptation* (New York: Doubleday, 1992), 108; in the same timeframe another priest of the Lafayette Diocese, John Engbers, was sued for abuse by five native American religious women. See Frank Bruni and Elinor Burkett, *A Gospel of Shame* (New York: HarperCollins, 2002), 31.

3. Bruni, *Gospel,* 31.

4. Thomas P. Doyle, "A Short History of the Manual," http://www.bishop-accountability.org/reports/1985_06_09_Doyle_Manual/Doyle_AShortHistory.htm, March 10, 2005; see also Thomas C. Fox, "What They Knew in 1985," *National Catholic*

Reporter (May 17, 2002): 1: "It was in January 1985 that [Father Michael] Peterson, then director of St. Luke Institute in Silver Spring, Md.; [Father Thomas] Doyle, a canonist at the office of the papal nuncio, or pope's representative, in Washington D.C.; and [F. Ray] Mouton, a civil attorney representing a priest, Fr. Gilbert Gauthe, then charged with pedophilia, began their collaboration. The collaboration continued over five months and resulted in the report, backed with more than 100 pages of supporting evidence. The report covered the civil, canonical, and psychological aspects of priest sexual involvement with children."

5. Bishop Quinn was later to gain some notoriety for a presentation that he gave to the Midwestern Regional Canon Law Society April 1990 meeting. In his talk on clergy sexual abuse cases, Quinn admonished chancery officials not to destroy or change the information in subpoenaed files. Then, however, he suggested, "If there's something you really don't want people to see you might send it off to the Apostolic Delegate, because they have immunity to protect something that is potentially dangerous." J. M. Hirsch, "2 Bishops on Abuse Panel Accused of Shielding Predators," *Nashua* (NH) *Telegraph*, April 13, 2002, http://www.nashuatelegraph.com/Main.asp?SectionID'25&Sub SectionID'378&ArticleID'54554, October 20, 2005. The incident is also reported in Bruni, *Gospel*, 161.

6. These and other details about the Doyle-Peterson-Mouton Report are taken from Doyle's "A Short History." The Ad Hoc Committee on Sexual Abuse of the NCCB, however, also states that "while the [Peterson-Mouton-Doyle] report was in process, two bishops also met informally with the drafters on at least one occasion." Ad Hoc Committee, "Brief History," 667. The two bishops evidently were Bishop Quinn and Archbishop Levada.

7. Doyle, "A Short History." The fact of Father Doyle's meeting with Bishop Bevilacqua is also documented in the *Report of the Grand Jury of September 17, 2003,* misc. no. 03-00-239, Court of Common Pleas, First Judicial District of Pennsylvania (Philadelphia), Criminal Trial Division: 44: "In 1985, he [Cardinal Bevilacqua] had been given a copy of a report, the Doyle-Mouton-Peterson 'Manual,' and had discussed it with one of the authors, Fr. Thomas Doyle, who testified before the Grand Jury."

8. Berry, *Lead Us Not,* 111–12. Berry misspells Issel (Issle) and Angell (Angelle).

9. Ad Hoc Committee, "Brief History," 667.

10. Monsignor Daniel F. Hoye, affidavit in *Spann et al. v. Thorne et al.,* Civil Action No. J87-0114 (B), S.D. Miss. 1989, p. 4.

11. Ad Hoc Committee, "Brief History," 667.

12. Michael R. Peterson, MD, December 9, 1985 letter to all diocesan bishops, http://www.bishop-accountability.org/reports/1985_12_09_Peterson_Guidelines/index.html, March 10, 2006.

13. Ad Hoc Committee, "Brief History," 667.

14. Michael R. Peterson, MD, August 27, 1986 letter to all diocesan bishops, http://www.bishop-accountability.org/reports/1985_12_09_Peterson_Guidelines/1986_08_27_Peterson_Revisions.pdf, March 10, 2006. Both pieces of Doyle's canonical advice are problematical. Suspension is a form of canonical penalty that can only be imposed after a warning is given and there is time for the offender to cease and desist. CIC, 1983, c. 1347, §1. Doyle's advice on the suspension of priests under investigation did not take into account the necessity for a canonical warning. His second alternative, "administrative leave," is not even a canonical concept. The term appears nowhere in the Code. Administrative leave has been defined as "a canonically flawed attempt to expand the circumstances in which the restrictions that can be imposed on the accused in the course of the penal process (c. 1722) to include situations when no penal process is in prospect." See John P. Beal, "At the Crossroads of Two Laws: Some Reflections on the Influence of Secular Law on the Church's Response to Clergy Sexual Abuse in the United States," *Louvain Studies* 25 (2000): 99–121, at 109; see also Bertram F. Griffin, "Canon 1722 Imposition of Administrative Leave Against an Accused," in *Roman Replies and CLSA Advisory Opinions 1988,* ed. William A. Schumacher and J. James Cuneo (Washington, D.C.: Canon Law Society of America, 1988), 103–8.

15. The path was evidently Father Doyle to Tom Fox, publisher of the *National Catholic Reporter,* to Jason Berry, the first reporter to break the Gauthe story in both Louisiana and the pages of *NCR.* See Philip Jenkins, *Pedophiles and Priests* (New York: Oxford University Press, 1996), 66.

16. David France, *Our Fathers* (New York: Broadway Books, 2004), 163.

17. Peterson was the founder and director of St. Luke's Institute; Mouton wanted to plea bargain Gauthe into a sentence at "an institution where Gauthe could have medical care." Berry, *Lead Us Not,* 45.

18. Michael R. Peterson, MD, F. Ray Mouton, and Thomas P. Doyle, *The Problem of Sexual Molestation by Roman Catholic Clergy: Meeting the Problem in a Comprehensive and Responsible Manner* (Privately published, 1985), 48; hereinafter referred to as Peterson, Mouton, and Doyle, Manual.

19. Ibid., 50–51.

20. Ibid., 52.

21. Ibid., 75.

22. Ibid., 46.

23. Ibid., 40.

24. Ibid., 62.

25. Ibid. Doyle is here referring to a form of laicization, requested not by the priest, but by his ordinary, that existed under the 1917 Code and the 1971 norms of the Congregation for the Doctrine of the Faith, but that was not included in 1980 norms published by the same congregation and was not accepted canonical praxis after then. See CIC, 1983, c. 290, 3°, and Francis J. Schneider, "Loss of the Clerical State," in *New Commentary on the Code of Canon Law,* ed. John P. Beal, James A. Coriden, and Thomas J. Green (New York: Paulist Press, 2000), 382–93. At 386, Schneider writes "The canon [290, §3] does not make explicit who must petition the Apostolic See—the cleric or the bishop or superior without the consent or knowledge of the cleric (*ex officio* petition). The 1980 norms [of CDF] do not contain the provision for the *ex officio* laicization procedure found in the 1971 norms, according to which the ordinary petitioned the Holy Father without the consent or at times the knowledge of the cleric. Whereas *ex officio* petitions had been accepted in the past, they are only rarely accepted now." (citing Private Reply of CDWDS in *Roman Replies 1995,* 7). See also John P. Beal, "Doing What One Can: Canon Law and Clerical Sexual Misconduct," *The Jurist* 52 (1992): 642–83, at 677: "Anecdotal evidence suggests that the Apostolic See has been willing to grant voluntary petitions for return to the lay state to clerics who have been guilty of serious sexual misconduct. These petitions also seem to be processed rather

expeditiously. However, the Apostolic See has, at least to date, been resistant to efforts to impose laicization on unwilling clerics even in cases of egregious sexual misconduct except pursuant to the canonical penal process."

26. Peterson, Mouton, and Doyle, Manual, 85 and 86, respectively.

27. See Nicholas P. Cafardi, "Stones Instead of Bread: Sexually Abusive Priests in Ministry," *Studia canonica* 27 (1993): 145–72, at 160–63. To be fair, the Manual does say (at 34) that "the extent of the responsibility of a Bishop or religious superior has in regard to tortious or felonious conduct of his priests/subjects has not been defined in the original sense by the higher courts of the civil law system, and thus, the exceptions to such original definition do not exist. There are absolutely no reported civil court decisions on the issues. This body of law is just beginning to develop with the filing of these cases."

28. See n. 14, *supra*.

29. Jonathan Friendly, "Roman Catholic Church Discusses Abuse of Children by Priests," *New York Times*, May 4, 1986, A26.

30. Ibid.

31. Ibid.

32. Canonical Affairs Committee of the NCCB, "Dismissal from the Clerical State in Cases of Sexual Crimes Against Minors" (Privately published, 1987). The members of the Canonical Affairs Committee were Bishop Adam J. Maida, Bishop Anthony J. Bevilacqua, Bishop James A. Griffin, Bishop John R. Keating, Bishop Daniel L. Ryan, and Bishop Edmund C. Szoka.

33. Ibid., 3.

34. Ibid., 4.

35. Ibid., 5.

36. Adam J. Maida, "A Focus for Canonical and Civil Law Issues in Pedophilia Cases" (Privately published, 1987), 4. This opinion of Maida's directly contradicts Doyle on administrative laicizations. See n. 14, *supra*.

37. Ibid., 4.

38. Ibid., 4–5.

39. Ibid., 6.

40. Ibid., 8.

41. Edwin J. Murphy, *Suspension Ex Informata Conscientia*,

Catholic University of America, Canon Law Studies, no. 76 (Washington, D.C.: Catholic University of America, 1932), 2–3.

42. Ibid., 1; citing Conc. Trid. Sess. XIV, de Reform., c. 1.— Mansi, *Sacrorum Conciliorum*, XXV, 357; see also H. J. Schroeder, *The Canons and Decrees of the Council of Trent* (Rockford, Ill.: Tan Books, 1978), 106.

43. The Latin reads: "Ordinariis licet ex informata conscientia clericos suos suspendere ab officio sive ex parte sive etiam in totum." CIC, 1917, c. 2186, §1.

44. The Latin reads: "Extraordinarium hoc remedium adhibere non licet, si Ordinarius potest sine gravi incommodo ad iuris normam in subditum procedere." CIC, 1917, c. 2186, §2.

45. Ibid., c. 2191, §1, §2.

46. The Latin reads: "Si testes probi et graves delictum quidem Ordinario patefaciant, sed nulla ratione induci possunt ut de eo testimonium in iudicio ferant, neque aliis probationibus delictum iudiciali processu evinci possit." Ibid., c. 2191, §3, 1°.

47. The Latin reads: "Si processu iudiciali conficiendo ferendaeque sententiae impedimenta exoriantur ex adversis civilibus legibus aut gravi scandali periculo." Ibid., c. 2191, §3, 3°.

48. Ibid., c. 2190.

49. Ibid., c. 2188.

50. Ibid., c. 2146.

51. Ibid., c. 2194.

52. Murphy, *Suspension*, 116–17; Murphy holds that, if the suspension *ex informata conscientia* is imposed as a form of vindictive penalty by the bishop, as opposed to a form of censure, the suspended priest's appeal would "suspend" the suspension.

53. One of the principles that was to govern the revision of the Code was, "In canon law we must, therefore, proclaim that the principle of the juridical protection of rights applies with equal measure to superiors and subjects alike, so that any suspicion whatsoever of arbitrariness in Church administration may completely disappear." Pontificia Commissio Codici Iuris Canonici Recognoscendo, *Communicationes* 1 (1969): 83. This is a slight restatement of the sixth principle for the revision of the Code of Canon Law approved by the 1967 Synod of Bishops: "The use of power in the Church should not, however, become arbitrary. The rights of all the Christian faithful

should be acknowledged and protected." John A. Alesandro, "General Introduction," in *The Code of Canon Law: A Text and Commentary,* ed. James A. Coriden, Thomas J. Green, and Donald E. Heintschel (New York: Paulist Press, 1985), 6.

54. It has been suggested that Norm 9 of the Dallas Norms, which allows a bishop to use his power of governance "to ensure that any priest who has committed even one act of sexual abuse of a minor...shall not continue in ministry," is a return to the *suspensio ex informata conscientia.* "The bishops' claim to this broad administrative power appears as a subliminal and nostalgic desire on their part to resurrect a provision of the Code of 1917 that was often used by bishops when confronted with a clerical disciplinary problem, *suspensio ex informata conscientia."* Kenneth E. Boccafola, "The Special Penal Norms of the United States and Their Application," in *The Penal Process and the Protection of Rights in Canon Law,* ed. Patricia M. Dugan (Montreal: Wilson & Lafleur, 2005), 257–85, at 280–81.

55. Canon 2222, §2 reads: "Pariter idem legitimus Superior, licet probabile tantum sit delictum fuisse commissum aut delicti certe commissi poenalis actio praescripta sit, non solum ius, sed etiam officium habet non promovendi clericum de cuius idoneitate non constat, et, ad scandalum evitandum, prohibendi clerico exercitium sacri ministerii aut etiam eundem ab officio, ad normam iuris, amovendi; quae omnia in casu non habent rationem poenae."

56. Congregation for the Doctrine of the Faith, January 13, 1971, *Acta Apostolicae Sedis* 63 (1971): 303–12.

57. Michael O"Reilly, "Recent Developments in the Laicization of Priests," *The Jurist* 52 (1992): 684–96, at 686. O'Reilly explains in a footnote that "this document was never officially published, but it has appeared, both in the original Latin and in English, in different collections. The English version can be seen in *CLD* 7: 1002–1015" (686, at n. 9). An earlier version of O'Reilly's article appears in *CLSA Proceedings* 44 (1982): 233–46. *CLD* 7 is a reference to volume 7 (VII) of the *Canon Law Digest.*

58. O'Reilly, "Recent Developments," 687.

59. *Canon Law Digest,* vol. VII, ed. James I. O'Connor (Chicago: Chicago Province S.J., 1975), 117.

60. CIC, 1917, cc. 122, 1923, §1, 2299, §3. In a timeframe after

that being written about here, the same principle was restated in CIC, 1983, c. 1350, §1.

61. O'Reilly, "Recent Developments," 687.

62. Congregation for the Doctrine of the Faith, October 14, 1980, *Acta Apostolicae Sedis* 72 (1980): 1132–37; also available at *Canon Law Digest,* vol. IX, ed. James I. O'Connor (Mundelein, Ill.: Chicago Province S.J., 1983), 92–101.

63. Ad Hoc Committee, "Brief History," 669; see also Thomas J. Green, "Clerical Sexual Abuse of Minors: Some Canonical Reflections," *The Jurist* 63 (2003): 366–425, at 370: "NCCB attention to this issue was intensified only in the early 1990's in such a way as to influence canonical changes."

64. John A. Alesandro, "Dismissal from the Clerical State in Cases of Sexual Misconduct: Recent Derogations," *CLSA Proceedings* 56 (1994): 28–67, at 29. The language describing these stages is based in part on Alesandro. His description of the first phase, "Proposals for an administrative penal procedure of dismissal," is, I believe, too narrow in describing what the bishops first asked for. There is no doubt that they wanted their old powers back. Also, I have separated out his fourth step, "The derogations as proposed by the NCCB and as promulgated," into two separate phases, the derogations as proposed by the bishops and as promulgated by the Holy See. Finally, his fifth step, "The publication of an Instruction by the NCCB to facilitate use of the process," is omitted.

65. Ibid., 29 (footnotes omitted); Alesandro is surely not correct when he says that the 1983 Code took away the bishops' ability to request a rescript of laicization for a sexually abusive priest. That ability was lost prior to the Code, in 1980, when the CDF's new norms on administrative laicizations did not include Section VII from the prior 1971 norms. In fact, the 1983 Code allows others to request rescripts. Canon 61 states: "Unless it is otherwise evident, a rescript can be requested for another even without the person's acceptance, without prejudice to contrary clauses." And Canon 290 on laicization by rescript contains no contrary language. What the bishops did lose with the 1983 Code was the ability to suspend sexually abusive priests without warnings and without a canonical penal process *ex informata conscientia* and the ability to impose nonpenal restrictions.

66. *Origins* 22:42 (April 1, 1993): 720–21.

67. Alesandro, "Dismissal from the Clerical State," 31.

68. The process for the removal of a pastor is found at CIC, 1983, cc. 1740–47.

69. Ibid., c. 1740.

70. Alesandro, "Dismissal from the Clerical State," 32.

71. Beal, "At the Crossroads," 114. Beal himself was a severe critic of an administrative process. See John P. Beal, "To Be Or Not To Be, That Is The Question: The Rights of the Accused in the Canonical Penal Process," *CLSA Proceedings* 53 (1991): 77–97, at 89: "One should not resort to an administrative penal process unless the judicial process is impossible even though the crime can be proved in the external forum, unless it is useless because the matter is already certain or unless it is harmful because in a particular case the demand for expedient action to protect the common good outweighs the rights of the accused to the fullest possible judicial protection."

72. National Conference of Catholic Bishops, *Canonical Delicts Involving Sexual Misconduct and Dismissal from the Clerical State* (Washington, D.C.: United States Catholic Conference, 1995), 1; hereinafter NCCB, *Canonical Delicts.* The copyright page states that "The document, *Canonical Delicts Involving Sexual Misconduct and Dismissal from the Clerical State,* was prepared by Monsignor John A. Alesandro with the assistance of canonists with expertise in the penal law." See also the narrative at Ad Hoc Committee, "Brief History," 669:

"Discussions with curial representatives about how canon law might be best adapted to deal with American circumstances continued. As noted, many of the claims that were coming to the attention of the U.S. bishops were beyond the five year time prescription in the Code of Canon Law. At this time, most claims involved conduct that occurred many years ago. In addition, because these claims involved psychological incapacity on the part of clerics, there was some question whether a sentence of dismissal from the clerical state could be sustained. Several consultations, supplemented by staff-level discussions, were held in 1992. Over the course of these deliberations we have offered expert opinion about the scope and trends of the problem in the United States and our own evaluation of the particular ways in which the canon law has been used in the United States. These discussions culminated in 1993 meetings, followed by a letter from the Holy Father. The Holy Father condemned child abuse and announced the formation of a joint study commission to address the NCCB/USCC concerns."

73. Pope John Paul II, June 11, 1993 letter to the American bishops, "Vatican-U.S. Bishops' Committee to Study Applying Canonical Norms," *Origins* 23:7 (July 1, 1993): 102–3, at 103.

74. Ibid., 102–3.

75. Alesandro, "Dismissal from the Clerical State," 35.

76. Angelo Cardinal Sodano, secretary of state, May 31, 1993 appointment letter, quoted in Alesandro, "Dismissal from the Clerical State," 35. Note the parallel terms in the pope's June 11, 1993 letter to the American bishops and the continued use of euphemisms.

77. Alesandro, "Dismissal from the Clerical State," 35.

78. John L. Allen Jr., "Canonist Criticizes U.S. Bishops Sex Abuse Norms," *National Catholic Reporter*, April 2, 2004, 1+.

79. NCCB, *Canonical Delicts*, 1.

80. *Origins* 23:25 (December 2, 1993): 436–37.

81. Alesandro, "Dismissal from the Clerical State," 36.

82. Ad Hoc Committee, "Brief History," 669.

83. Alesandro, "Dismissal from the Clerical State," 36–37.

84. Ibid.

85. William H. Woestman points out that while these changes are often referred to as "derogations," the more exact term is "exceptions" to the law. William H. Woestman, *Ecclesiastical Sanctions and the Penal Process: A Commentary on the Code of Canon Law*, 2nd ed. revised and updated (Ottawa: Faculty of Canon Law, St. Paul University, 2003), 270.

86. *Origins* 23:25 (December 2, 1993): 437. Cardinal Bevilacqua had in mind "temporary or permanent suspension" or "getting the priest to agree to seek a return to the lay state voluntarily." There are, of course, serious canonical difficulties with each of these alternatives.

87. NCCB, *Canonical Delicts*, 2.

88. Ibid.

89. Secretariat of State, April 25, 1994 rescript, protocol no. 346.053. The full text of the rescript is printed as Ex #1 to Alesandro, "Dismissal from the Clerical State," 63, and can also be found in *Roman Replies and CLSA Advisory Opinions 1994*, 20–21. See also Patrick R. Lagges, "The Use of Canon 1044, §2, 2° in the Removal of Parish Priests," *Studia canonica* 30 (1996): 31–69, at 32, n. 2: "in a letter from

the secretary of State, Cardinal Angelo Sodano, dated May 11, 1994 and addressed to Archbishop William Keeler, the president of the National Conference of Catholic Bishops (prot. No. 346.053) has issued some derogations from certain canons dealing with the penal process."

90. Secretariat of State, December 4, 1998 letter, protocol no. 445.119/G.N. The letter is available at *Studia canonica* 33 (1999): 211–12.

91. Congregation for the Doctrine of the Faith, May 18, 2001 letter *De delictis gravioribus, Acta Apostolicae Sedis* 93 (2001): 785–88.

92. Alesandro, "Dismissal from the Clerical State," 36.

93. See Rescript cited in n. 89, *supra*. Also renewed by the Secretariat of Sate in 1998. See n. 90, *supra*. Also extended to the universal Church by Substantive Norms, Article 5, §1 that accompanied *Sacramentorum sanctitatis tutela*. See *Sacraentorum sanctitatis tutela* in *Acta Apostolilca Sedis* 93 (2001): 73–79. See also Woestman, *Ecclesiastical Sanctions*, 305.

94. Secretariat of State, April 25, 1994 rescript, protocol no. 346.053.

95. Ibid.

96. Alesandro reports that there were discussions with representatives of the Apostolic See regarding the "speedier resolution of such appeals." Alesandro, "Dismissal from the Clerical State," 39–40.

97. CIC, 1983, c. 1324, §1, 1°, 2°.

98. This matter is discussed more fully in chapter 3, section C. 4, "The Crimes Were Covered by Prescription."

99. It should be noted that some penal processes were made more likely by the changes in the law approved by the Apostolic See in raising the age of the victim from sixteen to eighteen. According to the John Jay Report, Table 4.3.2, "Victim's Age at First Instance of Abuse," 15.1 percent of victims from 1950 to 2002 were in this category. Of course, the change in age approved by the Apostolic See only applies to instances of abuse committed after April 25, 1994.

100. Ad Hoc Committee, "Brief History," 668.

101. Ibid.

102. Mark Chopko, "USCC Pedophilia Statement," *Origins* 17:36 (February 18, 1988): 624.

103. Ibid. The assertion that "most offenders were themselves victims of abuse as children" turned out not to be the case when data

was finally collected sixteen years later. The John Jay Report found that "fewer than 7 percent of the priests [who abused children] were reported to have experienced physical, sexual or emotional abuse as children." Thomas J. Reese, "Facts, Myths and Questions," *America* (March 22, 2004): 13.

104. Chopko, "Pedophilia Statement," 624.

105. Ibid.

106. Ibid.

107. Ibid.

108. On the legislative authority of bishops' conferences, see Donald B. Murray, "The Legislative Authority of the Episcopal Conference," *Studia canonica* 20 (1986): 33–47 and Thomas J. Green, "The Authority of Episcopal Conferences: Some Normative and Doctrinal Considerations," *CLSA Proceedings* 51 (1989): 123–36. See also Pope John Paul II, apostolic letter *motu proprio, Apostolos suos,* "On the Theological and Juridical Nature of Episcopal Conferences," May 21, 1998, *Acta Apostolicae Sedis* 90 (1998): 655–56.

109. Administrative Committee, National Conference of Catholic Bishops, "Statement on Priests and Child Abuse," *Origins* 19:24 (November 16, 1989): 394–95.

110. Ibid., 394.

111. Ibid.

112. Ibid., 395.

113. Chopko, "Pedophilia Statement," 624.

114. Administrative Committee, "Statement," 395.

115. Office of Media Relations, "Policy on Priests and Sexual Abuse of Children," United States Catholic Conference, February 1992.

116. Washington Archdiocese, February 7, 1995 statement, *Origins* 24:35 (February 16, 1995): 590.

117. Ray Rivera, "High-profile Panelists Hearing Priest Case," *The Seattle Times,* May 17, 2002, Local News, http://archives.seattletimes. nwsource.com, November 6, 2005. The Seattle policy was adopted after the February 1988 statement by USCC general counsel and after charges of child sexual abuse against two priests of the archdiocese, Father Paul Conn and Father James McGreal, became public later that same year. It should be noted that the "independent" Seattle board was chaired by Auxiliary Bishop George Thomas.

118. Salt Lake City Diocese, "Child Abuse Policy," *Origins* 20:3 (May 3, 1990): 42–44, at 43; hereinafter Salt Lake City Policy.

119. Ibid., 43.

120. Ibid.

121. Diocese of Davenport, "Sexual Abuse Policy," *Origins* 20:6 (June 21, 1990): 93–94, at 94; hereinafter Davenport Policy. Bishop O'Keefe was himself to become the object of unfounded charges of sexual abuse in 1992. See "On File," *Origins* 23:8 (July 15, 1993): 114.

122. Davenport Policy, 94.

123. Ibid. There is a genuine canonical problem with this part of the policy. An August 6, 1976 letter of the Secretariat of State sent to "pontifical representatives" stated that such psychological evaluation could not be compelled. This principle was enshrined in CIC, 1983, c. 220, creating a canonical right to privacy. See Woestman, *Ecclesiastical Sanctions,* 228.

124. Davenport Policy, 94.

125. Ibid.

126. St. Cloud Diocese, "Sexual Misconduct Policy," *Origins* 21:12 (August 29, 1991): 194–96; hereinafter St. Cloud Policy.

127. Ibid., 195.

128. Ibid.

129. Ibid.

130. Ibid., 196.

131. Ibid.

132. Peter Steinfels, "Inquiry in Chicago Breaks Silence on Sex Abuse by Catholic Priests," *New York Times,* February 24, 1992, A1+. See also Cafardi, "Stones Instead of Bread," 148.

133. Steinfels, "Inquiry in Chicago." See also Julia Quinn Dempsey, John R. Gorman, and John P. Madden, *Report to Joseph Cardinal Bernardin, The Cardinal's Commission on Clerical Sexual Misconduct with Minors* (Chicago, Ill., June 1992), 5; hereinafter Report of the Cardinal's Commission.

134. Steinfels, "Inquiry in Chicago."

135. Cardinal Joseph Bernardin, October 25, 1991 letter to Chicago Catholics, Appendix A in Report of the Cardinal's Commission; see also Steinfels, "Inquiry in Chicago."

136. Cardinal Joseph Bernardin, "Child Sexual Abuse by Church Personnel," *Origins* 21:21 (October 31, 1991): 354–55, at 355.

137. *America* staff, "When the 'Unspeakable' Must Be Spoken," *America* (October 17, 1992): 267–68, at 267. See also Cardinal Joseph Bernardin, "Statement Announcing Policy on Clerical Sexual Misconduct with Minors," *Origins* 22:16 (October 1, 1992): 282–83; and Chicago Archdiocese, "Chicago Policy Regarding Clerical Sexual Misconduct with Minors," *Origins* 22:16 (October 1, 1992): 273–78.

138. Andrew M. Greeley, "How Serious Is the Problem of Sexual Abuse by Clergy?" *America* (March 20, 1993): 6–10, at 7.

139. Andrew M. Greeley, "Why?" *America* (May 27, 2002): 12–13, at 13.

140. Louise I. Gerdes, "Introduction," in *At Issue: Child Abuse in the Catholic Church*, ed. Louise I. Gerdes (San Diego: Greenhaven Press, 2003), http://wwwenotes.com/catholic-child-abuse-article/38969, December 14, 2005.

141. Ibid.

142. A. W. Richard Sipe, "Preliminary Expert Report," p. 83, http://www.bishop-accountablity.org/tx-dallas/resource-files/sipe-report.htm, March 12, 2006.

143. *USA Today*, "Bishops Who Have Resigned Amid Church Sex Scandals," December 12, 2002, http://www.usatoday.com/news/nation/2002-12-3-bishop-resignations_x.htm, March 12, 2006.

144. Canadian Bishops' Committee, "Fifty Recommendations: The Church and Child Sexual Abuse," *Origins* 22:7 (June 25, 1992): 97–107, at 99.

145. Ibid., Recommendation 99.

146. Ibid., Recommendation 6, at 100.

147. Ibid., Recommendations 6 and 41, at 100 and 106, respectively. The placement of the priest on "administrative leave" before the preliminary investigation called for by Canon 1717 is completed, as the Canadian bishops recommend, is canonically problematical. See text, *supra*, at n. 14.

148. Canadian Bishops' Committee, "Fifty Recommendations," Recommendation 7, at 100–101.

149. Ibid., Recommendation 8, at 101.

150. Ibid., Recommendation 20, at 102–3.

151. Ibid., Recommendation 17, at 102.

152. Ibid., Recommendation 15, at 102; the Canadian bishops' approach is not without criticism. See Jonathon Gatehouse, "Catholic

Church Sex Abuse Scandals," *Maclean's* (July 22, 2002): "'If there is a way in which the Canadian Church is better than the American Church, it's in getting away with the crime,' says David Gagnon, national director of SNAP-Canada, the Survivors' Network of Those Abused by Priests. 'The Church treats victims with contempt and malice.' Gagnon, who lives in Ottawa, says victims look at the American Church's steps towards a national 'zero tolerance' policy on sexual abusers and wonder why allegations, and even criminal convictions for sexual misconduct, seem to be taken so lightly in Canada. 'They recycle these guys over and over again,' Gagnon says of the Canadian Church's policy of 're-integrating' fallen priests back into active ministry after treatment. 'It's like asking an alcoholic to work at a liquor store.'" http://www.canadianencyclopedia.ca/index.cfm? PgNm'TCE&Params'M1ARTM0012306, January 11, 2006.

153. Chopko, "Pedophilia Statement," 624.

154. Canadian Bishops' Committee, "Fifty Recommendations," Preliminary Observation 3, at 99.

155. Ibid., Recommendation 17, at 102.

156. Ibid., Recommendation 12, at 101.

157. Ibid., Introductory Summary, at 99.

158. United States Conference of Catholic Bishops, Ad Hoc Committee on Sexual Abuse, "Efforts to Combat Clergy Sexual Abuse Against Minors—Chronology," in *Restoring Trust: A Pastoral Response to Sexual Abuse* (Washington, D.C.: National Conference of Catholic Bishops, 2002).

159. Thomas J. Reese, "Bishops Meet At Notre Dame," *America* (July 1, 1992): 4–6, at 6. See also *America* staff, "Editorial: Sexual Abuse by Priests," *America* (February 18, 2002): 3. See also Brooks Egerton and Michael D. Goldhaber, "Documents Show Bishops Transferred Known Abuser; Church Officials Say Policies Have Since Changed," *Dallas Morning News,* August 31, 1997, 1: "In 1992, the National Conference of Catholic Bishops first spoke with one voice about abusive priests; some bishops also met with a group of victims. That same year, Cincinnati Archbishop Daniel E. Pilarczyk, then president of the bishops' group, issued this statement: 'In the matter of priests and sexual abuse, undoubtedly mistakes have been made in the past....' He said new policies were already in place, 'notwithstanding the fact that such sexual misconduct has involved relatively few priests measured against 53,000 priests in our country.'"

160. *America* staff, "Editorial: Sexual Abuse by Priests," 3. In Archbishop Pilarczyk's public statement released by the NCCB on June 20, 1992, before stating the five steps of a recommended response to clergy sexual abuse of minors, he says, "For the last five years, strongly and consistently, the National Conference of Catholic Bishops has recommended the following course of action to our 188 dioceses." On the other hand, the Ad Hoc Committee on Sexual Abuse's "Brief History: Handling Child Sex Abuse Claims" in *Origins* 23:38 (March 10, 1994): 666–70, at 668, dates these five principles back to early 1988, not 1987: "At the request of the general secretary and the Executive Committee, the general counsel was directed to issue a statement in early February, 1988. Two months thereafter [which makes it April 1988] confidential documents were released to bishops and attorneys completing the conference's action on these matters. Dioceses were provided guidelines to develop personnel policies. Although the detail and specified advice remain confidential, the principles outlined remained the same through the present date [February 24, 1994]. As summarized by former NCCB president Archbishop Daniel Pilarczyk in June 1992, they are…" [there then followed the text of the five recommendations, verbatim, as in the text, *supra*].

161. Archbishop Daniel Pilarczyk, "Statement of Archbishop Pilarczyk, President of the National Conference of Catholic Bishops, on the Sexual Abuse of Children," June 20, 1992, reprinted in *Statements of the National Conference of Catholic Bishops and the United States Catholic Conference on the Subject of the Sexual Abuse of Children by Priests 1988–1992.* (Washington, D.C., 1992), 6–9. The language is exactly the same as reported by the Ad Hoc Committee, "Brief History," 668. See also Archbishop Daniel Pilarczyk, "Painful Pastoral Question: Sexual Abuse of Minors," *Origins* 22:10 (August 6, 1992): 177–78.

162. Pilarczyk, "Statement," 8. Eleven years later, on November 20, 2003, Archbishop Pilarczyk was in Common Pleas Court in Cincinnati admitting that from 1978 to 1982, at a time when Joseph Bernardin was archbishop of Cincinnati, the archdiocese had failed to report five sexual abuse accusations against its priests to the civil authorities, a fourth-degree misdemeanor. The archdiocese was fined the maximum $10,000. Laurie Goodstein, "Archdiocese of Cincinnati Fined in Sex Abuse Scandal," *New York Times,* November 21, 2003, A25.

163. Jason Berry, "Listening to the Survivors: Voices of People of God," *America* (November 13, 1993): 4–9, at 4.

164. Cardinal Roger Mahony, "Talk with Victims of Clergy Sexual Misconduct," *Origins* 22:24 (November 26, 1992): 405.

165. Ibid.

166. Ibid.

167. Ibid.

168. National Conference of Catholic Bishops, "Resolution on Clergy Sex Abuse," *Origins* 22:25 (December 3, 1992): 418.

169. National Review Board for the Protection of Children and Young People, *A Report on the Crisis in the Catholic Church in the United States* (Washington, D.C.: United States Conference of Catholic Bishops, February 27, 2004), 138; hereinafter NRB *Report*. It should not be inferred that Cardinal Law was the bishop who said, "No one is going to tell me how to run my diocese." He was not.

170. Peter Steinfels, "The Church's Sex-Abuse Crisis," *Commonweal* (April 19, 2002): 13–19, at 15.

171. Ad Hoc Committee, "Brief History," 669.

172. Ibid., 669–70.

173. For example, at the bishops' June 1993 meeting in New Orleans, Archbishop William H. Keeler, then-president of the National Conference of Catholic Bishops, told Father Thomas J. Reese, SJ, editor of *America* magazine, "We have discussed it [clergy sexual abuse of minors] every year for the last five years." Thomas J. Reese, "Bishops Speak in Public Session of Sexual Abuse," *America* (July 3, 1993): 4–6, at 4. This would mean that the topic was discussed by the bishops as a group at least since 1988. Before that, in 1987, the bishops had the presentation by Bishop Maida at their November 1987 meeting. Yet what was discussed, and which joint actions were proposed and rejected, is unknown.

174. Stephen J. Rossetti, "Child Sexual Abuse and the Church: How I Understand It," *Priest* (January 1994): 32–37, at 32–33.

175. Ad Hoc Committee, "Brief History," 670.

176. Ibid.

177. Canice Connors, "Subcommittee Head Introduces Think Tank Recommendations," *Origins* 23:7 (July 1, 1993): 105–7, at 105.

178. Peter Steinfels, "Bishops Struggle Over Sex Abuses by Parish Priests," *New York Times*, June 18, 1993, A1+.

179. Ibid.

180. The recommendations of the subcommittee are taken verbatim from "Child Sexual Abuse: Think Tank Recommendations," *Origins* 23:7 (July 1, 1993): 108–11.

181. Ibid., Recommendation 11, at 109–10.

182. Canice Connors, "Priests and Pedophilia: A Silence That Needs Breaking?" *America* (May 9, 1992): 400–401, at 400.

183. Reese, "Bishops Speak," 4.

184. Ibid.

185. Ibid.

186. Steinfels, "Bishops Struggle," A1+.

187. Archbishop William Keeler, "Remarks," *Origins* 23:7 (July 1, 1993): 104.

188. *Origins* 23:7 (July 1, 1993): 104.

189. United States Conference of Catholic Bishops, Ad Hoc Committee on Sexual Abuse, "Efforts to Combat Clergy Sexual Abuse," 3.

190. Steinfels, "Bishops Struggle," A1+.

191. Bishop John Kinney, "NCCB Establishes Committee on Sexual Abuse," *Origins* 23:7 (July 1, 1993): 104–5. See also Steinfels, "Bishops Struggle," A1+: "Bishop Kinney warned the 238 bishops gathered here that the process may 'involve uncomfortable listening, nationally as well as back home,' adding, 'It might be messy listening, but that might well be necessary if we are to lance the boil.'"

192. Berry, "Listening to the Survivors," 4: "In July [1993] Bishop Kinney met in Washington with Barbara Blaine and David Clohessy of SNAP, Jeanne Miller and a second Linkup member."

193. Thomas H. Stahel, "The 'Real Catholic Story': U.S. Bishops Meet," *America* (December 4, 1993): 4–5, at 4.

194. Ibid., 5.

195. The document states in an introductory footnote, "Developed in collaboration with the Leadership Conference of Women Religious, Conference of Major Superiors of Women, Conference of Major Superiors of Men, and the National Conference of Catholic Bishops." See "Proposed Guidelines on the Assessment of Clergy and Religious for Assignment, Approved by the National Conference of Catholic Bishops, November 18, 1993," *The Jurist* 54 (1994): 623–28; hereinafter referred to as Assignment Guidelines.

196. Ibid., 624.

197. Ibid., 625.

198. Ibid., 626.

199. Stahel, "The 'Real Catholic Story,'" 4.

200. Ibid.

201. See "Charges Against Chicago Archbishop Dropped," *Origins* 23:38 (March 10, 1994): 661–63. In the same number of *Origins,* Archbishop Keeler, bishops' conference president, said, "While this sad chapter comes to a close for Cardinal Bernardin, it continues to raise troubling questions which must be dealt with. Without impugning the seriousness of authentic cases of sexual abuse, important questions remain concerning the role of certain attorneys, psychiatrists and media in bringing reckless charges against innocent people." Archbishop William Keeler, "Reckless Charges Against Innocent People," *Origins* 23:38 (March 10, 1994): 665. See also, however, A. W. Richard Sipe, "View from the Eye of the Storm," keynote address, The Linkup National Conference, Louisville, Kentucky, February 23, 2003: "A sad, and as yet unsolved, chapter of the sexual abuse saga in the United States is the story of Cardinal Joseph Bernardin. This man probably did die a saint, as his close friends attest. Without doubt, he did many wonderful things for the Church in America. In the media flurry that surrounded the allegation of sexual abuse, an impertinent reporter asked the Cardinal, 'Are you living a sexually active life?' A simple 'no' would have been sufficient. But the Cardinal said, 'I am sixty-five years old, and I have always lived a chaste and celibate life.' However defensible in the arena of public assault, I knew that the statement was not unassailably true. Years before, several priests who were associates of Bernardin prior to his move to Chicago revealed that they had 'partied' together; they talked about their visits to the Josephinum to socialize with seminarians. It is a fact that Bernardin's accuser did not ever retract his allegations of abuse by anyone's account other than Bernardin's." http://www.bishop-accountability.org/resources/resource-files/time line/2003-02-23-Sipe-ViewEyeStorm.htm, November 9, 2005. Surely, however, Sipe is wrong in stating that the accusations were not retracted. See Anthony Lewis, "Abroad at Home; Savaging The Great," *New York Times,* May 27, 1994, A27: "Last November Steven Cook filed a Federal lawsuit claiming that he had been sexually abused as a teenager by Joseph Cardinal Bernardin, the Roman Catholic

prelate in Chicago. He asked for $10 million in damages. The charge attracted enormous media attention. CNN, which had a documentary scheduled on sexual abuse by priests, put in a segment on the suit including an exclusive and tearful interview with Mr. Cook. It made highly emotional television. It turned out that Mr. Cook had 'recovered' memories of the supposed abuse under hypnosis by an unlicensed therapist trained on weekends at a school founded by a New Age guru. In February Mr. Cook, saying his memory was not reliable, dropped the lawsuit." See also "Cook's Claims Against Cardinal Dismissed," *Origins* 23:38 (March 10, 1994): 663–64.

202. See "Cook's Claims Against Cardinal Dismissed," *Origins* 23:38 (March 10, 1994): 663–64. See also James Serritella, "Statement," *Origins* 23:38 (March 10, 1994): 662: "These proceedings today have affirmed Cardinal Joseph Bernardin's innocence. They also establish that it was a terrible mistake to have filed these accusations in the first place. By coming forward at this time, Mr. Cook and his attorneys have spared all involved the pain, anguish, time and public expense of an unnecessary trial. The action today appropriately concludes this unfortunate episode as a legal matter. Nonetheless, Mr. Cook's mistaken allegations and the worldwide attention given them unjustly called into question the cardinal's reputation. We hope that today's unequivocal withdrawal of those allegations will serve to correct that injustice and reaffirm Cardinal Bernardin's good name."

203. Canice Connors, "Psychological Perspective on Priesthood," *Colloquia* (March 1999), http://www.nfpc.org/COLLOQUIA/MARCH-1999/connors.htm, November 30, 2005.

204. Peter Steinfels, "The Church's Sex Abuse Crisis," *Commonweal* (April 19, 2002): 13–19, at 17.

205. Peter Steinfels, "Beliefs: A Catholic Bishop Looks Back," *New York Times*, June 22, 2002, A12+.

206. Ad Hoc Committee on Sexual Abuse, *Restoring Trust: A Pastoral Response to Sexual Abuse*, vol. I (Washington, D.C.: National Conference of Catholic Bishops, November 1994).

207. Bishop John F. Kinney, chairman, Bishops' Ad Hoc Committee on Sexual Abuse, November 14, 1994 introductory letter, in *Restoring Trust: A Pastoral Response to Sexual Abuse*, vol. I (1994).

208. See, for example, *Origins* 22:10 (August 6, 1992): 178–79, "Diocesan Policy: When a Cleric Is Accused of Sexually Exploiting a

Minor," for the policy of the diocese of Sioux City, Iowa; *Origins* 24:25 (February 16, 1993): 588–89, "Washington Archdiocese Removes Four Priests," for the policy of the Archdiocese of Washington, D.C.; *National Catholic Reporter,* April 2, 1993, 6 for the policy of the diocese of Joliet, Illinois; *National Catholic Reporter,* April 30, 1993, 6, for the policy of the diocese of Helena, Montana; *National Catholic Reporter,* July 16, 1993, 8, for the policy of the Archdiocese of New York; *Origins* 24:5 (June 16, 1994): 70–74, "Policy on Sexual Abuse by Priests," for the policy of the Archdiocese of Los Angeles.

209. Kinney, introductory letter.

210. Ad Hoc Committee on Sexual Abuse, "Policies," in *Restoring Trust: A Pastoral Response to Sexual Abuse,* vol. I (Washington, D.C.: National Conference of Catholic Bishops, November 1994); hereinafter referred to as "Policies." The twenty-eight guidelines proposed by the Ad Hoc Committee are also available at "Twenty-Eight Suggestions on Sexual Abuse Policies," *Origins* 24:26 (December 8, 1994): 443–44.

211. Recommendations 1, 14, 16, 22 in "Policies."

212. Recommendations 26–27 in "Policies."

213. Steinfels, "Beliefs: A Catholic Bishop Looks Back," A12+.

214. Frank Valcour, MD, "Expectations of Treatment for Child Molesters," in Bishops' Ad Hoc Committee on Sexual Abuse, *Restoring Trust: A Pastoral Response to Sexual Abuse,* vol. I (Washington, D.C.: National Conference of Catholic Bishops, November 1994), 9.

215. James J. Gill, MD, "Will Priests Sexually Abuse After Treatment?" in Bishops' Ad Hoc Committee on Sexual Abuse, *Restoring Trust: A Pastoral Response to Sexual Abuse,* vol. II (Washington, D.C.: National Conference of Catholic Bishops, November 1995), 9.

216. Steinfels, "Beliefs: A Catholic Bishop Looks Back," A-12+. This was not the first time that the bishops were asked to collect information that would be helpful to them in dealing with the clergy child sexual abuse crisis. John Allan Loftus, SJ, then-executive director of Southdown, wrote in 1990: "If there is a single, obvious, and immediate conclusion to be drawn from the present disillusionment over sexual matters among religious professionals, it is that we are in desperate need for more careful research....The church has repeatedly professed its interest in the more secure convictions of modern social science research. The time has come to transform that interest into practical commitment. Within our own house, there is too much we do not

know yet." Loftus, "A Question of Disillusionment: Sexual Abuse Among the Clergy," *America* (December 1, 1990): 426–29, at 429. See also Leslie M. Lothstein, "The Relationship Between the Treatment Facilities and the Church Hierarchy: Forensic Issues and Future Considerations," in *Sins Against the Innocents*, ed. Thomas G. Plante (Westport: Praeger, 2004), 123–37, at 133–34: "There are many voices calling for research into the pedophile-priest issue. However, the debate has been going on for a decade. Around 1990, I was part of a research team that made a petition to the National Council of Catholic Bishops (NCCB) to fund a national research study of priest pedophiles by a consortium of treatment facilities (The Institute of Living, St. Luke's Institute, and the Servants of the Paracletes *(sic)*, Southdown, and later, St. John Vianney). This research study was meant to address most of the core issues…except homosexuality.…There was a lot of enthusiasm about the study, and a research protocol was developed and consultation arranged with senior researchers, including experts from [the] National Institute of Mental Health. The study was designed to address the reasons for the 'epidemic' in the clergy of the sexual abuse of minors. However, at the last minute the study was quashed as the NCCB withdrew support. The bishops feared that any findings of the study were potentially discoverable in court and could be used in law-suits against the Church."

217. Peter Steinfels, "On Sexual Abuse by Catholic Clergy: A Time for Bishops to Seize 'the Moment after Suffering,'" *New York Times,* October 8, 1994, A30+.

218. Steinfels, "Beliefs: A Catholic Bishop Looks Back," A12+.

219. At their November 1999 meeting, the bishops adopted "Norms Concerning Applications for Priestly Formation for Those Persons Previously Enrolled in a Formation Program." While these norms did not specifically deal with issues of child sexual abuse, in 1993, the Think Tank had advised, at no. 6, that "the NCCB recommend standardized and improved methods of screening candidates for the priesthood and religious life." Interestingly, since these Norms were adopted in response to a special mandate from the Holy See (Canon 455, §1), they had the force of law in the United States.

220. Andrew Greeley, "Why?" *America* (May 27, 2002): 12–13, at 13. Greeley has his date wrong. The bishops adopted their guidelines, based on Archbishop Pilarczyk's June 1992 presentation at their

November 1992 meeting and not in 1993. Even *America* magazine's editorial writers got the date wrong: "Only in 1993 did the conference leadership go public with guidelines and discussion." *America* staff, "Editorial: Healing and Credibility," *America* (April 1, 2002): 3. Again, the "conference leadership," that is to say, Archbishop Pilarczyk, the conference president, went public with the suggested five-point program at the June 1992 meeting. For some reason, on the pages of *America*, the bishops get a year's grace on what they ought to have known and when.

221. Greeley, "Why?" 13. This was also the judgment of the National Review Board for the Protection of Children and Young People in their *Report on the Crisis in the Catholic Church in the United States:* "While there are many ways to view the current crisis, as a crisis of priestly identity or a crisis of episcopal leadership, the Board believes that the over-riding paradigm that characterizes this crisis is one of sinfulness. The actions of priests who sexually abused minors were grievously sinful. The inaction of those bishops who failed to protect their people from predators was also grievously sinful." NRB *Report*, 90.

222. Bishop John F. Kinney, chair, Ad Hoc Committee on Sexual Abuse, U.S. Conference of Catholic Bishops, statement of Bishop John F. Kinney, http://www.diocesetucson.org/restore3.htm, November 6, 2005; hereinafter Kinney Statement. See also Steinfels, "The Church's Sex Abuse Crisis": "The watershed years were almost certainly 1992–1993."

223. See Thomas J. Reese, "Bishops Meet at Notre Dame," *America* (July 1, 1992): 4–6, at 5. "Sexual abuse is caused by a disorder (in some cases an addiction) for which treatment is essential," [Pilarczyk] said. "Sometimes therapy may be successful; sometimes it is not." He refused to rule out the possibility of a priest returning to ministry after treatment, but "we realize we must seek sound medical advice as we make responsible pastoral judgments," he said. "The protection of the child is and will continue to be our first concern." See also *America* staff, "Editorial: Sexual Abuse by Priests," 3: "In 1992, Archbishop Pilarczyk refused to rule out the possibility of a priest returning to ministry after treatment."

224. Office of Media Relations, "Policy on Priests and Sexual Abuse of Children," United States Catholic Conference, February 1992.

225. See, for example, the Diocese of Pittsburgh, where Bishop Donald W. Wuerl refused to reassign Father Anthony Cipolla,

Apostolic Signatura, definitive sentence, March 3, 1993, P.N. 22571/91 CA, 3–4; and the Archdiocese of Washington, where Cardinal Hickey removed four priests, Father Thomas Schaeffer, Father Alphonsus Smith, Father Edward Pritchard, and Father Edward Hartel, from ministry, stating he could "never again place" the four priests in ministry. James Cardinal Hickey, "Washington Archdiocese Removes Four Priests," *Origins* 24:35 (February 16, 1995): 588–89; and of course, in 1992 the Archdiocese of Chicago had removed twenty-one priests from parishes after the review of personnel files by the cardinal's advisory board. Andrew M. Greeley, "How Serious Is the Problem of Sexual Abuse by Clergy?" *America* (March 20, 1993): 6–10, at 7.

226. Warren Wolfe, "St. Cloud Catholics Gather to Discuss Abuse Crisis," *Star Tribune,* May 22, 2002, http://www.startribune.com/stories/197/2851313.html, January 16, 2006.

227. Ron Russell, *New Times* (LA), "Holy Hypocrite," May 16, 2002, http://www.bishop-accountability.org/ca-la/mahony-2002-05-d.htm, January 16, 2006.

CHAPTER FIVE

1. John P. Beal, "At the Crossroads of Two Laws: Some Reflections on the Influence of Secular Law on the Church's Response to Clergy Sexual Abuse in the United States," *Louvain Studies* 25 (2000): 99–121, at 108.

2. Thomas J. Green, "Sanctions in the Church," in *The Code of Canon Law: A Text and Commentary,* ed. James A. Coriden, Thomas J. Green, and Donald E. Heintschel (New York: Paulist Press, 1985), 893–931, at 929.

3. John G. Proctor, "Clerical Misconduct: Canonical and Practical Consequences," *CLSA Proceedings* 49 (1987): 227–44, at 242.

4. Ibid., 239–40.

5. James H. Provost, "Some Canonical Considerations Relative to Clerical Sexual Misconduct," *The Jurist* 52 (1992): 615–41, at 616.

6. Francis G. Morrisey, "The Pastoral and Juridical Dimensions of Dismissal from the Clerical State and of Other Penalties for Sexual Misconduct," *CLSA Proceedings* 53 (1991): 221–39, at 235.

7. Canice Connors, "Clerical Sexual Abuse Priests and Their Victims Find Healing," *Ligourian* (November 1994): 22–27, at 24.

8. CIC, 1983, c. 1718, §1, 3°.

9. John P. Beal, "To Be or Not To Be, That is the Question: The Rights of the Accused in the Canonical Penal Process," *CLSA Proceedings* 53 (1991): 77–97, at 87.

10. Francis G. Morrisey, "Procedures to Be Applied in Cases of Alleged Sexual Misconduct by a Priest," *Studia canonica* 26 (1992): 39–73, at 62.

11. John P. Beal, "Administrative Leave: Canon 1722 Revisited," *Studia canonica* 27 (1993): 293–320, at 316–17.

12. Bertram F. Griffin, "The Reassignment of a Cleric Who Has Been Professionally Evaluated and Treated for Sexual Misconduct with Minors: Canonical Considerations," *The Jurist* 51 (1991): 326–39, at 336–37.

13. Bertram F. Griffin, "Canon 1722 Imposition of Administrative Leave Against an Accused," in *Roman Replies and CLSA Advisory Opinions 1988,* ed. William A. Schumaker and J. James Cuneo (Washington, D.C.: Canon Law Society of America, 1988), 103–8, at 105.

14. Ibid., 105.

15. Beal, "Administrative Leave," 315–16.

16. Ibid., 316.

17. John P. Beal, "Doing What One Can: Canon Law and Clerical Sexual Misconduct," *The Jurist* 52 (1992): 642–83, at 663.

18. Peter Cimbolic, "The Identification and Treatment of Sexual Disorders and the Priesthood," *The Jurist* 52 (1992): 598–614, at 599: "Paraphilias are characterized by arousal in response to sexual objects that are not part of normative arousal patterns *and* that in varying degrees may interfere with the capacity for *reciprocal* affectionate activity."

19. The difference between the two categories is that pedophilia is listed in the *Diagnostic and Statistical Manual of the American Psychiatric Association* as a specific mental disorder that involves "recurrent intense sexual urges and sexually arousing fantasies involving sexual activity with a prepubescent child," while ephebophilia is not listed as a mental disorder and does not involve sexual activity with prepubescent children, but describes an adult who is "sexually involved with

postpubescent children." As Rossetti and Lothstein explain, "Ephebophilia is not listed in DSM-III-R [now DSM-IV] because being attracted to teenagers, of itself, is not considered to be a mental illness." Stephen J. Rossetti and Leslie M. Lothstein, "Myths of the Child Molester," in *Slayer of the Soul*, ed. Stephen J. Rossetti (Mystic: Twenty-Third Publications, 1990), 9–18, at 14–15. Lothstein claimed that "more than 95% of the [priest] cases" at the Institute of Living, St. Luke Institute, and Servants of the Paraclete were ephebophiles, which meant that less than 5 percent of priest sexual abusers of children were true pedophiles. Leslie M. Lothstein, "Can a Sexually Addicted Priest Return to Ministry after Treatment? Psychological Issues and Possible Forensic Solutions," *Catholic Lawyer* 34 (1990): 89–113, at 102. When the John Jay numbers were finally released in February 2004, it turned out that 47.3 percent of victims from 1950 to 2002 were under the age of thirteen. John Jay College of Criminal Justice, *The Nature and Scope of Sexual Abuse of Minors by Catholic Priests and Deacons in the United States 1950–2002* (United States Conference of Catholic Bishops, February 2004), Table 4.3.2.

20. Craig A. Cox, "Irregularities and Impediments," in *Clergy Procedural Handbook*, ed. Randolph R. Calvo and Nevin J. Klinger (Washington, D.C.: Canon Law Society of America, 2002), 178–20, at 187; Cox cites Russell E. Smith, "Pedophilia and Church Law," *Ethics and Medics* 15 (December 1990): 3 for the proposition that "pedophilia or pederasty is clearly a psychic defect as envisioned by the canon." See also Robert J. Kaslyn, "The Sacrament of Orders: Irregularities and Impediments—An Overview," *The Jurist* 62 (2002): 159–94.

21. Woestman's position is developed in "Too Good To Be True: A Current Interpretation of Canons 1041, 1° and 1044, §2, 2°," *Monitor Ecclesiasticus* 120 (1995): 619–29; "Canons 1041, 1° and 1044, §2, 2°," in *Roman Replies and CLSA Advisory Opinions 1995*, ed. Kevin Vann and James Donlon (Washington, D.C.: Canon Law Society of America, 1995), 80–82; and "Restricting the Right to Celebrate the Eucharist," *Studia canonica* 29 (1995): 165–71.

22. Woestman, "Too Good To Be True," 624–25.

23. See also William H. Woestman, *The Sacrament of Orders and the Clerical State*, 2nd ed. revised and updated (Ottawa: Faculty of Canon Law, St. Paul University, 2001), 80–81, where he cites a 1996

definitive sentence of the Apostolic Signatura, c. Davino, May 4, 1996, protocol no. 23737/92 CA, which holds (paraphrasing Woestman) that a diagnosis of some mental disorder such as ephebophilia does not suffice, on its own and in every case, to prove a mental disorder or grave mental disturbance. Rather, "the gravity of the infirmity, its effect on the priest and his ministry, the outcome of therapy, the means used to limit the effects of the illness" must be considered in the determination of whether a disqualifying psychic illness is present. The Signatura's sentence cited by Woestman appeared after the exchange cited in the text above.

24. John P. Beal, "To Good To be True? A Response to Professor Woestman on the Interpretation of Canons 1041, 1º and 1044, §2, 2º," *Monitor Ecclesiasticus* 121 (1996): 431–63, at 462.

25. Ibid., 448–49, citing *Presbyterorum ordinis,* §§1–2.

26. Apostolic Signatura, definitive sentence, June 24, 1995, P.N. 22571/91 CA, ¶5. The Latin reads: "Sacerdotalis status seu condicio postulat capacitatem in subiecto exercendi ordines, i.e., ministerium recte implendi, quae capacitas exigit qualitates ordini congruentes. Qualitates vero huiusmodi illae habendae sunt quae sinunt utiliter, seu ex una parte absque damno ex altera efficaciter seu fructose, munera propria clerici adimplere. Si quae vero obstant quominus animarum saluti provideatur, non tantum ob amentiam sed et insuper ob cuiusvis generis mentalem deordinationem, et haec impedimentum constituere possunt pro rite exercendo clericorum ministerio." This, of course, is the second decision of the Signatura in the Cipolla case.

27. Beal, "Response to Woestman," 463.

28. Writing in the same year (1996), neither refers to the other, indicating that the works were created simultaneously. In accord with both Lagges and Beal is Ingels. See Gregory Ingels, "Protecting the Right to Privacy When Examining Issues Affecting the Life and Ministry of Clerics and Religious," *Studia canonica* 34 (2000): 439–66, at 452: "From our work in marriage cases when dealing with the question of 'psychic incapacities,' we all understand that the use of the term 'psychic infirmity' in the Code is not limited to a defined mental disorder but is intended to include any behaviors of a psychological, emotional or even social nature which would serve to disrupt seriously a priest's ability to exercise his ministry."

29. Patrick R. Lagges, "The Use of Canon 1044, §2, 2° in the Removal of Parish Priests," *Studia canonica* 30 (1996): 31–69, at 60.

30. Ibid., 60.

31. Ibid., 60–61. It has recently been suggested that a violation of Canon 1395, §2 could be established as a new irregularity in the Code, making any reliance on the existing Canons 1041, 1° or 1044, §2, 2° unnecessary. See Ronny E. Jenkins, "On the Suitability of Establishing Clerical Sexual Abuse of Minors (c. 1395 §2) as an Irregularity *Ex Delicto* to the Reception and Exercise of Orders," *Periodica* 94 (205): 275–340.

32. Decision of the Congregation for the Clergy, October 8, 1998. The entire decision is printed as an appendix to Ingels, "Protecting the Right to Privacy."

33. "Inoltre, a nostro parere, non è ammissibile che il chierico incriminato sia costretto a sottoporsi a indagini psicologiche volte a determinare se la sua personalita è incline a commettere i delitti in questione oppure volte a estorcere una sua confessione. Tale prassi è contro il c. 220, che tutela il diritto a difendere la propria intimita." Gianfranco Ghirlanda, "Doveri a Diritti Implicati nei Casi di Abusi Sessuali Perpetrati da Chierici," *Civiltà Cattolica* 2 (2002): 341–53, quaderno 3646 (18 maggio 2002), at 345.

34. See Peter Steinfels, "Giving Healing and Hope to Priests Who Molested," *New York Times,* October 12, 1992: A1+: "Few priests refer themselves to St. Luke or other centers. Most are ordered by religious superiors to undergo evaluation and treatment."

35. Apostolic Signatura, definitive sentence, March 9, 1993, P.N. 22571/91 CA, 9.

36. The Signatura itself overturned this 1993 decision in 1995. See Apostolic Signatura, definitive sentence, June 24, 1995, P.N. 22571/91 CA.

37. These treatment centers were: Johns Hopkins, Department of Psychiatry and Behavioral Sciences, Baltimore, Maryland; the Institute of Living, Hartford, Connecticut; the New Life Center, Middleburg, Virginia; St. Luke Institute, Suitland, Maryland; Servants of the Paraclete—St. Michael's Community, St. Louis, Missouri; Servants of the Paraclete—The Albuquerque Villa, Albuquerque, New Mexico; University of Minnesota Medical School, Program in Human Sexuality, Minneapolis, Minnesota; Southdown, Aurora, Ontario,

Canada; Villa St. John Vianney Hospital, Downingtown, Pennsylvania; Our Lady of Peace Hospital, Peace Ministry Centre, Louisville, Kentucky—all recommended in *Restoring Trust,* vol. I; and Behavioral Medicine Institute of Atlanta, Atlanta, Georgia; Isaac Ray Center, Chicago, Illinois; Our Lady of Guadalupe Retreat Center, Cherry Valley, California; Progressive Clinical Services, Cincinnati, Ohio; Shalom Center, Inc., Splendora, Texas; St. Louis Consultation Center, St. Louis, Missouri; the Menninger Clinic, Topeka, Kansas; Wounded Brothers Project, Dittmer, Missouri—all recommended in *Restoring Trust,* vol. II.

38. Deal Hudson, "Ten Myths About Priestly Pedophilia," Catholic Commentary website, http://www.catholicity.com/commentary/hudson/tenmyths.html, November 23, 2005.

39. Ellen Barry, "Priest Treatment Unfolds in Costly, Secretive World," *Boston Globe,* April 3, 2002, A1.

40. Almost 44 percent of priests with credible allegations of child abuse against them in the 1950–2002 time period were sent on spiritual retreat. John Jay College of Criminal Justice, *The Nature and Scope of Sexual Abuse of Minors by Catholic Priests and Deacons in the United States 1950–2002, A Research Study Conducted by the John Jay College of Criminal Justice* (Washington, D.C.: United States Conference of Catholic Bishops, 2004), 95; hereinafter referred to as John Jay Report.

41. *Report of the Grand Jury of September 17, 2003,* misc. no. 03-00-239, Court of Common Pleas, First Judicial District of Pennsylvania [Philadelphia], Criminal Trial Division, 101: "By the time Fr. Leneweaver was transferred for the fourth time, the Archdiocese Chancellor, Francis J. Statkus, noted in a September 1980 letter that 'he was appointed to this area of the diocese because it is one of the few remaining areas where his scandalous action may not be known.'"

42. Kathleen Burge, "Geoghan Receives 9–10 Year Sentence for Molesting Child," *Boston Globe,* February 22, 2002, A1.

43. Quoted in Thomas Farragher, "A Troubled Life Spent Exploiting Vocation," *Boston Globe,* August 24, 2003, B6.

44. He was hardly the only one. As the Philadelphia Grand Jury Report describes another situation:

"Between each of his last three assignments, Fr. Leneweaver underwent some type of psychological evaluation or therapy. But the actual diagnosis or treatment had no discernible effect on the priest's subsequent assignments. The Grand Jury finds that [Philadelphia] Archdiocese officials used Fr. Leneweaver's 'treatment' solely for public-relations purposes, that is, so they could justify to parishioners who might question them why a serial child molester and rapist kept being reassigned to new parishes."

Report of the Grand Jury, Court of Common Pleas, First Judicial District of Pennsylvania, Criminal Trial Division, misc. no. 03-00-239: 109; hereinafter referred to as Philadelphia Grand Jury Report.

Father Raymond Leneweaver was a serial rapist of young boys. "In response to specific complaints made in 1975 to the Archdiocese by victims or their families, he admitted that he had 'seriously' abused at least seven young boys. These sexual assaults began when the children were as young as 11 years old, usually lasted a few years, and included fondling, anal rape, and attempted oral sex." Philadelphia Grand Jury Report, 101. In a number of ways, the Leneweaver abuse, treatment, and reassignment facts parallel the Geoghan abuse, treatment, and reassignment facts.

45. This chronology of John Geoghan's career as a priest of the Archdiocese of Boston is taken from "Geoghan's Troubled History," compiled by the *Boston Globe* Spotlight Team. It originally ran in the January 7, 2002 *Globe*, accompanying the story, "Geoghan Preferred Preying On Poorer Children," written by the *Globe* Spotlight Team, which appeared on page A1; available at http://www.boston.com/globe/spotlight/abuse/print/010702-geoghan.htm, January 10, 2006; hereinafter referred to as *Globe* Timeline.

46. Robinson and Carroll, "Documents," A1+.

47. Ibid.; see also Pfeiffer, "Letters," A21. The question remains, of course, why the archdiocese itself did not make sure that the treating doctors had Geoghan's full history.

48. Pfeiffer, "Letters," A21.

49. In 1968, still under the 1917 Code, the *suspensio ex informata conscientia* of Canon 2186, §2 and the nonpenal restrictions of Canon 2222, §2 would have been available. Three years later, in 1971, under the norms of the Congregation for the Doctrine of the Faith, an administrative rescript of laicization was available. None of these was used on, or apparently even mentioned to Geoghan.

50. *Betrayal*, 29.

51. Ibid., 27.

52. Ibid., 29.

53. After being released from St. Luke's at the end of January 1995, Geoghan returned to Regina Cleri. He had been on administrative leave, forbidden to say public Mass or perform any form of public ministry since December 30, 1994, but evidently when he returned to Regina Cleri, he was still functioning as associate director of the Office for Senior Priests. In 1995 and 1996, while assigned to Regina Cleri, he allegedly molested a ten-year-old boy from Weymouth. One of the molestations is said to have occurred at the christening of the boy's baby sister while the young boy was putting on his altar boy vestments. *Globe* Timeline and Michael Rezendes, "Church Allowed Abuse by Priest for Years," *Boston Globe*, January 6, 2002, A1+. In an August 4, 1996 letter to Geoghan, in which he refers to his earlier December 30, 1994 letter, Cardinal Law says "Since December 30, 1994, you have been on Administrative Leave and I have indicated that you should refrain from all pastoral activity and public ministry." If Geoghan was still on administrative leave after he returned to Regina Cleri from his January 1995 stay at St. Luke's, it appears that the terms of that leave were neither honored nor policed. Certainly the 1995 christening at which another molestation was alleged was an act of "public ministry."

54. Bernard Cardinal Law, excerpts from deposition, Suffolk Superior Court, *Boston Globe*, May 9, 2002, B34, Metro/Region Section.

55. 2002 Editorial, http://www.archdiocese.no.org/archbishop/ah-archives/013002.html, Archbishop Alfred C. Hughes, "Clergy and the Molestation of Minors," *Clarion Herald*, January 30, February 7, 2006.

56. Philadelphia Grand Jury Report, 47.

57. Cardinal Edward Egan, March 23, 2002 statement, http://www.ny-archdiocese.org/statement0323.cfm, February 10, 2006.

58. Dave Newbart and Dan Rozek, "Deposition, Suits Stun Joliet Diocese," *Chicago Sun-Times*, February 5, 2006, http://www.suntimes.com/output/news/cst-nws-priests05.html, February 6, 2006.

The exact quotes from the deposition are:

[Plaintiff's attorney]: "If you were satisfied that it occurred then why didn't you remove the priest from ministry?"

Imesch: "A number of priests received therapy and were given a green light, if you want, to be returned to restricted ministry."

Ted Slowik, "Imesch Testimony Public," *The Herald News Online*,

February 3, 2006, http://suburbanchicagonews.com/heraldnews/top/ 4_1_JO03_DIOCESE_S1.htm, February 7, 2006.

59. Brooks Egerton and Reese Dunklin, "Two-Thirds of Bishops Let Accused Priests Work," *Dallas Morning News,* June 12, 2002, 1A+.

60. Ibid.

61. Ibid. The John Jay Report indicates that well over half of priests with credible allegations of child sexual abuses were sent away for treatment in the 1950–2002 time period. John Jay Report, 95.

62. Barry, "Priest Treatment," A1+.

63. John Bookster Feister, "How the Church Is Confronting Clergy Sexual Abuse," *St. Anthony Messenger* (February 1994): 28–35. See also Peter Steinfels, "Beliefs: Lessons from the Past," *New York Times,* February 9, 2002, A34+: "In the late 1980's even some of the therapists trying hardest to get the church authorities to weed out abusers were also saying that with successful therapy, proper supervision and continuing support, priests could be returned to many forms of pastoral work—and that this was better than simply cutting such individuals loose to become anonymous predators. Reading the fine print, one learned that in reassigning accused priests, bishops often had relied on medical and psychological authorities—some of them amateurish, it seems, but some with every appearance of being state of the art."

64. Leslie M. Lothstein, "Can A Sexually Addicted Priest Return to Ministry after Treatment? Psychological Issues and Possible Forensic Solutions," *Catholic Lawyer* 34 (1990): 89–113, at 89.

65. Rossetti and Lothstein, "Myths of the Child Molester," 16. Rossetti went on to become the chief operating officer of the St. Luke Institute.

66. Frank Valcour, "The Treatment of Child Sex Abusers in the Church," in *Slayer of the Soul,* ed. Stephen J. Rossetti (Mystic: Twenty-Third Publications, 1990), 45–66, at 45.

67. Canice Connors, "Clerical Sexual Abuse Priests and Their Victims Find Healing," *Ligourian* (November 1994): 23–27, at 27.

68. Leslie M. Lothstein, "The Relationship between the Treatment Facilities and the Church Hierarchy: Forensic Issues and Future Considerations," in *Sins Against the Innocents,* ed. Thomas G. Plante (Westport: Praeger, 2004), 123–37, at 125.

69. Philadelphia Grand Jury Report, 47.

70. Ibid., 47–48: "We saw this in the case of Fr. Dunne (one of

the few diagnosed pedophiles), who remained in ministry for seven and a half years after the Archdiocese learned he had abused several boys. Cardinal Bevilacqua first had Chancellor Samuel Shoemaker pressure a Saint John Vianney therapist to make an 'accommodation' in the hospital's initial recommendations that Fr. Dunne be removed from parish ministry and that he be supervised 24 hours a day. The therapist 'accommodated' by reversing himself on both recommendations."

71. Werth, "Fathers' Helper."

72. Ibid.

73. Curtis Bryant, "Psychological Treatment of Priest Sex Offenders," *America* (April 1, 2002): 14–17, at 16. "Treatment at St. Luke Institute, for example, lasts approximately six months and involves three phases."

74. See Curtis Bryant, "Psychological Treatment of Priest Sex Offenders," in *Bless Me Father for I Have Sinned,* ed. Thomas G. Plante (Westport: Praeger, 1999), 87–110, at 105: "The treatment of clergy sexual offenders can be a lengthy and costly exercise. In the current economic climate, program managers are under increasing pressure to justify such high levels of expenditure from a limited church treasury for whom treatment will not frequently enable priests to return to ministry." This chapter in *Bless Me Father* was abridged and rewritten for Bryant's April 1, 2002 article of the same title in *America* magazine.

75. Eric Rich and Elizabeth Hamilton, "Doctors: Church Used Us," *Hartford Courant,* March 24, 2002, A1+.

76. Ibid.

77. Ibid.

78. Ibid.

79. *Betrayal,* 175.

80. Ibid.

81. Rich and Hamilton, "Church Used Us," A1+.

82. Philadelphia Grand Jury Report, 46.

83. This was predicted by A. W. Richard Sipe. In 1995, he wrote, "In spite of all their limitations, psychiatry and psychology will help to shift the balance of the celibate/sexual system toward public disclosure rather than secrecy; what was sequestered in private will become increasingly open to public scrutiny." A. W. Richard Sipe, *Sex, Priests, and Power* (New York: Brunner/Mazel, 1995), 91–92.

84. "It was clear from the court documents that knowledge of past allegations made doctors less likely to recommend that a priest be returned to parish work." Rich and Hamilton, "Church Used Us," A1+.

85. Lothstein, "Sexually Addicted Priest," 111.

86. Cafardi, "Stones Instead of Bread," 168; citing the Restatement 2d of Torts, §§317, 321.

87. Congregation for the Doctrine of the Faith, *Declaration Inter Insigniores*, October 15, 1976, *Acta Apostolicae Sedis* 69 (1977): 98–116, at §5.

88. Pope John Paul II, apostolic letter *Ordinatio sacerdotalis*, May 22, 1994, *Acta Apostolicae Sedis* 86 (1994): 545–48; Congregation for the Doctrine of the Faith, "Concerning the Reply of the Congregation for the Doctrine of the Faith on the Teaching Contained in the Apostolic Letter 'Ordinatio Sacerdotalis,'" October 28, 1995, *Acta Apostolicae Sedis* 87 (1995): 1114. See also Pope Pius XII, encyclical letter Mediator Dei, November 20, 1947, *Acta Apostolicae Sedis* 39 (1947): 541, at §69: " The priest is the same, Jesus Christ, whose sacred Person His minister represents. Now the minister, by reason of the sacerdotal consecration which he has received, is made like to the High Priest and possesses the power of performing actions in virtue of Christ's very person. Wherefore in his priestly activity he in a certain manner 'lends his tongue, and gives his hand' to Christ" [citing Saint Thomas Aquinas, *Summa Theologica*, IIIa, q. 22, art. 4. and Saint John Chrysostom, *In Joann. Hom.*, 86:4]. See also §20: "Christ is present at the august sacrifice of the altar…in the person of His minister"; §40: "Only to the apostles, and thenceforth to those on whom their successors have imposed hands, is granted the power of the priesthood, in virtue of which they represent the person of Jesus Christ before their people"; "The priest is the ambassador of the divine Redeemer. He is God's vice-gerent in the midst of his flock precisely because Jesus Christ is Head of that body of which Christians are the members"; §42: "[Holy Orders] not only imparts the grace appropriate to the clerical function and state of life, but imparts an indelible 'character' besides, indicating the sacred ministers' conformity to Jesus Christ the Priest"; §84: "But we deem it necessary to recall that the priest acts for the people only because he represents Jesus Christ, who is Head of all His members and offers Himself in their stead. Hence, he goes to the

altar as the minister of Christ, inferior to Christ but superior to the people" [citing Saint Robert Bellarmine, *De Missa,* 2, c. 4].

89. George Weigel, *The Courage to Be Catholic* (New York: Basic Books, 2002), 192.

90. Pope John Paul II, "Address to Summit of Vatican, U.S. Church Leaders," *Origins* 31:46 (May 2, 2002): 757–59, at 759. See also John J. Coughlin, "The Clergy Sexual Abuse Crisis and the Spirit of Canon Law," *Boston College Law Review* 44 (2003): 977–97, at 993: "The horrendously disordered priest who sexually abuses a child has not only harmed the victim but the entire Mystical Body of Christ. While he may be forgiven his sin, a just ecclesial order may require that he no longer function as a priest."

91. Report of the Philadelphia Grand Jury, 43–44.

92. CIC, 1983, cc. 277, §2; 326, §1; 695, §1; 696, §1; 703, §1; 933; 990; 1132; 1184, §1, 3º; 1211; 1318; 1328, §2; 1339, §2; 1341; 1344, 2º, 3º; 1347, §2; 1352, §2; 1357, §2; 1361, §3; 1364, §2; 1394, §1; 1395, §1; 1399; 1455, §3; 1560, §2; 1722; 1727, §2.

93. Philadelphia Grand Jury Report, 111.

94. "In 1970, there were 6,426 students enrolled in Catholic seminary programs in the United States. By 1990, the number had dwindled to 3,609." Frank Bruni and Elinor Burkett, *Gospel of Shame* (New York: Perennial, 2002), 207. "Over the past 20 years, an estimated 100,000 men have left the priesthood worldwide—some 23,000 in the U.S. alone." Kathy Coffey, "A Priest Is a Terrible Thing to Waste," *U.S. Catholic* (September 2000): 41–42, at 41.

95. Rich and Hamilton, "Church Used Us," A1+.

96. Weigel, *Courage,* 102

97. Connors, "Clerical Sexual Abuse," 27.

98. Coughlin, "Clergy Sexual Abuse Crisis," 988.

APPENDIX: A TIMELINE

1917

The 1917 Code of Canon Law. Promulgated by Pope Benedict XV, it stated in Canon 2359, §2 that clerical sexual abuse of a minor under the age of sixteen was a canonical crime that could lead to the cleric's dismissal from the clerical state (laicization). The 1917 Code also allowed a diocesan bishop, without a canonical penal process, to suspend a priest *ex informata conscientia* (Canon 2186, §1) or to impose nonpenal restrictions (Canon 2222, §2) when he had reason to believe that the priest was sexually abusive.

1962

Crimen sollicitationis. Promulgated by the Holy Office (now Congregation for the Doctrine of the Faith) under the authority of Pope John XXIII, it gave the Holy Office jurisdiction over the canonical crime of the sexual abuse of minors by clergy and had the effect of abolishing the prescriptive period (a statute of limitations) for the prosecution of such crimes. It was mailed to all the bishops of the world and ordered to be kept in the secret archives of each diocese.

1971

The Congregation for the Doctrine of the Faith. Under Pope Paul VI, the Congregation promulgated norms for the administrative (nonpenal) laicization of priests that allowed a diocesan bishop to request the administrative laicization of a priest leading a "depraved life."

1980

The Congregation for the Doctrine of the Faith. Under Pope John Paul II, the Congregation revised the administrative norms for the laicization of priests and diocesan bishops were no longer able to request administrative laicizations for any reason.

1983

The 1983 Code of Canon Law. This revision and updating of the Church's law in light of the Second Vatican Council was promulgated by Pope John Paul II. It replaced the 1917 Code of Canon Law, and did away with the former Code's suspension *ex informata conscientia* and nonpenal remedies that bishops could impose on abusive priests. Canon 1395, §2 repeated the 1917 Code's provision (Canon 2359, §2) that clerical sexual abuse of a minor under the age of sixteen was a canonical crime that could lead to the cleric's dismissal from the clerical state (laicization).

1984

The Diocese of Lafayette, Louisiana. Father Gauthe pleaded guilty to molesting eleven boys and admitted to victimizing dozens more.

1985

NCCB meeting in Collegeville, Minnesota. At their annual June meeting, the assembled bishops heard in their executive session from three experts on the sexual abuse of children by clergy.

The Manual. Formally titled "The Problem of Sexual Molestation by Roman Catholic Clergy: Meeting the Problem in a Comprehensive and Responsible Manner" the Manual was written by Father Thomas Doyle, OP, a canon lawyer working at the Papal Nunciature; F. Ray Mouton, the civil lawyer defending Father Gauthe; and Father

Michael Peterson, MD, the head of St. Luke Institute. Fewer than twenty copies were distributed to the bishops at their national meeting in June in Collegeville, Minnesota. It was never formally presented to the NCCB, and so was neither adopted nor rejected by the body. In December, Father Peterson sent copies of the Manual, together with an "Executive Summary," to each of the bishops as a mailing from St. Luke Institute, clearly labeling the document as "confidential."

1986

Manual revisions. Father Peterson sent revisions of the Manual to the bishops.

1987

"Dismissal from the Clerical State in Cases of Sexual Crimes Against Minors." This text, a guide to the canonical process on how to dismiss a sexually abusive priest from the clerical state, was prepared by the Canonical Affairs Committee of the NCCB and sent to every bishop.

1988

Statement of general counsel. The general counsel for the United States Catholic Conference as a spokesperson for the bishops issued the first national statement on the clergy's sexual abuse of minors.

The Apostolic See. Individual American bishops began asking the Apostolic See for an expedited canonical process to deal with sexually abusive priests.

1989

Statement of the Administrative Committee. The executive committee of the NCCB, known as the Administrative Committee, issued the first joint statement by the bishops themselves on the clergy's sexual abuse of minors.

Newfoundland, Canada. Allegations became public of physical and sexual abuse of boys by the Irish Christian Brothers at an orphanage in the Newfoundland Archdiocese.

1990 (approximate)

Apostolic See. The NCCB officially raised the issue of expedited canonical norms with the Apostolic See.

1991

The Archdiocese of Santa Fe, New Mexico. Several priests sent to the Servants of the Paraclete rehabilitative center near Santa Fe for the treatment of their sexual abuse of minors were secretly continuing their abusive conduct during their weekend parish work.

The Archdiocese of Chicago, Illinois. After the public disclosure of his reassignment of a sexually abusive priest, Cardinal Bernardin appointed a commission to study the matter and make recommendations to him.

1992

Statement of the Office of Media Relations. This statement by the NCCB's Office of Media Relations in February was the first statement by the national body after the 1989 statement of the NCCB's Administrative Committee. It outlined an effective procedure for handling cases of sexual abuse of minors.

The Diocese of Fall River, Massachusetts. Laicized priest James Porter was found to have molested between fifty and a hundred children years earlier when he was a priest of the diocese.

From Pain to Hope. This document, issued by the Canadian Bishops' Conference in June, described the Church culture that created the problem of the clergy's sexual abuse of children. The document included fifty guidelines for dealing with accusations of child sexual abuse by clergy and publicly bound the Canadian bishops to follow the guidelines.

Archbishop Pilarczyk's statement. At the NCCB's June meeting, the president of the NCCB, Archbishop Pilarczyk of Cincinnati, revealed that in 1987 the conference had begun recommending a five-step program for dealing with sexual abuse by the clergy to the individual dioceses.

NCCB's adoption of the Pilarczyk statement. Without dissent, the entire NCCB adopted Pilarczyk's five steps as the position of the NCCB. The adoption had only an advisory effect, however, since the NCCB lacked the canonical authority to legislate on this matter nationally. Notably, the five steps did require that the abusive priest be removed from assignment, although the preference was the treatment model, and the five steps did not deal with the reassignment issue.

The Think Tank. A subcommittee of the NCCB was formed to study clergy sexual abuse. The subcommittee was to make recommendations for the June 1993 meeting of the NCCB.

The Archdiocese of Chicago, Illinois. Cardinal Bernardin's commission issued its report that recommended that no sexually abusive priests be returned to ministry. The report was sent to all diocesan bishops in the United States.

1993

The Think Tank's report. The subcommittee made its report to the NCCB at its June meeting. None of its recommendations was specifically adopted, but they did lead to the formation of the NCCB's Ad Hoc Committee on Sexual Abuse.

The Apostolic See. Pope John Paul II sent a letter to the American bishops, which was discussed at their June meeting, in which he stated that a joint committee of both Vatican personnel and American bishops had been created to deal with the canonical norms on the sexual abuse of children by clergy.

NCCB's Ad Hoc Committee on Sexual Abuse. At their June meeting, the bishops created an ad hoc committee, headed by Bishop John Kinney from Bismarck, to consolidate and build on steps previously taken by the bishops to confront the issue of sexual abuse by the clergy.

Chicago, Illinois. Cardinal Joseph Bernardin was sued by a former seminarian based on alleged "recovered" memories of sexual abuse. The charges, deemed to have been false and trumped up for litigation purposes, were withdrawn and the national media turned its attention away from the bishops and their handling of the issue of the clergy's sexual abuse of children for the next five to six years.

The Joint Commission. The joint commission of Vatican officials and representatives of the NCCB, established by Pope John Paul II, reported how canonical norms could be applied to the ongoing sexual abuse crisis in the United States.

NCCB's proposed changes in the law. As a result of the work of the Joint Commission, the NCCB asked the Apostolic See for three changes in the law for the United States regarding the age of the victim, the time period for prescription (statute of limitations), and the Roman appeals process.

1994

The Apostolic See. The Vatican approved changes in the law for the United States, on the age of the victims, raising it from under sixteen to under eighteen, and on the prescriptive period, enlarging it from five years after the offense to ten years after the offense. Although requested, no change was granted in the Roman appeals process.

Restoring Trust: A Pastoral Response to Sexual Abuse, the Ad Hoc Committee on Sexual Abuse. The Ad Hoc Committee published its first report, *Restoring Trust*. The report reviewed the sexual abuse policies of 157 dioceses. The report also proposed twenty-eight concrete guidelines to the bishops on how to handle allegations of sexual abuse of children by clergy. These recommendations, however, were never brought to the floor and were never acted on.

1995

Canonical Delicts Involving Sexual Misconduct and Dismissal from the Clerical State. The Canonical Affairs Committee of the NCCB published *Canonical Delicts Involving Sexual Misconduct and Dismissal from the Clerical State*, which explained how to implement the changes in the law approved by the Apostolic See in the prior year.

Restoring Trust: A Pastoral Response to Sexual Abuse, vol. II. The Ad Hoc Committee released volume II of *Restoring Trust*. It contained information on the care of victims, and material endorsing the treatment model.

1996

Restoring Trust: A Pastoral Response to Sexual Abuse, vol. III. The Ad Hoc Committee released volume III of *Restoring Trust*. It was a report on how the Ad Hoc Committee had met its charge, summarizing the activities of the committee.

1997

The Diocese of Dallas, Texas. Eleven sexual abuse victims of Father Rudolph Kos brought civil suit against Father Kos and the Dallas Diocese.

2001

Sacramentorum sanctitatis tutela. Pope John Paul II issued, *motu proprio*, his apostolic letter, *Sacramentorum sanctitatis tutela*, which promulgated norms for certain grave delicts, including the sexual abuse of minors by clergy, jurisdiction over which was reserved to the Congregation for the Doctrine of the Faith. *Sacramentorum sanctitatis tutela* extended to the universal Church the American derogations in the law, raising the age of minor victims of clergy sexual abuse to those under the age of eighteen and extending the prescriptive period to ten years after the minor's eighteenth birthday.

De delictis gravioribus. Then-Cardinal Joseph Ratzinger, prefect of the Congregation for the Doctrine of the Faith, issued an instructional letter on those delicts or canonical crimes reserved to the jurisdiction of the Congregation for the Doctrine of the Faith in which he stated that *Crimen sollicitationis* of 1962 was *hucusque vigens*—in force until then, that is, May 18, 2001.

2002

The Archdiocese of Boston, Massachusetts. It was publicly revealed by way of newspaper articles based on information disclosed in litigation that the archdiocese had kept on active assignment, long after the 1992 NCCB advisory, at least two priests, John Geoghan and Paul Shanley, whom it knew to be sexually abusive of children.

The Dallas Charter and Norms. Under the harsh glow of the media spotlight again, the USCCB (formerly the NCCB) adopted strong measures to deal with priests who sexually abuse children, including the zero tolerance policy that such priests will not be returned to ministry. With some minor changes, the Dallas Norms became canon law for the United States with the *recognitio* of the Apostolic See.

BIBLIOGRAPHY

OFFICIAL, SEMIOFFICIAL, AND OLDER SOURCES

Ad Hoc Committee on Sexual Abuse, National Conference of Catholic Bishops. *Restoring Trust: A Pastoral Response to Sexual Abuse.* Vol. I. Washington, D.C.: National Conference of Catholic Bishops, 1994.

———. *Restoring Trust: A Pastoral Response to Sexual Abuse.* Vol. II. Washington, D.C.: National Conference of Catholic Bishops, 1995.

———. "Twenty-Eight Suggestions on Sexual Abuse Policies." *Origins* 24:26 (December 8, 1994): 443–44.

Administrative Committee, National Conference of Catholic Bishops. "Statement on Priests and Child Abuse." *Origins* 19:24 (November 16, 1989): 394–95.

Apostolic Signatura. Definitive sentence. March 9, 1993, P.N. 22571/91 CA.

———. Definitive sentence. June 24, 1995, P.N. 22571/91 CA.

Bernardin, Cardinal Joseph. October 25, 1991 letter to Chicago Catholics. Appendix "A" in Julia Quinn Dempsey, John R. Gorman, and John P. Madden. *Report to Joseph Cardinal Bernardin, The Cardinal's Commission on Clerical Sexual Misconduct with Minors.* Chicago, Ill., June 1992.

———. "Child Sexual Abuse by Church Personnel." *Origins* 21:21 (October 31, 1991): 354–55.

———. "Statement Announcing Policy on Clerical Sexual Misconduct with Minors." *Origins* 22:16 (October 1, 1992): 282–83.

Burchard of Worms. *Decretum*. In *Patrologiae*. Ed. J. P. Migne. Vol. 140. Paris, 1853.

Canadian Bishops' Committee. "Fifty Recommendations: The Church and Child Sexual Abuse." *Origins* 22:7 (June 25, 1992): 97–107.

Canon Law Digest. Vol. VII. Ed. James I. O'Connor. Chicago: Chicago Province S.J., 1975.

————. Vol. IX. Ed. James I. O'Connor. Mundelein, Ill.: Chicago Province S.J., 1983.

Canon Law Society of America. *Code of Canon Law, Latin-English Edition, New English Translation*. Washington, D.C.: Canon Law Society of America, 1998.

————. *Code of Canons of the Eastern Churches, Latin-English Edition*. Washington, D.C.: Canon Law Society of America, 1992.

The Canons and Decrees of the Council of Trent. Ed. H. J. Schroeder. Rockford, Ill.: Tan Books, 1978.

The Canons and Decrees of the Sacred and Ecumenical Council of Trent. Ed. and Trans. J. Waterworth. London: Dolman, 1848.

Chicago Archdiocese. "Chicago Policy Regarding Clerical Sexual Misconduct with Minors." *Origins* 22:16 (October 1, 1992): 273–78.

"Child Sexual Abuse: Think Tank Recommendations." *Origins* 23:7 (July 1, 1993): 108–11.

Chopko, Mark. "USCC Pedophilia Statement." *Origins* 17:36 (February 18, 1988): 624.

Codex Canonum Ecclesiarum Orientalium Auctoritate Ioannis Pauli Promulgatus. Vatican City: Libreria Editrice Vaticana, 1995.

Codex Iuris Canonici auctoritate Ioannis Pauli PP. II promulgatus. Vatican City: Typis Polyglottis Vaticanis, 1983.

Codicis Iuris Canonici Fontes. Ed. Petrus Card. Gasparri. *Concilia Generalia—Romani Pontifices usque ad annum 1745*. Rome: Typis Polyglottis Vaticanis, 1947.

Congregation for the Doctrine of the Faith. "Concerning the Reply of the Congregation for the Doctrine of the Faith on the Teaching Contained in the Apostolic Letter 'Ordinatio Sacerdotalis.'" October 28, 1995. *Acta Apostolicae Sedis* 87 (1995): 1114.

————. *De delictis gravioribus eidem Congregationi pro Doctrina Fidei riservatis*. May 18, 2001. *Acta Apostolicae Sedis* 93 (2001): 785–87.

_____.*Declaration Inter Insigniores*. October 15, 1976. *Acta Apostolicae Sedis* 69 (1977): 98–116.

_____. "Norms for Preparing in Diocesan and Religious Curias Cases of Reduction to the Lay State Together with a Dispensation from the Obligations Connected with Sacred Ordination." January 13, 1971, *Acta Apostolicae Sedis* 63 (1971): 303–12.

_____. "On the Modes of Procedure in the Examination and Resolution of Petitions Which Look to a Dispensation from Celibacy." October 14, 1980. *Acta Apostolicae Sedis* 72 (1980): 1132–37.

Corpus Iuris Canonici. Editio Lipsiensis Secunda. Ed. Aemilius Friedberg. Leipzig: Tauchnitz, 1879.

Damian, Peter. *Letters 31–60, Fathers of the Church—Mediaeval Continuation Series*. Trans. Owen P. Blum. Washington, D.C.: Catholic University of America Press, 1990.

Davenport Diocese. "Sexual Abuse Policy." *Origins* 20:6 (June 21, 1990): 93–94.

Decrees of the Ecumenical Councils. Ed. Norman Tanner. London and Washington, D.C.: Sheed and Ward and Georgetown University Press, 1990.

Decretales Gregorii IX (Extravagantium Liber). *Corpus Iuris Canonici*. Editio Lipsiensis Secunda. Ed. Aemilius Friedberg. Leipzig: Tauchnitz, 1879.

Decretalium Collectiones. Lateran Council IV. Editio Lipsiensis Secunda. Ed. Aemilius Friedberg. Leipzig: Tauchnitz, 1879.

"The Didache or the Teaching of the Twelve Apostles." Trans. James A. Kleist. In *Ancient Christian Writers*, no. 6. Ed. Johannes Quasten and Joseph C. Plumpe. Washington, D.C.: Catholic University of America. Republished, New York: Paulist Press, 1948.

"The Epistle of Barnabas." Trans. James A. Kleist. In *Ancient Christian Writers*, no. 6. Ed. Johannes Quasten and Joseph C. Plumpe. Washington, D.C.: Catholic University of America. Republished, New York: Paulist Press, 1948.

Gratian. *Concordia Discordantium Canonum ac Primum de Iure Naturae et Constitutionis*. *Corpus Iuris Canonici*. Editio Lipsiensis Secunda. Ed. Aemilius Friedberg. Leipzig: Tauchnitz, 1879.

Keeler, Archbishop William. "Remarks." *Origins* 23:7 (July 1, 1993): 104.

Kinney, Bishop John F. "NCCB Establishes Committee on Sexual Abuse." *Origins* 23:7 (July 1, 1993):104–5.

————. November 14, 1994 introductory letter. In Ad Hoc Committee on Sexual Abuse, National Conference of Catholic Bishops. *Restoring Trust: A Pastoral Response to Sexual Abuse*. Vol. I. Washington, D.C.: National Conference of Catholic Bishops, 1994.

Los Angeles Archdiocese. "Policy on Sexual Abuse by Priests." *Origins* 24:5 (June 16, 1994): 70–74.

Mahony, Cardinal Roger. "Talk with Victims of Clergy Sexual Misconduct." *Origins* 22:24 (November 26, 1992): 405.

National Conference of Catholic Bishops. "Resolution on Clergy Sex Abuse." *Origins* 22:25 (December 3, 1992): 418.

Office of Media Relations, United States Catholic Conference. "Policy on Priests and Sexual Abuse of Children." In *Statements of the National Conference of Catholic Bishops and the United States Catholic Conference on the Subject of the Sexual Abuse of Children by Priests 1988–1992*. Washington, D.C.: United States Catholic Conference, 1992.

Pilarczyk, Archbishop Daniel. "Painful Pastoral Question: Sexual Abuse of Minors." *Origins* 22:10 (August 6, 1992): 177–78.

————. "Statement of Archbishop Pilarczyk, President of the National Conference of Catholic Bishops, on the Sexual Abuse of Children." June 20, 1992, reprinted in *Statements of the National Conference of Catholic Bishops and the United States Catholic Conference on the Subject of the Sexual Abuse of Children by Priests 1988–1992*. Washington, D.C.: United States Catholic Conference, 1992.

Polycarp. "Letter to the Philippians." In *Apostolic Fathers:* Vol. I. I Clement. II Clement. Ignatius. Polycarp. Didache. Barnabas. Trans. Kirsopp Lake. Loeb Classical Library no. 24. London: Harvard University Press, 1975.

Pontificia Commissio Codici Iuris Canonici Recognoscendo. *Communicationes* 1 (1969).

Pope John Paul II. "Address to Summit of Vatican, U.S. Church Leaders." *Origins* 31:46 (May 2, 2002): 757–59.

———.Apostolic letter *motu proprio Apostolos suos.* "On the Theological and Juridical Nature of Episcopal Conferences." May 21, 1998. *Acta Apostolicae Sedis* 90 (1998): 655–56.

———. Apostolic letter *motu proprio Sacramentorum sanctitatis tutela. Acta Apostolicae Sedis* 93 (2001): 737–39.

———. Apostolic letter *Ordinatio sacerdotalis.* May 22, 1994. *Acta Apostolicae Sedis* 86 (1994): 545–48.

———. June 11, 1993 letter to the American bishops. "Vatican-U.S. Bishops' Committee to Study Applying Canonical Norms." *Origins* 23:7 (July 1, 1993): 102–3.

———. *Pastor bonus.* Apostolic constitution on the Roman Curia. June 28, 1988. Reprinted in *Code of Canon Law, Latin-English Edition.* Washington, D.C.: Canon Law Society of America, 1998: 681–751.

Pope Pius XII. Encyclical letter *Mediator Dei.* November 20, 1947. *Acta Apostolicae Sedis* 39 (1947): 541.

"Proposed Guidelines on the Assessment of Clergy and Religious for Assignment." Approved by the National Conference of Catholic Bishops, November 18, 1993. *The Jurist* 54 (1994): 623–28.

Roman Rota. *Coram Colagiovanni.* April 9, 1994.

Sacred Congregation for the Council. *Lavellana seu Romanum,* June 8 and July 6, 1726. In *Codicis Iuris Canonici Fontes.* Ed. Petrus Card. Gasparri. *Concilia Generalia—Romani Pontifices usque ad annum 1745.* Rome: Typis Polyglottis Vaticanis, 1947: V:763–64.

St. Cloud Diocese. "Sexual Misconduct Policy." *Origins* 21:12 (August 29, 1991): 194–96.

Salt Lake City Diocese. "Child Abuse Policy." *Origins* 20:3 (May 3, 1990): 42–44.

Secretariat of State. April 25, 1994 rescript. Protocol no. 346.053. *Roman Replies and CLSA Advisory Opinions 1994:* 20–21.

———. December 4, 1998 letter. Protocol no. 445.119. G.N. *Studia canonica* 33 (1999): 211–12.

Sioux City Diocese. "Diocesan Policy: When a Cleric Is Accused of Sexually Exploiting a Minor." *Origins* 22:10 (August 6, 1992): 178–79.

Suprema Sacra Congregatio Sancti Officii. "Crimen Sollicitationis." March 16, 1962. Typis Polyglottis Vaticanis.

United States Conference of Catholic Bishops, Ad Hoc Committee on Sexual Abuse. "Efforts to Combat Clergy Sexual Abuse Against Minors—Chronology." In *Restoring Trust: A Pastoral Response to Sexual Abuse*. Washington, D.C.: National Conference of Catholic Bishops, 2002.

Washington Archdiocese. February 7, 1995 Statement. *Origins* 24:35 (February 16, 1995): 590.

TREATISES

Prummer, Domenicus M. *Manualis Iuris Canonici*. Freiburg-i-Br: Herder, 1922.

Wernz, F. X. *Ius Decretalium*. Prato: Giachetti, Filii et Soc., 1913 (rev. ed.).

BOOKS, DISSERTATIONS, AND REPORTS

American Psychiatric Association. *Diagnostic and Statistical Manual of Mental Disorders*. 4th ed. Washington, D.C.: American Psychiatric Association, 1994.

Berry, Jason. *Lead Us Not Into Temptation*. New York: Doubleday, 1992.

Boston Globe investigative staff. *Betrayal: The Crisis in the Catholic Church*. Boston: Little, Brown, 2002.

Brundage, James A. *Law, Sex and Society in Medieval Europe*. Chicago: University of Chicago Press, 1987.

Bruni, Frank, and Elinor Burkett. *A Gospel of Shame*. New York: HarperCollins, 2002.

Canon Law Society of America. *The Art of the Good and Equitable*. Ed. Frederick C. Easton. Washington, D.C.: Canon Law Society of America, 2002.

_____. *Clergy Procedural Handbook*. Ed. Randolph R. Calvo and Nevin J. Klinger. Washington, D.C.: Canon Law Society of America, 2002.

_____. *The Code of Canon Law: A Text and Commentary*. Ed. James A. Coriden, Thomas J. Green, and Donald E. Heintschel. New York: Paulist Press, 1985.

————. *New Commentary on the Code of Canon Law.* Ed. John P. Beal, James A. Coriden, and Thomas J. Green. New York: Paulist Press, 2000.

————. *Revised Guide to the Implementation of the U.S. Bishops' Essential Norms for Diocesan/Eparchial Policies Dealing with Allegations of Sexual Abuse of Minors by Priests or Deacons.* Washington, D.C.: Canon Law Society of America, 2004.

Dempsey, Julia Quinn, John R. Gorman, and John P. Madden. *Report to Joseph Cardinal Bernardin, Archbishop of Chicago, The Cardinal's Commission on Clerical Sexual Misconduct with Minors.* Chicago: Archdiocese of Chicago, 1992.

Dilexit Justitiam. Ed. Zenon Grocholewski and Vincenzo Carcel Orti. Vatican City: Libreria Editrice Vaticana, 1984.

France, David. *Our Fathers.* New York: Broadway Books, 2004.

Jenkins, Philip. *Pedophiles and Priests.* New York: Oxford University Press, 1996.

John Jay College of Criminal Justice. *The Nature and Scope of Sexual Abuse of Minors by Catholic Priests and Deacons in the United States 1950-2002, A Research Study Conducted by the John Jay College of Criminal Justice.* Washington, D.C.: United States Conference of Catholic Bishops, 2004.

McNeil, John T., and Helena M. Gamer. *Medieval Handbooks of Penance: A Translation of the Principal "Libri Poenitentiales" and Selections from Related Documents.* New York: Columbia University Press, 1990.

Murphy, Edwin J. *Suspension Ex Informata Conscientia.* The Catholic University of America, Canon Law Studies, no. 76. Washington, D.C.: Catholic University of America, 1932.

National Conference of Catholic Bishops. *Canonical Delicts Involving Sexual Misconduct and Dismissal from the Clerical State.* Washington, D.C.: United States Catholic Conference, 1995.

National Review Board for the Protection of Children and Young People. *A Report on the Crisis in the Catholic Church in the United States.* Washington, D.C.: United States Conference of Catholic Bishops, 2004.

Payer, Peter. *Sex and the Penitentials.* Toronto: Toronto University Press, 1984.

Peters, Edward N. *Penal Procedural Law in the 1983 Code of Canon Law.* Washington, D.C.: Catholic University of America, 1991.

Il Processo Penale Canonico. Ed. Zbigniew Suchecki. Rome: Lateran University Press, 2003.

Rossetti, Stephen J. *A Tragic Grace.* Collegeville: Liturgical Press, 1996.

Sexual Abuse in the Catholic Church: Scientific and Legal Perspectives. Ed. R. Karl Hanson, Friedemann Pfafflin, and Manfred Lutz. Vatican City: Libreria Editrice Vaticana, 2004.

Sipe, A. W. Richard. *Sex, Priests, and Power.* New York: Brunner/ Mazel, 1995.

Slayer of the Soul. Ed. Stephen J. Rossetti. Mystic: Twenty-Third Publications, 1990.

von Hefele, Carl Joseph. *Histoire des Conciles d'apres Les Documents Originaux.* Tome I. Paris: Letouzey et Ane, 1907.

Weigel, George. *The Courage to Be Catholic.* New York: Basic Books, 2002.

Woestman, William H. *Ecclesiastical Sanctions and the Penal Process: A Commentary on the Code of Canon Law.* 2nd ed. Revised and updated. Ottawa: Faculty of Canon Law, St. Paul University, 2003.

————. *The Sacrament of Orders and the Clerical State.* 2nd ed. Revised and updated. Ottawa: Faculty of Canon Law, St. Paul University, 2001.

SCHOLARLY ARTICLES

Alesandro, John. "Dismissal from the Clerical State in Cases of Sexual Misconduct." *CLSA Proceedings* (1994): 29–67.

————. "General Introduction." In *The Code of Canon Law: A Text and Commentary.* Ed. James A. Coriden, Thomas J. Green, and Donald E. Heintschel. New York: Paulist Press, 1985.

Ballotta, Karen Ann. "Losing Its Soul: How the Cipolla Case Limits the Catholic Church's Ability to Discipline Sexually Abusive Priests." *Emory Law Journal* 43 (1994): 1431–65.

Beal, John P. "Administrative Leave: Canon 1722 Revisited." *Studia canonica* 27 (1993): 293–320.

————. "At the Crossroads of Two Laws: Some Reflections on the Influence of Secular Law on the Church's Response to Clergy

Sexual Abuse in the United States." *Louvain Studies* 25 (2000): 99–121.

————. "Doing What One Can: Canon Law and Clerical Sexual Misconduct." *The Jurist* 52 (1992): 642–83.

————. "To Be or Not To Be, That Is the Question: The Rights of the Accused in the Canonical Penal Process." *CLSA Proceedings* 53 (1991): 77–97.

————. "To Good To Be True? A Response to Professor Woestman on the Interpretation of Canons 1041, 1º and 1044, §2, 2º." *Monitor Ecclesiasticus* 121 (1996): 431–63.

Bryant, Curtis. "Psychological Treatment of Priest Sex Offenders." In *Bless Me Father for I Have Sinned*. Ed. Thomas G. Plante. Westport: Praeger, 1999: 87–110.

Cafardi, Nicholas P. "Stones Instead of Bread: Sexually Abusive Priests in Ministry." *Studia canonica* 27 (1993): 145–72.

Choli, Roman M. T. "The *lex continentiae* and the Impediment of Orders." *Studia canonica* 21 (1987): 391–418.

Cimbolic, Peter. "The Identification and Treatment of Sexual Disorders and the Priesthood." *The Jurist* 52 (1992): 598–614.

Cipriotti, Pio. "De consumatione delictorum attento eorum elementum obiectivo: Caput IV." *Appolinaris* 9 (1936): 404–12.

Coughlin, John J. "The Clergy Sexual Abuse Crisis and the Spirit of Canon Law." *Boston College Law Review* 44 (2003): 977–97.

Cox, Craig A. "Irregularities and Impediments. In *Clergy Procedural Handbook*. Ed. Randolph R. Calvo and Nevin J. Klinger. Washington, D.C.: Canon Law Society of America, 2002: 178–20.

de Paolis, Velasio. "Processo Penale nel Nuovo Codice." In *Dilexit Justitiam*. Ed. Zenon Grocholewski and Vincenzo Carcel Orti. Vatican City: Libreria Editrice Vaticana, 1984: 473–94.

Doyle, Thomas J. "The Canonical Rights of Priests Accused of Sexual Abuse." *Studia canonica* 24 (1990): 335–56.

————. "Roman Catholic Clericalism, Religious Duress, and Clergy Sexual Abuse." *Pastoral Psychology* 51 (2003).

Ferme, Brian E. "*Graviora delicta:* The Apostolic Letter M.P. sacramentorum sanctitatis tutela." In *Il Processo Penale Canonico*. Ed. Zbigniew Suchecki. Rome: Lateran University Press, 2003: 365–82.

Gill, James J., MD. "Will Priests Sexually Abuse After Treatment?" In Ad Hoc Committee on Sexual Abuse, National Conference of Catholic Bishops. *Restoring Trust: A Pastoral Response to Sexual Abuse.* Vol. II. Washington, D.C.: National Conference of Catholic Bishops, 1995.

Gonsiorek, John C. "Barriers to Responding to the Clergy Sexual Abuse Crisis within the Roman Catholic Church." In *Sins Against the Innocents.* Ed. Thomas G. Plante. Westport: Praeger, 2004: 139–53.

Grabowski, John S. "Clerical Sexual Misconduct and Early Traditions Regarding the Sixth Commandment." *The Jurist* 55 (1995): 527–91.

Green, Thomas J. "The Authority of Episcopal Conferences: Some Normative and Doctrinal Considerations." *CLSA Proceedings* 51 (1989): 123–36.

———. "Book VI: Sanctions in the Code." In *New Commentary on the Code of Canon Law.* Ed. John P. Beal, James A. Coriden, and Thomas J. Green. New York: Paulist Press, 2000: 1527–1605.

———. "Canon 1342, §2 Involuntary Dismissal from the Clerical State." In *Roman Replies and CLSA Advisory Opinions 1991.* Ed. Kevin W. Vann and Lynn Jarrell. Washington, D.C.: Canon Law Society of America, 1991: 118–21.

———. "Clerical Sexual Abuse of Minors: Some Canonical Reflections." *The Jurist* 63 (2003): 366–425.

———. "Sanctions in the Church." In *The Code of Canon Law: A Text and Commentary.* Ed. James A. Coriden, Thomas J. Green, and Donald E. Heintschel. New York: Paulist Press, 1985: 893–931.

Griffin, Bertram F. "Canon 290 Penal Dismissal from the Clerical State." In *Roman Replies and CLSA Advisory Opinions 1988.* Ed. William A. Schumacher and J. James Cuneo. Washington, D.C.: Canon Law Society of America, 1988: 66–71.

———. "Canon 1722: Imposition of Administrative Leave Against an Accused." In *Roman Replies and CLSA Advisory Opinions 1988.* Ed. William Schumacher and J. James Cuneo. Washington, D.C.: Canon Law Society of America, 1988: 103–8.

———. "The Reassignment of a Cleric Who Has Been Professionally Evaluated and Treated for Sexual Misconduct with

Minors: Canonical Considerations." *The Jurist* 51 (1991): 326–39.

Ingels, Gregory. "Dismissal from the Clerical State: An Examination of the Penal Process." *Studia canonica* 33 (1999): 169–212.

————. "Protecting the Right to Privacy When Examining Issues Affecting the Life and Ministry of Clerics and Religious." *Studia canonica* 34 (2000): 439–66.

Isely, Paul J. "Child Sexual Abuse and the Catholic Church: An Historical and Contemporary Review." *Pastoral Psychology* 45 (1997): 277–99.

Jenkins, Ronny E. "On the Suitability of Establishing Clerical Sexual Abuse of Minors (c. 1395 §2) as an Irregularity *Ex Delicto* to the Reception and Exercise of Orders." *Periodica* 94 (205): 275–340.

Kaslyn, Robert J. "The Sacrament of Orders: Irregularities and Impediments—An Overview." *The Jurist* 62 (2002): 159–94.

Lagges, Patrick R. "The Use of Canon 1044, §2, 2º in the Removal of Parish Priests." *Studia canonica* 30 (1996): 31–69.

Lothstein, Leslie M. "Can a Sexually Addicted Priest Return to Ministry after Treatment? Psychological Issues and Possible Forensic Solutions." *Catholic Lawyer* 34 (1990): 89–113.

————. "The Relationship Between the Treatment Facilities and the Church Hierarchy: Forensic Issues and Future Considerations." In *Sins Against the Innocents*. Ed. Thomas G. Plante. Westport: Praeger, 2004: 123–37.

Lynch, John E. "The Obligations and Rights of Clerics (cc. 273-289)." In *New Commentary on the Code of Canon Law*. Ed. John P. Beal, James A. Coriden, and Thomas J. Green. New York: Paulist Press, 2000: 343–81.

Maida, Adam J. "The Selection, Training and Removal of Diocesan Clergy." *Catholic Lawyer* 33 (1990): 53–60.

McDonough, Elizabeth. "Sanctions in the 1983 Code: Purpose and Procedures; Progress and Problems." *CLSA Proceedings* 52 (1990): 206–21.

Mendonca, Augustine. "Justice and Equity: At Whose Expense?" In *The Art of the Good and Equitable*. Ed. Frederick C. Easton. Washington, D.C.: Canon Law Society of America, 2002: 189–235.

Miragoli, E. "Il confessore e il 'de sexto.'" *Quaderni di diritto ecclesiale* 4 (1991): 238–58.

Morrisey, Francis G. "Addressing the Issue of Clergy Abuse." *Studia canonica* 35 (2001): 403–20.

———. "The Pastoral and Juridical Dimensions of Dismissal from the Clerical State and of Other Penalties for Sexual Misconduct." *CLSA Proceedings* 53 (1991): 221–39.

———. "Procedures to Be Applied in Cases of Alleged Sexual Misconduct by a Priest." *Studia canonica* 26 (1992): 39–73.

Murray, Donald B. "The Legislative Authority of the Episcopal Conference." *Studia canonica* 20 (1986): 33–47.

O'Reilly, Michael. "Recent Developments in the Laicization of Priests." *The Jurist* 52 (1992): 684–96.

Paulson, Jerome E. "The Clinical and Canonical Considerations in Cases of Pedophilia: The Bishop's Role." *Studia canonica* 22 (1988): 77–124.

Proctor, John G. "Clerical Misconduct: Canonical and Practical Consequences." *CLSA Proceedings* 49 (1987): 227–44.

Provost, James H. "The Christian Faithful." In *The Code of Canon Law: A Text and Commentary.* Ed. James A. Coriden, Thomas J. Green, and Donald E. Heintschel. New York: Paulist Press, 1985: 117–73.

———. "Offenses Against the Sixth Commandment: Towards a Canonical Analysis of Canon 1395." *The Jurist* 55 (1995): 632–63.

———. "Some Canonical Considerations Relative to Clerical Sexual Misconduct." *The Jurist* 52 (1992): 615–41.

Rochet, Jean-Claude. "Efficacité Du Droit Pénal Canonique." *Année Canonique* 38 (1996): 137–39.

Rossetti, Stephen J., and L. M. Lothstein. "Myths of the Child Molester." In *Slayer of the Soul.* Ed. Stephen J. Rossetti. Mystic: Twenty-Third Publications, 1990: 9–18.

Schneider, Francis J. "Loss of the Clerical State." In *New Commentary on the Code of Canon Law.* Ed. John P. Beal, James A. Coriden, and Thomas J. Green. New York: Paulist Press, 2000: 382–93.

Scicluna, Charles J. "Sexual Abuse of Children and Young People by Catholic Priests and Religious: Description of the Problem from a Church Perspective." In *Sexual Abuse in the Catholic Church:*

Scientific and Legal Perspectives. Ed. R. Karl Hanson, Friedemann Pfafflin, and Manfred Lutz. Vatican City: Libreria Editrice Vaticana, 2004: 13–22.

Taub, Sheila. "The Legal Treatment of Recovered Memories of Child Sexual Abuse." *Journal of Legal Medicine* 17 (1996): 183–214.

Tuohey, John. "The Correct Interpretation of Canon 1395: A Study of the Sixth Commandment in the Moral Tradition from Trent to the Present Day." *The Jurist* 55 (1995): 592–631.

Urru, Angelo G. "Natura e Finalità della Pena Canonica." In *Il Processo Penale Canonico*. Ed. Zbigniew Suchecki. Rome: Lateran University Press, 2003: 61–73.

Valcour, Frank, MD. "Expectations of Treatment for Child Molesters." In Ad Hoc Committee on Sexual Abuse, National Conference of Catholic Bishops. *Restoring Trust: A Pastoral Response to Sexual Abuse*. Vol. I. Washington, D.C.: National Conference of Catholic Bishops, 1994.

––––––. "The Treatment of Child Sex Abusers in the Church." In *Slayer of the Soul*. Ed. Stephen J. Rossetti. Mystic: Twenty-Third Publications, 1990: 45–66.

Woestman, William H. "Canons 1041, 1o and 1044, §2, 2o." In *Roman Replies and CLSA Advisory Opinions 1995*. Ed. Kevin Vann and James Donlon. Washington, D.C.: Canon Law Society of America, 1995: 80–82.

––––––. "Restricting the Right to Celebrate the Eucharist." *Studia canonica* 29 (1995): 165–71.

––––––. "To Good To Be True: A Current Interpretation of Canons 1041, 1o and 1044, §2, 2o." *Monitor Ecclesiasticus* 120 (1995): 619–29.

Wrenn, Lawrence G. "Book VII Processes, Part I." In *New Commentary on the Code of Canon Law*. Ed. John P. Beal, James A. Coriden, and Thomas J. Green. New York: Paulist Press, 2000: 1607–54.

JOURNAL ARTICLES

Ad Hoc Committee on Sexual Abuse. "Brief History: Handling Child Sex Abuse Claims." *Origins* 23:38 (March 10, 1994): 666–70.

America staff. "Editorial: Healing and Credibility." *America* (April 1, 2002): 3.

———. "Editorial: Sexual Abuse by Priests." *America* (February 18, 2002): 3 http://www.americamagazine.org/.

———. "Signs of the Times, Boston Priest Advocated Sex with Boys." *America* (April 22, 2002): 5.

———. "Signs of the Times, Diocese Sues Archdiocese Over Priest Accused of Sexual Abuse." *America* (April 14, 2003): 5.

———. "When the 'Unspeakable' Must Be Spoken." *America* (October 17, 1992): 267–68.

"Archbishop Sanchez Submits Resignation." *Origins* 22:42 (April 1, 1993): 722–24

Berry, Jason. "Listening to the Survivors: Voices of People of God." *America* (November 13, 1993): 4–9.

Bryant, Curtis. "Psychological Treatment of Priest Sex Offenders." *America* (April 1, 2002): 14–17.

"Charges Against Chicago Archbishop Dropped." *Origins* 23:38 (March 10, 1994): 661--63.

Coffey, Kathy. "A Priest Is a Terrible Thing to Waste." *U.S. Catholic* (September 2000): 41–42.

Congregation for the Doctrine of the Faith. "De delictis gravioribus." English translation. *Origins* 31:32 (January 24, 2002): 528–29.

Connors, Canice. "Clerical Sexual Abuse Priests and Their Victims Find Healing." *Ligourian* (November 1994): 22–27.

———. "Priests and Pedophilia: A Silence That Needs Breaking?" *America* (May 9, 1992): 400–401.

———. "Subcommittee Head Introduces Think Tank Recommendations." *Origins* 23:7 (July 1, 1993): 105–7.

"Cook's Claims Against Cardinal Dismissed." *Origins* 23:38 (March 10, 1994): 663–64.

Feister, John Bookster. "How the Church Is Confronting Clergy Sexual Abuse." *St. Anthony Messenger* (February 1994): 28–35.

Greeley, Andrew M. "How Serious Is the Problem of Sexual Abuse by Clergy?" *America* (March 20, 1993): 6–10.

————. "Why?" *America* (May 27, 2002): 12–13.

Keeler, Archbishop William. "Reckless Charges Against Innocent People." *Origins* 23:38 (March 10, 1994): 665.

Keneally, Thomas. "Cold Sanctuary." *New Yorker* (June 17–24, 2002): 58–66.

Loftus, John Allen. "A Question of Disillusionment: Sexual Abuse Among the Clergy." *America* (December 1, 1990): 426–29.

Reese, Thomas J. "Bishops Meet At Notre Dame." *America* (July 1, 1992): 4–6, http://www.americamagazine.org/reese/america/nc9206.

————. "Bishops Speak in Public Session of Sexual Abuse." *America* (July 3, 1993): 4–6.

————. "Facts, Myths and Questions." *America* (March 22, 2004): 13.

Rossetti, Stephen J. "The Catholic Church and Child Sexual Abuse." *America* (April 22, 2002): 13–16.

————. "Child Sexual Abuse and the Church How I Understand It." *Priest* (January 1994): 32–37.

Serritella, James. "Statement." *Origins* 23:38 (March 10, 1994): 662.

Sheehan, Michael. "Archbishop's Letter Explains Bankruptcy Risk." *Origins* 23:30 (January 13, 1994): 529–30.

Stahel, Thomas H. "The 'Real Catholic Story': U.S. Bishops Meet." *America* (December 4, 1993): 4–5.

Steinfels, Peter. "The Church's Sex-Abuse Crisis." *Commonweal* (April 19, 2002): 13–19.

"Washington Archdiocese Removes Four Priests." *Origins* 24:25 (February 16, 1993): 588–89.

NEWSPAPER ARTICLES

Allen, John L., Jr. "1962 Document Orders Secrecy in Sex Cases: Many Bishops Unaware Obscure Missive Was in Their Archives." *National Catholic Reporter,* August 7, 2003, 1+.

————. "Canonist Criticizes U.S. Bishops Sex Abuse Norms." *National Catholic Reporter,* April 2, 2004, 1+.

Barry, Ellen. "Priest Treatment Unfolds in Costly, Secretive World." *Boston Globe,* April 3, 2002, A1+.

Boston Globe staff. "James Porter—Key Dates." *Boston Globe,* July 16, 1992, A14+ (National News).

Boston Globe staff (Spotlight Team). "Geoghan Preferred Preying on Poorer Children." *Boston Globe,* January 7, 2002, A1+.

————."Geoghan's Troubled History." *Boston Globe,* January 7, 2002, A1+ (Geoghan Timeline).

Burge, Kathleen. "Appeals Court Ruling Sought." *Boston Globe,* September 6, 2002, A15.

————. "Geoghan Receives 9–10 Year Sentence for Molesting Child." *Boston Globe,* February 22, 2002, A1.

Egerton, Brooks, and Reese Dunklin. "Two-Thirds of Bishops Let Accused Priests Work." *Dallas Morning News,* June 12, 2002, 1A+.

Egerton, Brooks, and Michael D. Goldhaber. "Documents Show Bishops Transferred Known Abuser; Church Officials Say Policies Have Since Changed." *Dallas Morning News,* August 31, 1997, 1A+.

Farragher, Thomas. "A Troubled Life Spent Exploiting Vocation." *Boston Globe,* August 24, 2003, B6.

Finer, Jonathan, and Alan Cooperman. "Catholic Church Settles in Boston: Alleged Victims to Share $85 Million." *Washington Post,* September 10, 2003, A1+.

Fouhy, Beth. "US Priest on Abuse Charge." AP Wire, May 25, 2003.

Fox, Thomas C. "What They Knew in 1985." *National Catholic Reporter,* May 17, 2002, 1.

Franklin, James L. "Porter Says Church to Blame." *Boston Globe,* December 8, 1993, B33 (Metro Section).

Friendly, Jonathan. "Roman Catholic Church Discusses Abuse of Children by Priests." *New York Times,* May 4, 1986, A26.

Goodstein, Laurie. "Archdiocese of Cincinnati Fined in Sex Abuse Scandal." *New York Times,* November 21, 2003, A25.

Housewright, Ed. "Dallas Bishop Testifies He Warned Kos." *Dallas Morning News,* July 2, 1997, 1A.

Law, Bernard Cardinal. Excerpts from deposition, Suffolk Superior Court. *Boston Globe,* May 9, 2002, 34, Metro/Region Section.

Lewis, Anthony. "Abroad at Home; Savaging The Great." *New York Times,* May 27, 1994, A27.

Liptak, Adam. "Religion and the Law." *New York Times,* April 14, 2002, A30.

Matachan, Linda. "Ex-Priest Accused in Minnesota." *Boston Globe*, July 14, 1992, A1+ (National News).

———. "Porter Guilty of Molesting Baby Sitter." *Boston Globe*, December 12, 1992, A1+.

Matachan, Linda, and Stephen Kurjian. "Porter's Treatment Questioned." *Boston Globe*, July 16, 1992, A1+.

Pfeiffer, Sacha. "Letters Exhibit Gentle Approach Toward Priest." *Boston Globe*, January 24, 2002, A21.

Rezendes, Michael. "Critics Blast Law for Comment on Archdiocese Files." *Boston Globe*, April 13, 2002, A1.

Rich, Eric, and Elizabeth Hamilton. "Doctors: Church Used Us." *Hartford Courant*, March 24, 2002, A1+.

Robinson, Walter V., and Matt Carroll. "Documents Show Church Long Supported Geoghan." *Boston Globe*, January 24, 2002, A1+.

Rodgers-Melnick, Ann. "Bishops Torn by Cipolla Decision." *Pittsburgh Post-Gazette*, June 21, 1993, A1.

———. "Rare Sanction Imposed on Priest." *Pittsburgh Post-Gazette*, November 16, 2002, A1.

———. "Vatican Clears Priest, Wuerl Rejects Verdict." *Pittsburgh Post-Gazette*, March 21, 1993, A1.

Shaw, Kathleen A. "Vatican Document Instructed Secrecy in Abuse Cases." *Worcester Telegram & Gazette*, July 29, 2003, 1.

Steinfels, Peter. "Beliefs: A Catholic Bishop Looks Back." *New York Times*, June 22, 2002, A12+.

———. "Beliefs: Lessons from the Past." *New York Times*, February 9, 2002, A34+.

———. "Bishops Assail Press on Sex Charges." *New York Times*, November 16, 1993, A24.

———. "Bishops Struggle Over Sex Abuses by Parish Priests." *New York Times*, June 18, 1993, A1+.

———. "Giving Healing and Hope to Priests Who Molested." *New York Times*, October 12, 1992, A1+.

———. "Inquiry in Chicago Breaks Silence on Sex Abuse by Catholic Priests." *New York Times*, February 24, 1992, A1+.

———. "On Sexual Abuse by Catholic Clergy: A Time for Bishops to Seize 'the Moment after Suffering.'" *New York Times*, October 8, 1994, A30+.

AFFIDAVITS, ATTORNEY GENERAL, AND GRAND JURY REPORTS

Hoye, Monsignor Daniel F. Affidavit in *Spann et al. v. Thorne et al.* Civil Action No. J87-0114 (B), S.D. Miss. 1989,¶ 4.

Office of the Attorney General Commonwealth of Massachusetts. *The Sexual Abuse of Children in the Roman Catholic Archdiocese of Boston.* July 23, 2003.

Report of the Grand Jury of September 17, 2003, Misc. No. 03-00-239, Court of Common Pleas, First Judicial District of Pennsylvania [Philadelphia], Criminal Trial Division: 101.

Stradley, Ronon, Stevens & Young, LLP. *Response of the Archdiocese of Philadelphia to the Report of the Investigating Grand Jury Pursuant to 42 PA. C.S. § 4552(e).*

PRIVATELY PUBLISHED AND UNPUBLISHED MATERIALS

Canonical Affairs Committee of the NCCB. "Dismissal from the Clerical State in Cases of Sexual Crimes Against Minors." Privately published, 1987.

Ingels, Gregory. "Examination of the Rights of Priests Accused of Misconduct." Presentation to National Federation of Priests' Councils, April 17, 2002. Unpublished manuscript, 1.

Maida, Adam J. "A Focus for Canonical and Civil Law Issues in Pedophilia Cases." Privately published, 1987.

Peterson, Michael R., F. Ray Mouton, and Thomas P. Doyle. *The Problem of Sexual Molestation by Roman Catholic Clergy: Meeting the Problem in a Comprehensive and Responsible Manner.* Privately published, 1985.

ELECTRONIC SOURCES

AP Wire. "Pedophile Ex-Priest Goes Free, Heads for Texas." *Detroit News,* February 4, 2000, Religion Section. http://www.detnews.com/2000/religion/0002/05/02050012.htm.

Athenagoras of Athens. "A Plea for Christians." Trans. B. P. Pratten. http://www.earlychristianwritings.com/athenagoras.html.

Banks, Bishop Robert J. November 30, 1989 letter to Vincent M. Stephens, MD. http://www.bishop-accountability.org/ma-boston/archives/PatternAndPractice/0328-Banks-Exhibit-44.pdf.

Berry, Jason. "The Man Who Keeps the Secrets." *San Francisco Magazine,* September 2005. http://www.sanfranmag.com/archives/view_story/998.

Boston Globe staff. "Geoghan's Troubled History." http://www.bishop-accountability.org/service-records/service-archive/supporting docs/Geoghan-John-J-History.htm.

Boston Globe website. "Sexual Scandals Strike at Highest Level of US Catholic Church." http://www.boston.com/globe/spotlight/abuse/extras/bishops-map.htm.

Brennan, John H., MD. December 7, 1990 letter to Bishop Robert J. Banks. http://www.bishop-accountability.org/ma-boston/archives/PatternAndPractice/0301-Geoghan-II-06703.pdf.

CBS News. "The Church on Trial, Part 1." *Sixty Minutes.* June 12, 2003. Transcript. http://www.cbsnews.com/stories/2002/06/11/60II/printable511845.shtml.

Connors, Canice. "Psychological Perspective on Priesthood." *Colloquia* (March 1999). http://www.nfpc.org/COLLOQUIA/MARCH-1999/connors.htm.

Court TV Crime Library. "Father James Porter: Pedophile Priest." Ch. 4 "Cured Again." http://crimelibrary.com/serialkillers/predators/porter/index_1.html.

Doyle, Thomas J. *Memorandum to Sylvia Demarest,* May 16, 1996, In re: Does v. Diocese of Dallas. http://www.bishop-accountability.org/tx.dallas/resources-files/doyle-memo.

———. "A Short History of the Manual." http://www.bishop-accountability.org/reports/1985_06_09_Doyle_Manual/Doyle_AShortHistory.htm.

Dunklin, Reese. "Convicted Priest Helped Abusers Stay in Ministry." *Dallas Morning News,* January 19, 2004. http://www.dallasnews. com/spe/2002/bishops/stories/071302dnpriest.d1a3.html.

Egan, Cardinal Edward. March 23, 2002 statement. http://www.ny-archdiocese.org/statement0323.cfm.

Gatehouse, Jonathon. "Catholic Church Sex Abuse Scandals." *Maclean's* (July 22, 2002). http://www.canadianencyclopedia.ca/ index.cfm?PgNm+TCE& Params=M1ARTM0012306.

Geoghan, John J. Letter of October 19, 1996 to Cardinal Law. http://www.bishop-accountability.org/ma-boston/archives/ PatternAndPractice/0235-Geoghan-II-01923.pdf.

Gerdes, Louise I. "Introduction." In *At Issue: Child Abuse in the Catholic Church.* Ed. Louise I. Gerdes. San Diego: Greenhaven Press, 2003. http://www.enotes.com/catholic-child-abuse-article/38969.

Hirsch, J. M. "2 Bishops on Abuse Panel Accused of Shielding Predators." *Nashua* (NH) *Telegraph,* April 11, 2002. http://www. nashuatelegraph.com/Main.asp?SectionID=25&SubSectionID= 378&ArticleID=54422.

Housewright, Ed. "Ex-priest's Siblings Tell of Sex Abuse Diocese Denies It Knew of Molestation Charges." *Dallas Morning News,* May 17, 1997. http://nl.newsbank.com/nl-search/we/Archives?.

———. "Trial Opens Against Ex-Priest, Diocese." *Dallas Morning News,* May 16, 1997. http://nl.newsbank.com/nl-search/we/ Archives?.

———. "Victim Says Kos Phoned From Center." *Dallas Morning News,* May 29, 1997. http://nl.newsbank.com/nl-search/we/ Archives?.

Hudson, Deal. "Ten Myths About Priestly Pedophilia." Catholic Commentary website. http://www.catholicity.com/commentary/ hudson/tenmyths.html.

Hughes, Archbishop Alfred C. "Clergy and the Molestation of Minors." *Clarion Herald,* January 30, 2002 editorial. http://www. archdiocese.no.org/archbishop/ah-archives/013002.html.

Johnson, Allen, Jr. "Deposing the Archbishop." bestofneworleans.com News Feature, May 21, 2002. http://www.bestofneworleans.com/ dispatch/2002-05-21/news-feat.html.

Kinney, Bishop John F. November 6, 2005 statement. http://www.diocese tucson.org/restore3.htm.

Lavoie, Denise. "Defrocked Priest Sentenced to 12 to 15 Years for Child Rape." *Associated Press Boston.com News,* February 15, 2005. http://boston.com/Boston.com/news/local/massachusetts/articles/2005/02/15.

Law, Bernard Cardinal. January 6, 1993 letter to Reverend John J. Geoghan. http://www.bishop-accountability.org/ma-boston/archives/PatternAndPractice/0314-Geoghan-II-07370.pdf.

————. January 23, 1996 letter to Reverend John J. Geoghan. http://www.bishop-accountability.org/ma-boston/archives/PatternAndPractice/0247-Geoghan-II-01935.pdf.

————. August 4, 1996 letter to Reverend John J. Geoghan. http://www.bishop-accountability.org/ma-boston/archives/PatternAndPractice/0239-Geoghan-II-01927.pdf.

————. December 12, 1996 letter to Reverend John J. Geoghan. http://www.bishop-accountability.org/ma-boston/archives/PatternAndPractice/0233-Geoghan-II-01921.pdf.

Lennon, Monsignor Richard. May 8, 1998 memorandum to Reverend James McCarthy. http://www.bishop-accountability.org/ma-boston/archives/PatternAndPractice/0232-Geoghan-II-01919.pdf.

Martinez, Demetria. "Lawyers' Strategies Vie in Bankruptcy Case— Santa Fe, New Mexico Archdiocese Priest Sexual Misconduct Suits." *National Catholic Reporter,* January 14, 1994; *Find Articles* website. http://www.findarticles.com/p/articles/mi-m1141/is_n11_v30/ai_14760028.

Nashua (NH) *Telegraph,* April 13, 2002. http://www.nashuatelegraph.com/Main.asp?SectionID=25&SubSectionID=378&ArticleID=54554.

Newbart, Dave, and Dan Rozek. "Deposition, Suits Stun Joliet Diocese." *Chicago Sun-Times,* February 5, 2006. http://www.suntimes.com/output/news/cst-nws-priests05.html.

O'Neill, Robert. "Former Priest John Geoghan Killed in Prison; Was Center of Church Abuse Scandal." *Associated Press Boston.com News,* August 23, 2003. http://www.boston.com/news/daily/23/mass-geoghan.htm.

Peterson, Michael R., MD. December 9, 1985 letter to all diocesan bishops. http://www.bishop-accountability.org/reports/1985_12_09_Peterson_Guidelinesindex.html.

————. August 27, 1986 letter to all diocesan bishops. http://www.bishop-accountability.org/reports/1985_12_09_Peterson_Guidelines/1986_08_27_Peterson_Revisions.pdf.

Rezendes, Michael, and Matt Carroll. "Doctors Who OK'd Geoghan Lacked Expertise, Review Shows." *Boston Globe*, January 16, 2002. http://www.boston.com/globe/spotlight/abuse/print/011602-doctors.htm.

Rivera, Ray. "High-profile Panelists Hearing Priest Case." *The Seattle Times*, May 17, 2002, Local News. http://archives.seattletimes.nwsource.com.

Russell, Ron. "Blind Eye Unto the Holy See." *SF Weekly*, July 13, 2005. http://www.sfweekly.com/Issues/2005-07-13/news/feature.html.

————. "Camp Ped." *Los Angeles New Times*, August 15, 2002. http://www.bishop-accountability.org/ca-la/mahony-2002-08-a.htm.

————. "Fast Times at Marin Catholic High." *SF Weekly*, January 19, 2005. http://www.sfweekly.com/Issues/2005-01-19/news/sidebar.html.

————. "Holy Hypocrite." *Los Angeles New Times*, May 16, 2002. http://www.bishop-accountability.org/ca-la/mahony2002-05-d.htm.

Saul, Michael. "Kos Gets Life Term for Molesting Boys." *Dallas Morning News*, April 2, 1998. http://www.bishop-accountability.org.tx-dallas/Dallas-1998-04-05.htm.

Schaeffer, Pamela. "Reporter's Trial Notes." *National Catholic Reporter*, August 15, 1997. http://natcath.org?NCROnline/archives2/1997c/081597/081597f.htm.

Sipe, A. W. Richard. "Preliminary Expert Report." http://www.bishop-accountablity.org/tx-dallas/resource-files/sipe-report.htm.

————. "View from the Eye of the Storm," keynote address, The Linkup National Conference, Louisville, Kentucky, February 23, 2003. http://www.bishop-accountability.org/resources/resource-files/timeline/2003-02-23-Sipe-ViewEyeStorm.htm.

Slowik, Ted. "Imesch Testimony Public." *The Herald News Online*, February 3, 2006. http://suburbanchicagonews.com/heraldnews/top/4_1_JO03_DIOCESE_S1.htm.

Swords, Robert F., MD. December 13, 1989 letter to Bishop Robert J. Banks. http://www.bishop-accountability.org/ma-boston/archives/PatternAndPractice/0329-1989-12-13-Swords.pdf.

USA Today. "Bishops Who Have Resigned Amid Church Sex Scandals." December 12, 2002. http://www.usatoday.com/news/nation/2002-12-13-bishop-resignations_x.htm.

Werth, Barry. "Fathers' Helper." *The New Yorker* (June 9, 2003); (January 12, 2006). http://www.newyorker.com/printables/fact/030609fa-fact.htm.

Wolfe, Warren. "St. Cloud Catholics Gather to Discuss Abuse Crisis." *Star Tribune,* May 22, 2002. http://wwwstartribune.com/stories/1697/2851313.html.